ANTECEDENTS OF LEADERSHIP BEHAVIOUR

Its Influences on Quality of Work Life and Organisational Commitment

ANTECEDENTS OF LEADERSHIP BEHAVIOUR

Its Influences on Quality of Work Life and Organisational Commitment

DR. UPASNA JOSHI

DEEP & DEEP PUBLICATIONS PVT. LTD.
F-159, Rajouri Garden, New Delhi - 110 027

ANTECEDENTS OF LEADERSHIP BEHAVIOUR
Its Influences on Quality of Work Life
and Organisational Commitment

ISBN 978-81-8450-153-7

Typeset by RAHUL COMPOSERS
358, Pocket-B, Phase-II, Sector-16B, Dwarka, New Delhi - 110 075

Printed in India at MAYUR ENTERPRISES
WZ Plot No. 3, Gujjar Market, Tihar Village, New Delhi - 110 018

Published by DEEP & DEEP PUBLICATIONS PVT. LTD.,
F-159, Rajouri Garden, New Delhi - 110 027 • Phone : 25435369, 25440916
E-mail : ddpubs@gmail.com • ddpbooks@yahoo.co.in
Showroom :
2/13, Ansari Road, Daryaganj, New Delhi - 110 002 • Teléfax : 23245122

Contents

DR. JASPAL SINGH
Vice Chancellor
PUNJABI UNIVERSITY, PATIALA

ਡਾ. ਜਸਪਾਲ ਸਿੰਘ
ਵਾਈਸ ਚਾਂਸਲਰ
ਪੰਜਾਬੀ ਯੂਨੀਵਰਸਿਟੀ, ਪਟਿਆਲਾ

Foreword

The intent as well as the content of leadership is undergoing a transformation with the advent of various forces of globalization. Managers of today are beset with radically different sets of challenges than those encountered by our forefathers. The astounding pace of these changes makes it imperative that the managers of today develop strategic-orientation in their decision-making. In the era of rapid change and unparalleled opportunity, the profitable and sustainable growth is possible in only those organizations whose leaders can delineate possibilities and opportunities beyond traditional mind sets and ways of operations. To meet these challenges, organizations must broaden the scope of leadership responsibility and empower them for strategic thinking and engage larger number of people in the process of leadership. Such leadership envisions delegation, decentralization, team building and a paradigm shift in the employer-employee relationship.

Punjabi University, Patiala has been in the forefront in encouraging young researchers in their academic pursuits. It gives me immense pleasure to note that Dr. Upasna Joshi, a

Ph. : (Off.) 0175-2286418, 3046001 (Resi.) 2282478, 3046005, Fax : 0175-2286682
E-mail : drjaspalsingh@yahoo.com, vc@pbi.ac.in, Telegram : UNIVERSITY PATIALA 147 002

young researcher has worked tirelessly to undertake research in the area of leadership. As leadership is situational and there is scarcity of researches in this area in Indian context, I am sure this effort of Dr. Upasna will be of immense academic interest and motivate similar other researchers.

I wish her all success in all her future endeavours.

DR. JASPAL SINGH

Preface

Organisations have realized that to excel in the era of volatile business environment, there is a need to ensure a fit between the various stakeholders. A proper alignment of management philosophy, business strategy and human resource policies can mutually benefit all the key stakeholders. The nature of employee-organisation inter-relationship is important to individual employee, business organisation and society as a whole. Organisational performance is often dependent upon managerial and leadership traits of its top management. Management and Leadership are separate, while equally important, organisational processes. Management is predominantly responsible for creating organisation, order and stability whereas leadership is creating thrust, vision, ensuring commitment, aligning individual and organisational goals. Strategy execution is regarded as one of the critical sources of sustainable competitive advantage. Therefore, leadership effectiveness in organisational performance is often regarded as being the outcome of skillfulness of ensuring employee commitment and aligning individual goal orientations towards that of the organisation. Early work on leadership focused on leadership traits, leadership styles, and contingency theories.

However, it has been strongly felt that there is a need for a paradigm shift in emphasis towards thinking about the followers in leadership, to the extent that leadership is now often defined as the process of leaders and followers engaging in reciprocal influence to achieve a shared purpose. Thus, leaders' behavioural patterns have gained prominence. This transformational approach ensures that leaders and followers raise one another to higher levels of motivation and morality. Leaders set high expectations, use symbolism to focus efforts, and communicate a vision to followers. Manager's role in handling conflicts, building supportive work relationships, communicating effectively: all contribute to the formulation of positive attitudes towards the organisation and, therefore, to its success. Followers react by willingly increasing their efforts to attain the vision. Leaders being role models, their behaviour and extent of achievement of goals will be interrelated because the climate established by leadership behaviour provides individuals with focus and feedback regarding organisational goals.

Organisations must have committed members if they are to prosper or even survive. Organisational commitment is a multi-dimensional construct that reflects relative strength of an individual's identification with and involvement in a particular organisation. Conceptually, it is characterized by three factors: (a) a strong belief in and acceptance of the organisation's goals and values; (b) a willingness to exert considerable effort on behalf of the organisation; and (c) a strong desire to maintain membership in the organisation. Organisational commitment is determined by a range of organisational and individual factors such as personal characteristics, structural characteristics, work experience and role-related features, etc.

Thus, Organisational commitment is an attitude that reflects the nature and quality of the linkage between an employee and an organisation. It is a state in which an individual identifies with a particular organisation and its goals and wishes to maintain membership in order to facilitate these goals. It is argued that commitment often establishes an exchange relationship in which individuals attach themselves to the organisation in return for certain rewards from the organisation. Individuals come to organisations with certain needs, skills, expectations and they hope to find a work environment where they can use their abilities and satisfy their needs. When an organisation can provide these opportunities, the likelihood of increasing commitment is increased. Employees with high organisational commitment are more willing to put more effort and are more likely to develop positive attitudes towards organisational performance.

It was thought prudent to explore whether leadership behaviour influenced organisational commitment among his subordinates. Majority of the existing studies have treated organisation commitment as an independent variable influencing work outcomes, i.e. turnover, absenteeism or as a dependent variable on demographic variables, role conflict, organisational size, etc. However, behavioural patterns of the manager could also influence commitment of the subordinates. For the present study, Organisation commitment was considered a better measure to reflect the total causal effects of positive affectivity, job security, job satisfaction and motivation.

Quality of Work Life (QWL) has been perceived as a process by which an organisation responds to employee needs by developing mechanisms to allow them to share fully in making the decisions that design their lives at work and include job security, better reward systems, higher pay, and opportunity for growth, participative groups and increased organisational productivity, among others. It is set of favorable conditions and environment of a workplace that supports and promote employee satisfaction by providing them with rewards, job security and growth opportunities. The basic objectives of an effective QWL program are improved working conditions (mainly from an employee's perspective) and greater organisational effectiveness (from organisational perspective). Not only does QWL contribute to a company's ability to recruit quality people, but also it enhances a company's competitiveness. Leadership strongly influences and motivates employees to change and accommodate to their jobs and environment. This may entail not only altering structures but also the processes, systems, attitudes, leadership philosophy and style. Higher QWL emanates from job satisfaction, intrinsic nature of the work, autonomy, democratic and supportive peers and an organisational climate which supports open communication and autonomy.

As the manager is responsible for developing these variable constructs of QWL, it was considered worthwhile to study influence of a manager's leadership behavioural patterns and ability to create, sustain, and improve organisational cultures and environment on enhancing QWL.

Present study is a humble effort to study the impact of leadership behaviour on organisational commitment and quality of work life. The study was conducted in consumer durable industry, which is an important segment of Indian industry. The introductory chapter highlights approaches to leadership and critical evaluation of leadership styles. The existing theories of leadership have been examined so as to delineate emerging trends in leadership behaviour. Similarly, various determinants and approaches to measurement of organisational commitment and quality of work life have been critically examined.

A review of existing literature has been presented in Chapters 6, 5 and 6 wherein studies on leadership behaviour in general and Indian context in particular, besides emerging trends in the behavioural research on leadership have been critically examined. A critique on existing literature on organisational commitment has been also undertaken to develop the conceptual framework of role of firm's human resource management practices on developing organisational commitment among employees. A salient features is the appraisal of quality of work life practices in business organisations.

Chapter 7 outlines the gaps in existing studies and the rationale for undertaking the present study. The research objectives and hypotheses have been outlined as well as the details about the three research instruments and research design used in the study.

Chapters 8, 9, 10 and 11 are devoted to presentation, analysis and interpretation of findings regarding leadership behaviour, organisational commitment, quality of work life as well as inter-relationship between them.

Conclusions and recommendations as well as implications for future research have been delineated in Chapter 12. A distinctive feature is the attempt to provide linkages of the findings of the present research with similar researches carried out elsewhere to give overall perspective.

It is fervently hoped that the present study will act as a useful addition to the exciting field of human resource management and leadership. It will be of immense benefit to not only the academicians and researchers but also to the practitioners and business organisations keen on developing organisational commitment and enhancing work life of their employees.

UPASNA JOSHI

Acknowledgements

The most pleasurable aspect of writing a manuscript is the opportunity it provides to express gratitude to all the persons who have contributed their might and have been a source of encouragement and enlightenment.

Prof. Jaspal Singh, esteemed Vice-Chancellor, Punjabi University always had an inspiring attitude and excellent spirit towards academic endeavours of faculty members. His academic leadership, benevolence and quest for research orientation have been highly encouraging. *His Foreword has inspired me to achieve still higher levels of academic excellence.*

Professor R.C. Sobti, esteemed Vice-Chancellor, Panjab University and a Biotechnologist of international repute has been encouraging, kind hearted and benevolent to all my academic pursuits. His personal academic achievements and pursuit for excellence have been a source of motivation to academicians and teachers like me. His academic excellence inculcated in us a habit of hard work.

Professor Satish Kapoor, the then Chairman, University Business School, Panjab University has always been a source of inspiration and guidance. He was extremely cooperative in taking care of all my research material requirements and placed all his facilities at my disposal.

The patronage of Prof. K.K. Uppal and Dr. Sanjeev K. Sharma of University Business School, Panjab University, Chandigarh during my research has been tremendous. They have been highly supportive during my research at Panjab University.

I am obliged to the Professor A.S. Chawla, Director, Punjabi University Regional Centre for Information Technology and Management (PURCITM), Mohali for their whole-hearted encouragement and cooperation. I am beholden to the faculty for refining my knowledge of the challenging and rewarding field of management.

The library staff of Panjab University, Punjabi University, Indian Institute of Management at Ahmedabad and Faculty of Management Studies, Delhi University was highly supportive to my requirements and indulgent enquiries. I owe a debt of gratitude to them.

My family members have been extremely accommodating and constantly encouraging me in my research. My special thanks to my husband and son. I owe them a debt of gratitude.

Chandigarh UPASNA JOSHI

CHAPTER

1

Conceptual Framework of Leadership Behaviour

1.1 STRATEGIC ROLE OF LEADERSHIP, QUALITY OF WORK LIFE AND ORGANISATIONAL COMMITMENT

In recent years, businesses have transformed the way in which they conduct their operations in order to respond to the competitive challenges of global markets, rapid technological developments and the transition from an industrial to an information economy. Although it is recognized that managers in these businesses need to develop new skills and management techniques, there is no consensus on what these are. *Barney* (1991) developed a resource-based view of the firm which premises that companies generate sustainable competitive advantages by effectively controlling and manipulating their resources and/or capabilities that are: (1) valuable, (2) rare, (3) that cannot be perfectly imitated, and (4) for which no perfect substitute is available. Human resource activities including those that improve employee attitudes on workplace quality meet these four characteristics. As a result, human resource activities can create a competitive advantage by developing a skilled workforce that effectively carries out the company's business strategy. This competitive advantage leads to improved performance, higher profitability and greater market value. Thus, one of the most challenging tasks for an organization is to create, sustain and improve through an authentic teamwork-based environment. For an organization to change from a traditional classical structure to an organic team-based structure requires changes not only in structure, but in processes, systems, attitudes, leadership philosophy and style. This calls for a paradigm shift.

This is an age of fundamental and accelerated changes characterised by the globalisation of markets, ubiquitous presence of information technology, dismantling of hierarchical structures and the creation of new organisational forms and networks. Growing around these is a new information age economy whose fundamental sources of wealth are knowledge and communication rather than natural resources and physical labour. Whereas the second half of the 20th century was about the revolution in technology, the challenge of the 21st century is to keep pace with the international time element as businesses move from local and regional to a truly global environment.

Given the ever-increasing demand to become more competitive and effective, today's employers are not simply interested in ensuring the legal defensibility of their policies, practices and procedures; rather they are also interested in "managing diversity" to ensure that employees reach their full potential. Organizations are interested in implementing management initiatives in order to create an environment that supports and retains a diverse work force while capitalizing on individual differences as a competitive advantage. There is growing recognition that in order to create organizations that are effective with a diverse employee base, the organizational climate must be appropriate. Such a *conducive environment is predominantly dependent on the leader's behaviour and is reflected in the improved quality of work life and organizational commitment manifested by the employees.*

Organization-wide policies, practices and procedures send implicit and explicit messages to employees about the organization's stance toward the allocation of opportunities. For example, the existence of a family leave policy, an affirmative action policy, a sexual harassment training program and employee grievance process are examples of policies that may influence these perceptions. Likewise, an organization's compensation, promotion and hiring systems can negatively impact climate of members of identifiable groups. Organizational performance is the organization's ability to realize its mission and obtain its goals. Work group effectiveness is the output or productive quality and quantity of the group as a collective unit. It is believed that climate for opportunity does not directly impact the organizational level, but instead is mediated by individual outcomes (e.g., turnover, performance). Since the organization is comprised of individuals and work groups, any negative impacts that occur at those levels will eventually be transmitted to the larger organization. Employees who perceive a negative climate for opportunity are likely to be less committed and more likely to quit. If several individuals quit, work groups and organizations will experience the direct costs and possible performance decrement resulting from time lost and other expenses associated with replacing employees. The organization and the individuals contribute to the fulfilment of needs of the other (i.e., complementary congruence) or the organization and the individual share similar characteristics (i.e., supplementary congruence) (*Kristof*, 1996).

Committed employees are considered necessary to build better relationships with clients and customers, to learn more effectively, to be more adaptable to change and generally to work more efficiently. From the employee's perspective, organizational commitment can lead to career advancement, increased compensation and more intrinsically rewarding jobs.

A Visionary leader is also required to manage competing goals that may occur between quality and efficiency, between short- and long-term benefits to the organization, between various departments differing in focus (e.g., production, marketing, or sales) or between an individual orientation and a more global, organization-wide orientation. When constructing a problem, individuals may chose to ignore these competing goals, or may not even be aware that multiple goals exist. The latter is more likely to occur when problem construction occurs automatically and a more simple construction of the problem results. A business leader is required to reconcile these competing goals, redefining the problem in a way that would take these competing goals into account. Awareness of the existence of the competing goals will result in higher quality solutions as well as more creative solutions. The need to integrate multiple goals and take into account the restrictions that are placed because of conflicting goals may result in a more complex and innovative problem construction, leading to higher quality and more original solutions.

Strategy scholars have argued that managing knowledge effectively can provide firms with sustainable competitive advantages. Leaders are central to the process of managing knowledge effectively. Managing knowledge includes three key processes: creating, sharing and exploiting knowledge. Leaders are central to each of these processes at multiple levels of the firm. Examining the role of leadership in converting knowledge into competitive advantages is important to our understanding of leaders and organizations. Transformational leadership may be more effective at creating and sharing knowledge at the individual and group levels, while transactional leadership is more effective at exploiting knowledge at the organizational level. Leaders play a pivotal role in the process of managing organizational knowledge. Leaders provide vision, motivation, systems and structures at all levels of the organization that facilitate the conversion of knowledge into competitive advantages. Managing knowledge requires a conscious effort on the part of leaders at all levels of the organization to manage three key knowledge processes: creating, sharing and exploiting knowledge.

Leadership is usually defined as the process of influencing people to achieve organizational objectives (*McShane,* 2003). Successful leaders tend to create a climate within the work environment where they are able to assist employees to set and achieve individual, team and ultimately organizational objectives. Creating that climate involves working with employees to develop goals, celebrating the achievement of those goals and inculcating a positive performance ethic into the work environment. Thus the leadership climate in a workplace is a function of employee perceptions of leader behaviours.

The dimensions of climate for opportunity are also proposed to have a direct influence on work group cohesiveness (i.e., the unity or connectedness among group members). To the extent that work group members perceive that the distribution and processes for allocating rewards are fair, they are likely to be more attracted to the group. In contrast, negative climate for opportunity may lead individuals to withdraw from the group, reducing their connectedness to others and the overall cohesiveness of the group. The limited empirical work in this area supports this direct influence as is reflected in the review of related literature undertaken in Chapters 4, 5 and 6.

Organizational leaders are under pressure to find ways to increase creativity in their organizations due to increasing globalization, competition and pace of technological change. Leaders have at their disposal various means to influence creativity in their organizations.

With the shift from hierarchical organizations to flatter and team-based structures, the role of leaders has changed so as to become less concerned with the day-to-day work activities and more focused on the procurement of needed resources and developing and supporting a work environment that facilitates team success. Employees are increasingly working in locations separated by time and geographical location; this presents leaders with a new level of complexity when trying to foster creativity. In virtual work, the social and climate components of the organizational context are stripped away.

There has been a decline in the quest for universal leadership principles that apply equivalently across all cultures and focus has shifted on the increasing application of the dimensions of culture identified by *Hofstede* (1991) and others to describe variation in leadership styles, practices and preferences. The emergence of the field of cross-cultural leadership as a legitimate and independent field of endeavor is also reflected in this present research work.

1.2 DETERMINANTS OF LEADERSHIP

A number of forces affect the process of leadership, which can be enumerated as under:

1. *Organization structure*: It plays central role in facilitating and impeding leadership. In a centralized structure, where reporting is to one chair, leadership is going to make a lot of difference depending upon the quality of leadership. On the other hand, in a decentralized structure, where various departments work at cross-functional interests, synergy is difficult to achieve.
2. *Culture*: Culture is also a powerful enabler or blocker of leadership. Culture is norms of behaviour and shared values among a group of people. Values define how people live as they pursue their goals. Inconsistencies between shared values and values in practice destroy morale and commitment and leads to preventing effective leadership.
3. *Systems*: Organizations are complex living systems. The relationship between many parts is as important as the parts themselves. Information technology is also vital to make effective leadership.
4. *People:* People are the most critical component of effective leadership. People create new ideas, courage and passion. Organizational values and structures are created by people. Their values and norms constitute the organisation's culture. People produce resources and allocate them. It is the relationship between people that actually makes leadership happen.

1.2.1 Approaches to Leadership

There have been numerous approaches to leadership. However, *leadership can be thought of as a process whereby an individual influences a group of individuals to achieve a common goal* (*Northouse,* 1997). Thus, primary function of a leader is motivating, inspiring and empowering their employees. Leadership can be described in terms of quality, quantity and spread.

1. Trait Approach

This approach began in the early 1900's. It attempted to identify personal characteristics of effective leaders. The most identified leadership properties are urgency, conscientiousness, agreeableness, adjustment and intelligence. This approach was first mentioned by Sir Francis Gatton in his book "Hereditary Genius" (1860). He believed that leaders possessed the same qualities which are due to generic characteristics or hereditary of family. Specific personality traits were investigated including 'wisdom' and 'courage'. However this approach was short-lived.

2. Behavioural Approach

This approach was characterized by research conducted at Personal Research Board at Ohio State University and the University of Michigan. This approach categorized the leadership behaviour on two dimensions: one on human relations and other on job itself. Blake & Mouton named it as 'Managerial Grid' and later on as 'Leadership Grid.' Behavioural Approach suggests that the ideal leader is one who has high concern for the work that needs to be done and the people who accomplish that work.

However these two types of behaviour, task-oriented and people-oriented were not sufficient to explain important organizational outcomes. *Lewin et. al.* (1939) studied the impact of three different styles ranging from autocratic to democratic. Morale was best under democratic but productivity was greatest under autocratic leadership.

3. Situational Contingency Approach

This approach was developed in 1960s. This approach holds that situation is also responsible for making any leadership behaviour effective. For a leader to be effective there must be an appropriate fit between the leader's behaviour and conditions of the situation. Situation plays a vital role in determining leader effectiveness. Leader must behave differently in different situations. Fiedler's LPC (least preferred co-worker) construct tries to explain this approach. The same leader produces greater or lesser effectiveness depending upon three situational factors: Quality of leader-member liking, the degree of task structure and the position power of the leader.

But the researches, however, were inclusive. After LPC; 'path goal' and 'decision-making' theories of leadership were developed. Path goal theory is derived from *Varoom's* (1964) expectancy motivation theory. It explains how leaders motivate followers to achieve personal and organizational goals by striking a balance between the characteristics of subordinates and the tasks. According to *Northouse* (1997) leaders motivate employees by selecting an appropriate leadership style that provides necessary stimulation to employees in a particular work setting.

These theories suggested that effectiveness of the leader depends upon his judgment of situation rather than continuing a single style. It proposed that it is the responsibility of leader to evaluate the situation and then motivate subordinates to exert maximum to achieve organizational goals. This approach recognizes the subordinates' self-control depending upon the characteristics of followers and situation.

Tannenbaum & Schidmt (1958) developed the situational contingency approach. Their findings indicated that an effective leadership style in a given situation depends upon the characteristics of leader, manager and the situation.

Path goal theory suggests that leader's attitude affect subordinates' job satisfaction. Leadership style is dependent upon the task to be done and characteristics of the employee who has to do the task.

Yukl (2002) devised multiple linkage models to demonstrate the effect of leadership styles and situational factors on work performance. These models tried to explain leadership process in a group setting.

The most recent contingency theory was developed by *Fiedler* (1967). According to this theory, effectiveness of leadership style is a function of leader's character and the leadership situation.

4. Reciprocal Approach to Leadership

This approach focuses on the interaction between leaders

and the followers. It has two types of leadership styles: Transactional and Transformational.

Transactional approach focuses on behaviours used to influence followers. It uses rewards and punishment to influence employee behaviour. Transactional leadership focuses on exchanges between leaders and followers. Leader achieves their goals while followers receive award for job performance. It helps organization to run smoothly and efficiently. It emphasizes compliance with rules to control and maintain stability rather than promoting change. Satisfied followers have high morale are confident and more productive.

Transactional leadership is measured with two dimensions: contingent reward and management by exertion. Transactional leadership is the exchange of something valued between leader and the follower. "Leaders approach followers with an eye towards exchanging" (*Burns,* 1978). Transactional leader "mostly consider, how to marginally improve and maintain the quantity and quality of performance, how to reduce resistance to particular action and how to implement decisions" (*Bass,* 1985).

Transactional leaders .aspire to achieve consistent performance that meets agreed upon goals. According to *Bass* (1985), transactional leaders have three characteristics:

1. They work to develop clear, specific goals and ensure that workers get the reward for achieving these goals.
2. They exchange reward for workers' efforts.
3. They are responsive to the needs of workers only if they could be met while getting the work done.

On the other hand, transformational approach is focused on effect of leader on followers. It involves shifts in the beliefs, needs and the values of followers. Transformational leadership raises the efforts and moral aspirations of followers. Transformational leaders are attentive to the needs and motives of the followers and inspire them to go beyond their self-interests for the betterment of organizations. Transformation leader make vision of the future and communicate that vision to followers to achieve it without resenting the painful process of change. They inspire followers to identify with the mission while motivating them to work together to achieve higher performance.

Transformational leadership is measured through three dimensions: charisma, individualized consideration and intellectual stimulation. *Bass* (1985), *Schein* (1985) and *Khunert and Lewis* (1987) investigated the interaction between leaders and followers and concluded that transformational leadership results in leader effectiveness. The leader meets the needs of the follower and helps followers to grow both professionally and emotionally.

Transformational leaders "attempt and succeed in raising colleagues, subordinates and followers to a greater awareness about the issues of consequences. This heightening of awareness requires a leader with vision, self-confidence and inner strength to agree successfully for what he or she sees as right or good, not for what is popular or is acceptable according to established wisdom of the time" (*Bass*, 1985).

Transformational leadership "results in a high level of follower motivation and commitment and well above-average performance, especially under the condition of crisis or uncertainty" (*House & Aditya*, 1977).

Transformational leaders are able to rise their subordinates above their own self-interest and give extra efforts to achieve the organization's mission.

Conger & Kanungo (1998) defined transformational leadership as a behaviour and effect that motivate subordinates for exceptional performance. They create an atmosphere to create and share knowledge.

1.2.2 Leadership Styles

Pearce & Conger (2003) outlined four types of leadership styles, namely *Directive Leadership, Transactional Leadership, Transformational Leadership and Empowering Leadership.*

1. Directive Leadership

Leaders establish followers as compliant subordinate. They give command and direction to achieve assigned goals and rely on fear of punishment to get work done. Followers are not allowed to participate in decision-making and have no discretion over the tasks to be performed. These leaders are self-centered and power-oriented. They keep tight control over subordinates. They keep all information to themselves. They are insensitive to their subordinates' need and try to manipulate them. These leaders are generally ineffective in the long-run.

This style is based on theory X management style (*McGregor,* 1960), initiating structure behaviour of Ohio state studies and punishment research (*Arvey & Ivancevitch,* 1980). Directive leadership is the process of commanding others to do what the leader wishes them to do (*Sims & Manz,* 1996). The leader possesses full authority and is the fountain source of wisdom and direction. The followers are just instruments of the leaders through which he ensures task completion. The leaders make the followers aware of what is expected from them in terms of organizational obligation. Employees do not realize the contribution of their work to the firm's goals, but they blindly follow the direction of the leaders.

Transactional Leadership: *Howell & Avdio* (1993) defined this as "leader-follower relationship based on series of exchanges or bargains between leader and followers." Here the followers obey the wishes of leaders in expectation of economic and social rewards. The main focus of this leadership style is on setting goals, clarifying the link between performance and rewards and providing timely and accurate feedback to the followers on tasks. This style is based on expectancy theory (*Vroom,* 1964), path-goal theory (*House,* 1971), exchange-equity theory (*Adams,* 1963) and reinforcement theory (*Luthans & Kreitner,* 1985).

Lepak & Snell (1999) suggested that this type of relationship is reciprocal in which both sides act on a give and take principle. This relationship is continued as long as both sides benefit from each other. Transactional leader tries to motivate employees through incentives. Incentives are performance boosters. The essence of transactional leadership stems from providing appropriate rewards to followers who perform the work.

According to *Hollander & Julian* (1969), the transactional leaders fulfil the expectations and achieves group goal by providing rewards to the employees. Employees in return show heightened responsiveness to the leaders. This style is an effective way as it meets the employee's expectation for a fair reward and efficiently achieves the organization's objectives.

2. *Transformational Leadership*

Such leaders stimulate followers to transcend their own self-interest for a higher collective purpose, mission or vision. Transformational leaders concentrate their efforts on long-term goals, emphasize the vision and inspire followers to pursue the vision and induce trust and commitment. This style is based on sociology of charisma (charismatic leadership theory).

Effective transformational leaders articulate ideological goal, communicate high expectations and confidence in subordinates. They transform followers to seek higher levels of needs such as self-actualization. According to *Bass* (1999), transformational leaders achieve alignment with leader's vision through consensus inspiration, identification and individualization.

These leaders want to change the way the group works. They are interested in doing things in a better way. They do so by motivating subordinates to give their best to the organization. They make subordinates sacrifice their personal interest for the sake of organizational interests. They bring about growth and effectiveness in the organization.

Transformational leaders vision, plan and frame activities of their organization to give meaning and purpose to action they demand from followers. They take risk to reach unconventional goals. They are high on self-esteem, self-confidence and have high degree of concern for employees' needs. They have an ability to read reactions of followers quickly and accurately.

3. *Empowering Leadership*

These leaders consult their subordinates; encourage them for participation and decision-making. They treat them on equal footings and prefer to work in teams. Here leader empowers the followers to make their own decision, develop their self-control, innovate and act on their own. The leader fosters constructive thinking pattern and habits through self-discipline, enjoyment and motivation at work. They promote mutual trust and cooperation. This style is effective when subordinates are trained and experienced, prefer to work on their own and have respect and trust for others. This style is based on social cognitive theory (*Bandura,* 1986) participative goal setting (*Locke & Latham,* 1990) and self-leadership theory (*Manz & Sims,* 1980).

The empowering leadership emphasizes the development of self-management skills. The empowering leader makes the followers discover their own capabilities and develop the required ones to the fullest. Such empowering leaders (i) encourage opportunity thinking, (ii) emphasize self-leadership, (iii) employ participative decision-making (iv) foster decision-making, and (v) facilitate the transition of follower to self-leader. Employees become more competent in organization. They develop a spirit of continuous improvement, have a strong sense of ownership and responsibility in their work and are highly committed to organization.

As there is less control and more autonomy at work, employees are internally motivated in their work. Due to culture of self-leadership, there are agreed upon values, believes and norms that give rise to imitativeness, responsibility-taking and self-improvement. Empowering leadership also encourage participation which ensures commitment and involvement at work.

1.2.3 Leadership Styles as a Function of Emotional Competence

Joseph (2003) identified nine leadership styles as a function of the emotional competencies of the leader.

1. *Principle centered leadership:* This style lays emphasis on compliance with the proven principles, rules and regulations. It is also labeled as 'bureaucratic style' where leaders want all the rules and procedures to be followed. They don't believe in any quick fix or ready-made solution to organizational and human relation problem. There are fundamental statements for every problem based on some principles which are as real as natural laws.

2. *Entrepreneurial leadership:* These leaders take risks to achieve organizational goals. They want to bring changes in existing styles to increase productivity and increase satisfaction of the subordinates. They believe in management by objectives. They provide proper feedback to the subordinates so that they can proceed along the chosen path.
3. *The servant leader*: This concept was developed by *Greenleaf* (1988). Here the basic purpose of the leader is to provide service to the followers as well as organization. He works with a natural feeling of serving others.
4. *Transformational leader*: *Burns* (1978) identified this style. These leaders raise subordinates to revolutionary heights to bring about change. They yearn for constant innovation. They are ambitious by nature.
5. *Transactional leaders:* Such leaders provide contingent reward to reinforce desirable behaviour and to curb undesirable behaviour. They are responsible and reliable. They minutely check the details to ensure that everything goes as desired. They consult rules and procedures for handling conflicts and problems based on past experience. But in case of new problems they are not desirable.
6. *Empowering leadership:* This style evolved from Japanese style of management and is based on the concept of power sharing and participation of the subordinates in decision-making. The head does not act as the boss but helps in coordinating and facilitating decision-making in a group.
7. *Charismatic leaders:* They have emotional effect on the followers. They are heroes and role models for the subordinates and gain a position of higher than life by the followers. They become the leader effortlessly and without any legitimate authority. Gandhi Ji can be cited as an embodiment of charismatic leadership.
8. *Visionary leaders:* According to *Bennis* (1992) visionary leaders are appropriate for the organization at the time of change. They set standards of excellence and reflect high targets. They give direction to subordinates to

achieve those standards. They reflect the uniqueness of the ideas to the subordinates and win their acceptance.

9. *Strategic leadership:* An organization maintains position in a competitive environment through strategic leadership. It includes all the basic managerial functions of planning, organizing, leading and controlling. The leader plans organization's strategies, organize, execute and control them. It involves the process of strategy formulation, implementation and evaluation.

1.2.4 Theories of Leadership

1. *Implicit leadership theory*: This theory is propounded by *Lord, Foti & De Vader* (1984). According to this theory there are certain traits that differentiate leaders from leaders and followers. In essence implicit leadership theories are mental models or schemes of leadership. An individual is labeled as 'leader' if he has close resemblance to traits like sensitivity, dedication, tyranny, charisma, attractiveness, masculinity, intelligence and strength (*Offerman et. al.*, 1994). These leadership schemes may cause individuals to selectively attend to, encode and retrieve schema consistent information.
2. *Attachment theory*: According to this theory proposed by *Bowlby* (1969), treatment of child during infancy period and afterwards is responsible for his behaviour as a leader. Three types of leader behaviours are expected because of attachment theory:

   (a) *Secure attachment style*: Consistent parental attachment and responsiveness gives rise to secure adults who perceive themselves as worthy of love. They mature into high self-esteemed individual and are liked by co-workers.

   (b) *Anxious ambivalent style*: Results from inconsistent parental attachment. Such children do no receive constant attention of their parents or guardian. They devise strategies to hold their attention.

They mature into adults who attempt to hold on to others. They have low self-esteem. Followers some time find this clinginess aversive and seek to distance themselves from the leader.

(c) *Avoidant style*: This type of individual's results when there is consistent non-availability and responsiveness of the parents. These types of adults prefer to work alone and get bored and distant during interaction. They develop self-reliance strategies that result in hostile and conflictual relations with peers.

1.2.5 Leadership Behaviour

Stordeur et. al. (2001) opined that leaders who enable employees to participate in decision-making and encourage communication among subordinates generate favourable work culture. QWL among such organization is highly characterized by less interpersonal conflicts and hostility and less non-cooperative relationships. Leader makes things happen. He relies on commitment not on control. He needs to be a change leader. Moving people towards adaptive work will be the mark of leadership. He creates an awareness and feeling of belongingness among the employs that each and every employee is an invaluable asset to the organization. Leaders are required for inspiration, goal and need for improvement.

Leadership is about making things happen. It is about change or getting other people creates change. It occurs at all levels of organizational process. Leadership is a function of time and environmental complexity and uncertainty. External factors demand certain attributes at a given point of time to be a successful leader and entirely different set of attributes at some other time. Choosing right people and having faith in their capabilities are two essential factors of a successful leader.

Leadership is a process that moves people in direction that is genuinely in their real long-term interest. It is a human activity that involves building and maintaining relationships. Leadership is the result of interaction among leader, the follower and leadership situation. The main challenge for leaders are to build a long-term vision, to increase commitment, to build teams and coalitions in order to create required organisational changes.

Leader is a person who is able to unite people and under whose influence people willingly come together to achieve common organizational goals in the best possible way. He is a role model for his followers. The yardstick for the leader's character is how he uses those powers vested in him for which he will never be questioned. He should have the ability to change and shape things and rise up to the occasion.

Leaders' behaviour has a profound impact on developing organisation's culture and to exert a direct influence upon subordinates' behaviour. Superiors who enable employees to participate more in decision-making and who encourage a two-way communication process tend to generate a favourable climate among their team, characterised by less interpersonal conflict and hostility and fewer non-cooperative relationships (*Stordeur et. al.*, 2001).

Within the vast body of leadership literature, four major themes have emerged. Some researchers have concentrated on leader traits or competencies, while others have considered the behaviour of leaders. In the 1970s, situational or contingency approaches to understanding leadership became popular and more recently researchers have investigated the antecedents and consequences of transformational leadership.

Each of these streams of research has made and continues to make, a valid contribution to the understanding of leadership. Attempts to identify particular traits or competencies common to effective leaders have not always produced consistent results, but some competencies such as integrity and emotional intelligence continue to attract the attention of researchers. An understanding of leader traits and competencies is necessary for leaders to apply the most effective leadership strategies in different contingencies or situations. Transformational leadership which involves creating, communicating and modeling an organizational vision and generating commitment to that vision among followers, has helped to clarify the dynamics of leadership during strategic organizational change activities.

Until the 1980s most leadership research focused on transactional leadership. Today transformational leadership is viewed as the most prominent topic in the current research and theories of leadership (*Bass*, 1998). *Burns* (1978) used the term transforming leadership to refer to individuals who not only recognize the existing needs of potential followers, but go further; seeking to satisfy higher needs to engage the full person of the follower in terms of Maslow's hierarchy of needs. By definition, transformational leadership involves strong personal identification with the follower (*Bass*, 1985). Such leaders create a shared vision with the follower by articulating new opportunities, inspiring members and obtaining their commitment to the leader's vision of the group and organization.

Bass's (1985) transformational leadership has four components: charisma, inspirational motivation, intellectual stimulation and individualized consideration.

Charismatic leaders are extraordinarily gifted people who gain the respect, pride, trust and confidence of followers by transmitting a strong sense of vision and mission. Such leaders excite, arouse and inspire their followers, such that the relationship between the leader and follower is one based on personal understanding as opposed to one based on formal, institutional rules, regulations, rewards or punishments. Their communication style is effective because it encompasses powerful non-verbal tactics that mobilize followers into action by linking present behaviour to past events.

Inspirational motivation is concerned with a leader setting higher standards, thus becoming a sign of reference. Such leaders provide an emotional appeal to increase awareness and understanding of mutually desired goals among followers. Inspirational leaders behave in ways that motivate and inspire those around them by providing meaning and challenge to followers' work. Such leaders also demonstrate self-determination and commitment to attaining objectives and present an optimistic and achievable view of the future.

Intellectually stimulating leaders challenge followers to think critically. Such leaders provide followers with challenging new ideas and encourage them to break away from the old ways of thinking. As a result, followers under intellectually stimulating leaders who are likely to alter their ways of thinking, are critical in their problem-solving and tend to have enhanced thought processes (*Dubinsky et. al.*, 1995).

Individualized consideration is concerned with developing followers by coaching and mentoring. A leader displaying individualized consideration pays special attention to each individual's abilities, aspirations and needs to enhance followers' confidence in responding to problems facing them and their organizations. By providing mentoring and one-to-one communication such leaders are able to build a sense of determination, self-confidence and affective organizational commitment, which describes an individual's psychological attachment to an organization through such feelings as loyalty, affection and belonging in their followers.

Leadership behaviour is defined as the ability of a leader to influence subordinates in performing at the highest level within an organizational framework (*Ivancevich & Matteson*, 1993). *Weierter* (1997) noted in addition that attribution processes are situationally bound. The leader behaviours previously described may be perceived and interpreted differently depending on the political norms of the situation. Since leadership is a process, it can be viewed as ongoing, where members are continuously perceiving their leaders and reevaluating their relationship based on prior and current interactions as they occur.

Fleishman et. al. (1953) at The Ohio State University isolated two styles for measuring leadership behaviour: initiating structure and consideration. The initiating structure leadership style involves behaviour in which the leader organizes and defines the relationships in the group. The leader dictates how the job is performed. The consideration leadership style involves behaviour indicating friendship and respect between the leader and other subordinates.

Consideration is the degree to which a leader acts in a friendly and supportive manner, shows concern for subordinates and looks out for their well-being. Initiating structure is the degree to which a leader defines and structures his or her own role and the roles of subordinates toward attainment of the group's formal goals. Transformational or charismatic leadership adds to these behaviours by introducing the visionary aspect of leadership as well as the emotional involvement of employees within the organization.

Some of the conditions that appear to moderate leader effects include : (1) the creativity of followers; (2) work group processes including clarity of objectives, emphasis on quality, emphasis on participation and support for innovation; (3) leader control of rewards; (4) job characteristics such as job complexity and challenge; and (5) organizational climate and structure.

Holdnak et. al. (1993) found two correlations between a leader's behaviour style and job satisfaction. They found a positive relationship between the consideration style and job satisfaction, suggesting that a leader who uses consideration in leadership has a positive impact on subordinates' job satisfaction. They also found a negative relationship between initialing structure behaviour and job satisfaction, suggesting that leaders who use an initiating structure style will see a decrease in their employees' level of job satisfaction.

Thus, leaders who work by assigning tasks, specifying procedures and clarifying expectations help in reduced role ambiguity and increased job satisfaction among employees. Leaders who are perceived to closely monitor their subordinates in order to prevent mistakes tend to evoke higher levels of emotional exhaustion among their staff (*Stordeur et. al.*, 2001).

Childers et. al. (1990) illustrated a strong and positive relationship between the consideration style and job satisfaction. Highly significant positive relationship between consideration leadership behaviour and job satisfaction and a negative relationship between initiating structure leadership behaviour and job satisfaction was reported.

Conger & Kanungo (1998) and *Yukl* (2002) identified five elements of effective leadership, namely : (1) develop collective goals; (2) instill knowledge and appreciation of work; (3) generate motivation and build trust; (4) encourage flexibility; and (5) maintain meaningful organizational identity.

McGregor (1960) summed up two opposing attitudes managers may have towards their subordinates. One view is that people only work in the ways and to the extent that they are induced to do so by their managers. McGregor argued that this was the prevailing management attitude and "the principles of organization which comprise the bulk of the literature of management could only have been derived from assumptions such as these". The opposing view is that work is a primary source of satisfaction and fulfilment for most people. Managers who hold these assumptions will naturally behave very differently in their interactions with employees, creating a climate of 'integration' in which members of an organisation can "achieve their own goals best by directing their efforts toward the success of the enterprise."

Singh & Pestonjee (1974) studied the detrimental effect of supervisory behaviour on job satisfaction of workers. Supervisor's orientation schedule determines the production-oriented and employees-oriented style of supervision. Job satisfaction scores, social relations area scores and management area scores were higher under employee centered supervision. Job and personal adjustment areas are not influenced by supervisory orientation.

Rao (1975) investigated the relationship between interpersonal trust and leadership style, job satisfaction and performance in small-scale industries. Interpersonal trust of owner manager is related with consideration and structure. Interpersonal trust is also related with employee's satisfaction with motivation and hygiene factors. It is also positively related to employee's performance. Both employees and management are agreed upon the consideration style of leadership.

Northouse (1997) defined leadership "as a process whereby an individual influences a group of individuals to achieve a common goal." The leader builds long-team vision, increase commitment, build teams and alliances to achieve organizational objectives. Leaders motivate, inspire and empower their subordinate.

Ivancevich & Matteson (1993) defined leadership as the "ability of a leader to influence subordinates in performing at the highest level with an organizational framework".

Adler (1991) has defined leadership "as the ability to inspire and influence the thinking, attitudes and behaviours of other people." It is the ability to help others meet their goals.

According to *Rost* (1991), "leadership is a particular form of social relationships." It is process of people working together to benefit the common goal. Leadership is about motivating people to change.

For the present study, leadership behaviour as manifested by *Kouzes & Pozner* (1995) was considered appropriate. According to these authors, "leadership is the art of mobilizing others to want to struggle for shared aspirations." Thus leadership behaviour is exhibited in establishing a culture with values that influences others to strongly desire, mobilize and struggle for a shared vision.

Yukl (1994) has opined that leadership is independent set of behaviours, namely, consideration and initiating structure. This classification of leadership behaviour forms the basis of the present study. Consideration is a people-related behaviour, defined as "the degree to which a leader act in a friendly and supportive manner, shows concern for subordinates and looks out for their welfare" (*Yukl,* 1994). Leaders high on consideration index have been found to concentrate on the physical and psychological needs of the employees. Initiating structure behaviours are more task-oriented and have been defined as "the degree to which a leader defines and structures his or her own role and the role of subordinates towards the attainment of the group's formal goals." Leaders high on initiating structure provide direction and describe goals. This style focuses less on employee's feelings and more on creating efficiently performing job tasks.

The initiating structure involves behaviour in which leader organizes and defines relationships in the group (*Fleishman,* 1973). Leader dictates how the job is performed. The consideration leadership style involves behaviour indicating friendship and respect between the leader and the subordinate.

References

Adams, J.S. (1963): "Wage Inequities, Productivity and Work Wet Quality." *Industrial Relations,* Vol. 3, pp. 916.

Adler, N.J. (1991): *International Dimensions of Organizational Behaviour,* Boston, MA: Kent.

Arvey, R.D. & Ivancevitch, J.M. (1980): "Punishment in Organizations: A Review, Propositions and Research Suggestions", *Academy of Management Review,* Vol. 5, pp. 123–32.

Bandura, A. (1986): *Social foundations of thought and Action: A Social Cognitive Theory,* Englewood Cliffs, New Jersy: Prentice-Hall.

Barney, J.B. (1991):."Firm Resources and Sustained Competitive Advantage." *Journal of Management,* Vol. 17, pp. 99-120.

Bass, B.M. (1985): *Leadership and Performance Beyond Expectations,* New York: The Free Press.

Bass, B.M. (1998): *Transformational Leadership: Industrial, Military and Educational Impact,* Lawrence Erlbaum, Mahwah, New Jersy.

Bass, B.M. (1999): "On the Taming of Charisma: A Reply to Janice Beyer." *Leadership Quarterly,* Vol. 10, pp. 541–53.

Bennis, W. (1992): *Visionary Leadership,* Jossey-Bass Publishers, San Francisco, p. 29.

Bowlby, J. (1969): "Attachment and Loss." Vol. 1, New York: Basic Books.

Burns, J.M. (1978): *Leadership,* New York: Harper & Row.

Childers, T.L., Dubinsky, A.J. and Skinner, S.J. (1990): "Leadership Substitutes as Moderators of Sales Supervisory Behaviour", *Journal of Business Research,* Vol. 21, pp. 363-82.

Conger, J.A. and Kanungo, R.N. (1998): *Charismatic Leadership in Organizations,* Thousand Oaks, CA: Sage.

Dubinsky, A.J., Yammarino, F.J., Jolson, M.A. and Spangler, W.D. (1995): "Transformational Leadership: An Initial Investigation in Sales Management", *Journal of Personal Selling and Sales Management,* Vol. 15, pp. 17-31.

Fiedler, F.E. (1967): *A Contingency Model of Leadership Effectiveness,* New York: McGraw-Hill.

Fleishman, E.A. (1953): "The Measurement of Leadership Attitude in Industry", *Journal of Applied Psychology,* Vol. 38, pp. 153-58.

Fleishman, E.A. (1973): "Twenty Years of Consideration and Structure", In: Fleishman, E.A. and Hunt, J.G. Editors, *Current Developments in the Study of Leadership,* Southern Illinois University Press, Carbondale, IL, pp. 1–37.

Greenleaf, R. (1988): *Spirituality as Leadership,* Greenleaf Center for Servant-Leadership, Indiana Polis.

Greenleaf, R. (1988): *Spirituality as Leadership,* Greenleaf Center for Servant-Leadership, Indiana Polis.

Hofstede, G. (1991): *Culture and Organizations: Software of the Mind.* London: McGraw-Hill.

Holdnak, B.J., Harsh, J. and Bushardt, S.C. (1993): "An Examination of Leadership Style and its Relevance to Shift Work in an Organizational Setting", *Health Care Management Review,* Vol. 18, pp. 21-30.

Hollander, E.P. and Julian, J.W. (1969): "Contemporary Trends in the Analysis of Leadership Process", *Psychological Bulletin,* Vol. 71, pp. 387-97.

House, R.J. (1971): "A Path-goal theory of Leadership Effectiveness", *Administrative Science Quarterly,* Vol. 16, pp. 321-38.

House, R.J. and Aditya, R.N. (1997): "The Social Scientific Study of Leadership: Quo vadis?" *Journal of Management,* Vol. 23, pp. 409-73.

Howell, J.M. and Avolio, B.J. (1993): "Transformational Leadership, Transactional Leadership, Locus of Control and Support for Innovation: Key Predictors of Consolidate–business-unit Performance", *Journal of Applied Psychology,* Vol. 78, pp. 891-902.

Ivancevich, J.M. and Matteson, M.T. (1993): *Organisational Behaviour and Management* (3rd ed.), Boston: Irwin.

Joseph, P.T. (2003): "Leadership Styles and Emotional Competencies: An Exploratory Study", *Journal of Academy of Business and Economics*, 1 April.

Khunert, R. and Lewis, G. (1987): "Transactional and Transformational Leadership: A Constructive/Developmental Analysis", *Academy of Management Review*, Vol. 12 (4), pp. 648-57.

Kristof, A.L. (1996): "Person-organization fit: An Integrative Review of its Conceptualizations, Measurements and Implications", *Personnel Psychology*, Vol. 49, pp. 1-49.

Kouzes, J.M. and Pozner, B.Z. (1995): *The Leadership Challenges: How to Keep Getting Extraordinary Things Done in Organisations*, San Francisco: Jossey-Bass.

Lepak, D.P. and Snell, S.A. (1999): "The Human Resource Architecture: Towards a Theory of Human Capital Allocation and Development", *Academy of Management Review*, Vol. 24, pp. 31-48.

Lewin, K., Lippit, R. and White, R.K. (1939): "Patterns of Aggressive Behaviour in Experimentally Created Social Climates." *Journal of Social Psychology*, Vol. 10, pp. 271-99.

Locke, E.A. and Latham, G.P. (1990): *A Theory of Goal Setting and Task Performance*, Englewood Cliffs, New Jersy: Prentice-Hall.

Lord, R.G., Foti, R.J. and De Vader, C.L. (1984): "A Test of Leadership Categorization Theory: Internal Structure, Information Processing and Leadership Perceptions", *Organisational Behaviour and Human Performance*, Vol. 34, pp. 343-78.

Luthans, F. and Kreitner, R. (1985): *Organizational behaviour modification and beyond*, Glenview, IL: Scott-Foresman.

Manz, C.C. and Sims, H.P. Jr. (1980): "Self-management as a substitute for leadership: A Social Learning Theory Perspective", *Academy of Management Review*, Vol. 5, pp. 361-67.

McGregor, D. (1960): *The Human Side of Enterprise*, (25th Anniversary ed.) McGraw-Hill, New York.

McShane, S.L. and Travaglione, A. (2003): *Organisational Behaviour on the Pacific Rim*, McGraw-Hill Australia Pty. Ltd., Roseville, pp. 466–82.

Northouse, P.G. (1997): *Leadership: Theory and Practice*, USA: SAGE Publications.

Offermann, L.R., Kennedy, J.K. and Wirtz, P.W. (1994): "Implicit Leadership Theories: Content, Structure and Generalizability", *The Leadership Quarterly*, Vol. 5(1), pp. 43-58.

Pearce, C.L. and Conger, J.A. (2003): *Shared leadership: Reframing the hows and whys of Leadership*, Thousand Oaks, CA: Sage.

Rao, S.G.V. (1975): "Interpersonal Trust and Correlates as Perceived By Superior And Subordinates", *Indian Journal of Industrial Relations*, Vol. 10(3), pp. 359-69.

Rost, J.C. (1991): *Leadership for the Twenty-first Century*, New York, Praeger.

Schein, E.H. (1985): *Organizational Culture and Leadership: A Dynamic View*, San Francisco: Jossey-Bass.

Sims, H.P. Jr. and Manz, C.C. (1996): *Company of heroes: unleashing the power of self-leadership*, Wiley, New York.

Singh, A.P. and Pestonjee, D.M. (1974): "Supervisory Behaviour and Job Satisfaction", *Indian Journal of Industrial Relations*, Vol. 9(3), pp. 407-16.

Stordeur, S., D'hoore, W. and Vandenberghe, C. (2001): "Leadership, Organizational Stress and Emotional Exhaustion among Nursing Hospital Staff", *Journal of Advanced Nursing,* Vol. 35 (4), pp. 533-42.

Tannenbaum, R. and Schmidt, W.H. (1958): "How to Choose A Leadership Pattern", *Harvard Business Review,* Vol. 36(2), pp. 95-101.

Vroom, V.H. (1964): *Work and Motivation,* Wiley, New York.

Weierter, S.J.M. (1997): "Who Wants to Play Follow the Leader? A Theory of Charismatic Relationships based on Routinized Charisma and Follower Characteristics", *The Leadership Quarterly,* Vol. 8, pp. 171-93.

Yukl, G.A. (1994): *Leadership in organizations* (3rd ed.), Englewood Cliffs, New Jersy, Prentice-Hall.

Yukl, G.A. (2002): *Leadership in Organizations,* (5th ed.), Upper Saddle River, New Jersy, Prentice-Hall.

CHAPTER

2

Dynamics of Developments in Organisational Commitment

2.1 ORGANISATIONAL COMMITMENT

". . . The basic philosophy, spirit and drive of an organization have far more to do with its relative achievements than do technological or economic resources, organizational structure, innovation and timing. All these things weigh heavily in success. But they are, I think, transcended by how strongly the people in the organization believe in its basic precepts and how faithfully they carry them out."

—Thomas J. Watson, Jr.,
(A Business and its Beliefs—
The ideas that helped build IBM).

2.2 NEED AND IMPORTANCE OF DEVELOPING ORGANISATIONAL COMMITMENT

Organizational commitment is characterized by an individual's: (1) belief in and acceptance of organizational goals and values; (2) willingness to exert effort towards organizational goal accomplishment; and (3) strong desire to maintain organizational membership (*Porter et. al.*, 1974). Commitment research has shown that people are more likely to develop higher levels of commitment when they can identify with the values and standards of the organization (*Wiener*, 1982). Retaining talent requires a strong dedication to not only understanding the needs of employees, but also to aligning staff needs with the mission and vision of the organisation so as to ensure employee commitment.

Commitment is an advance agreement to a contract; strong support by employees to their company and its goals. Organizational Commitment is the extent to which an employee is committed to an organisation. It has both *attitudinal component* (i.e. the degree to which individual identify with the goals of the firm) and *behavioural aspect* (i.e. the likelihood of an employee leaving the firm) and as such has been criticized for being a muddled concept. There are a number of standard scales for measuring commitment and they are employed using survey method *(Collin's Dictionary).*

However, managers have to realize that organizational commitment is not a substitute for good management. Organisational Commitment is a relative term and is based on the assumption that workers want more responsibility. Commitment is the result of sustained good people management. This means communicating organisational values clearly, ensuring support staff for line managers, training appropriately, managing fairly and paying equitably, etc.

Organizations that can successfully harness the commitment of their employees enjoy several distinct competitive advantages. They are able to execute their business strategies more successfully and are more flexible and adaptive to changing market conditions. They have an enhanced reputation in the market place and hence can attract and retain the best talent. They produce superior shareholder value through lower operating costs and higher revenues and profits. Their employees demonstrate higher levels of integrity, support customers and colleagues more effectively and align with the corporate strategies. Organisational and managerial support, commitment to developing individual potential, culture and values alignment as well as organisational competence are the top four drivers for engendering and maintaining employee commitment. Commitment has several components: compatibility of values, pride in the organisation, loyalty, job satisfaction and feeling fairly rewarded. Commitment must also be understood as a two-way process, involving responsibilities on the employer to develop and value employees.

The concept of organisational commitment envisions a positive relationship between a series of important organisational behaviours and outcomes such as intention to stay in an organisation and willing cooperation to organisational change. Further evidence indicates that organisational commitment scores can predict absenteeism (*Tett & Meyer,* 1993) and actual employee turnover trends (*Whitner & Walz,* 1993). The work of *Meyer, Allen & Smith* (1993) has broadened our understanding of the concept of organisational commitment from a one-dimensional concept to a multi-dimensional construct. According to them organisational commitment is conceptually made up of Affective, Normative and Continuance commitment.

Organizational commitment refers to "the relative strength of an individual's identification and involvement in a particular organization" (*Fierman,* 1994). Committed individuals identify with the company and are loyal to it. Organizational citizenship is the willingness of employees to engage in behaviours that help the organization achieves its goals. Such behaviours include helping co-workers with job-related activities, accepting orders willingly, tolerating temporary impositions without fussing and making sacrifices for the good of the company. Providing employees with the support they expect—effectively reciprocating their loyalty and trust—is fundamental to maintaining a committed workforce. Employees need to know that they have the support and trust of their employer, their efforts are recognized and rewarded and they have access to flexible work practices, if and when they need them.

Organization commitment is defined as the strength of an employee's identification with and involvement in the goals and values of an organization (*McNeese-Smith,* 2001). The greater the extent to which the organization can understand and fulfil employee's needs, the greater will be their motivation and commitment and their potential impact on business success.

Management commitment makes a difference to employment outcomes. Commitment to employment requires a change in the day-to-day behaviour of individual managers and management teams. Having committed and consistent manager results in organisational change that is quicker, deeper and more sustainable. This occurs particularly because management commitment is more likely to lead to greater loyalty and commitment being demonstrated by the subordinates.

Probably the most popular method of examining the concept is through an individual's attitudes and feelings towards his or her employing organization. *Legge* (1995) states that, "virtually all the research conducted on organizational commitment, *per se*, has used the attitudinal conceptualization". This conceptualization suggests that committed employees have a strong belief in and acceptance of the organization's goals and values, show a willingness to exert considerable effort on behalf of the organization and have a strong desire to maintain membership with the organization.

Organizational commitment is at the heart of human resource management and is a "central feature that distinguishes HRM from traditional personnel management" (*Guest*, 1995). Commitment is an internalized employee belief, often associated with 'soft HRM' and a high-trust organizational culture. It is thus, necessary that issues concerning employees must be integrated into core business activities, bringing changes in systems, work practices and expectations from the employees. Organisations have to ensure that the best people are employed and receive opportunities for advancement. Employees pay particular attention to management behaviour linked to respect, fairness, support, etc. These are key drivers of their own commitment and loyalty to the organisation. It is often said that an employee leaves a (bad) boss, not an organisation. Research shows that when managers demonstrate commitment, these get reflected in higher levels of organisational commitment among the subordinates. Managers need to understand the considerations that are most important for each employee and each employee group, in order that they can create a relationship that meets the employees' needs and hence create the basis for commitment. Behaviour is a function of an individual's underlying *motives* and the *situation* they find themselves in, Stress and dysfunctional, unproductive behaviours arise when there is fundamental mismatch between the two.

Organisational commitment is a multi-dimensional concept that has been interpreted in a variety of different ways. The main approaches appear to be affective, or attitudinal (*Buchanan,* 1974; *Mowday et. al.,* 1982; *Porter et. al.,* 1974), normative (*Allen & Meyer,* 1990; *Wiener & Vardi,* 1980), behavioural (*Staw & Salancik,* 1977) and calculative (*Becker,* 1960; *Ritzer & Trice,* 1969).

Committed employees approach work with high degree of enthusiasm. Employee commitment has a direct impact on productivity as committed employees create committed customers who are far more beyond customer loyalty. Organization commitment is more than a passive attachment to an organization. It is more stable and more global than employee satisfaction and is more related to the achievement of organization goals. Committed employees go beyond normal job requirement to achieve organizational objectives. The positive indicators of commitment are productivity and health. The more satisfied employees are with the job, the more they will produce and healthier they will be. The negative indicators of organizational commitments are absenteeism, sabotage and violence. These factors indicate low commitment towards organization.

It has been noted that those organizations wherein employees exhibit higher levels of organisational commitment, employees contribute in three distinct ways:

(a) *Persistence*—longer tenure, reduced absence, improved punctuality and reduced stress.
(b) *Citizenship*—more ethical behaviours, spontaneous ambassadorship, more proactive support for others and increased discretionary effort.
(c) *Performance*—greater productivity, enhanced customer service, improved quality and higher outputs.

Organizational commitment is the degree, attitude and personal property of the organizations resources to fulfil the group goal.

Perusal of existing literature has led to identification of ten fundamental needs that the majority of the employees are looking to satisfy through their occupations:

1. *Achievement*—performing to a high standard of excellence and meeting goals.
2. *Power*—having influence and control over others.
3. *Affiliation*—developing close harmonious relationships.
4. Meaning—operating in line with one's values and *making* a difference.
5. *Growth*—acquiring new skills, knowledge and building own capability.
6. *Status*—being recognized, admired and respected.
7. *Creativity*—being innovative and creative.
8. *Wealth*—acquiring possessions and having a high standard of living.
9. *Security*—having a solid and predictable future.
10. *Autonomy*—being independent and having decision-making responsibility.

Organizational commitment – efforts × ability and attributes × organizational support

2.3 DEFINING ORGANISATIONAL COMMITMENT

Organisational commitment is characterised by a belief in and acceptance of the organisation's goals and values, a willingness to exert considerable effort on behalf of the organisation and a strong desire to maintain membership in the organisation (*Mowday, Porter & Steers,* 1982). It also means practising the organisation's beliefs consistently. There are two fundamental conditions for organisational commitment. The first is having a sound set of beliefs. The second is faithful adherence to those beliefs with one's behaviour, i.e. "persistence with a purpose."

Johnston et. al. (1990) defined commitment as the degree that individuals attach themselves to, identify with and become part of an organisation. The positive effects of organisational commitment include personal sacrifice for the organisation, persistence in behaviours not dependent on rewards and a preoccupation with the organisation (*Scholl,* 1981) as well as a desire to see the firm prosper and be more effective (*Lawler,* 1979).

According to *Becker* (1960), organisational commitment is defined as "a structural phenomenon which occurs as a result of individual's organisational transactions and alterations in side-bets or investments over time."

Organizational commitment has been defined as the relative strength of an individual's identification and involvement in a particular organization (*Steers,* 1977).

Organizational commitment has been defined by *Mowday et. al.* (1982) as "the relative strength of an individual's identification with and involvement in a particular organization." *Mowday et. al.* (1979) see organizational commitment as a stable attitude, reflecting a general affective response towards the organization as a whole and consider behaviours that exceed formal or normative expectations to be overt manifestations of that commitment. Organizational commitment is more than just a passive attachment to an organization. Committed employees feel the need to go beyond normal job requirements in order to make a significant personal contribution to the organization.

Kobasa (1982) argues that commitment is a crucial personal resource that acts as a stress buffer by enabling individuals to attach direction and meaning to their work and to resist the effects of tension in their environments.

Commitment has four dimensions:

(a) *Needs fit*: the extent to which organization fulfills the respective needs affects commitment.
(b) *Extent of detachment*: extent to which employees are attracted towards outside options. More they are attracted, less is the commitment.
(c) *Extent of involvement*: it is the degree to which the employee cares about work. More is the involvement, more is commitment.
(d) *Ambivalence*: it is the confusion between alternatives available. Ambivalent employees are less committed to organization.

2.4 COMPONENTS OF ORGANISATIONAL COMMITMENT

The most popular recently cited theory is the three-factor model developed by *Meyer & Allen* (1991). These authors developed the construct of organizational commitment by bringing together three components of affective commitment, continuance commitment and normative commitment. Employees with strong affective commitment stay with an organization because they are emotionally attached to the organization. Employees with strong continuance commitment stay with an organization out of necessity and those with strong normative commitment because they feel obliged to do so.

Affective Organizational Commitment: It describes an individual's emotional attachment to an organization. The stronger the affective commitment, the more an individual identifies with, is involved in and enjoys membership in the organization. Affective commitment summarizes an individual's psychological state of "wanting to stay" with an organization (*Meyer & Allen,* 1997). *Affective Commitment (AC)* also includes the concept of involvement and identification with the organisation. Implicit in the concept is an acceptance of the organisation's goals and a willingness to exert effort and energy on behalf of the organisation. *Affective commitment* refers to the degree to which the employee identifies with, is involved in and is emotionally attached to the organisation. Affectively committed employees believe in the goals and values of the organisation and enjoy being a member of it. Employees with strong affective commitment remain with the organisation because they want to do so.

Alignment of values between employer and employee is true reflection of this type of commitment. "Where there is misalignment, employees become dissatisfied as they feel they are compromising their personal values relative to those of the organisation—a belief that can result in unnecessary emotional turmoil and angst. People need to fit the culture of the company—that is, they need to fit the organisation by virtue of their values and work preferences." It was crucial for an organisation's core values and behaviour to be clearly explained at the time of engagement and reinforced at every step of the employment relationship. Commitment results from a mutually fulfilling relationship between employer and employee. Commitment is not static but changes over time. Commitment needs to be established and maintained. Companies create a compelling employer brand and deliver it consistently and honestly. High commitment leads to superior performance.

Perceptions of organisation competence are also closely linked to employee commitment. People like to be proud of where they work but given that most of us work for organisations which aren't exactly household names, pride comes from the way the organisation is run, the way it handles change and its effectiveness at implementing projects.

Continuance Organizational Commitment: It describes the commitment that results from the perceived cost associated with leaving the organization. Continuance commitment summarizes an individual's psychological state of "having to stay" with an organization (*Meyer & Allen*, 1997). *Continuance Commitment (CC)* results from an employee's estimation of the cost to them of changing the employer and it is mediated by their perception of the availability of alternative suitable work elsewhere. *Continuance commitment* refers to the degree to which the employee recognizes that costs associated with leaving the organisation tie him or her to the organisation. Such employees remain within the organisation because they have to do so. Employees need to know that their organisation is committed to maximising their potential and know that their contribution is making a meaningful difference to the organization. The skill of a manager is to continuously set the level of challenge slightly above the level of the skill of the employee which means they are never in their comfort zone but always in a greater performance zone.

Normative Organizational Commitment: It describes an individual's feeling of obligation to remain with the organization. It can be summarized as an individual's psychological state of "moral obligation to stay" with an organization (*Meyer & Allen,* 1997). It is frequently seen as a personal value orientation rather than one which is influenced greatly by the actions of the organisation (*Finegan,* 2000). *Normative commitment* refers to the degree to which the employee feels an obligation to the organisation; staying within the organisation is the right and moral thing to do. Employees remain within the organisation because they feel they *ought* to do so. All components of commitment are positively related to the decision whether to stay or leave the organisation.

Professional commitment: Commitment to one's profession has not been studied as extensively as organisational commitment. However, it has been found to be an important component of different types of work-related commitment (*Cohen,* 1998). *Gardner* (1992) emphasized the importance of occupational commitment because it relates to the attractiveness of a profession as a lifelong occupational choice and valued career option.

In arriving at these definitions, *Meyer & Allen* (1997) examined the differences and similarities of descriptions from other researchers. In arguing for three separate types of commitment, *Allen & Meyer* (1990) offered: Affective, continuance and normative commitment are best viewed as disguisable components rather than types of attitudinal commitment; that is, employees can experience each of these psychological states to varying degrees. Some employees might feel both a strong need and a strong obligation to remain, but no desire to do so; others might feel neither a need nor obligation but a strong desire, and so on. The 'net sum' of a person's commitment to the organization, therefore, reflects each of these separable psychological states.

All three dimensions are relevant for judging the performance of a strategic change process because they tend to be positively related to organizational efficiency and effectiveness by contributing to resource transformations, innovativeness and adaptability (*Williams & Anderson,* 1991). According to procedural justice theory, members' commitment to an organization is heavily influenced by their perception of to what degree they receive fair treatment.

Sharma (1978) opined that tension and conflict in the industrial relation is due to the alienation of the Indian industrial worker. Workers' attitude and orientation towards company and job is not related to their socio-cultural background. However, worker attitude is influenced by industrial work, personal policies and practices, work technology and union involvement. Commitment was found not to be related to socio-cultural background or rural agricultural origin of the workers.

ISR research (2005) suggested that employee commitment is a binary concept, comprising two elements, one of which is a necessary condition for commitment, the other a sufficient condition. The *necessary* condition is *Retention.* That is, for whatever reason, employees intend to remain with their current employer rather than seeking employment elsewhere. The *sufficient* condition is *Recommendation.* That is, employees are not only motivated to stay with their current employer but also think highly enough of it to recommend to others that they join. ISR carried out a Cluster Analysis of their global database to see how these two elements of commitment interact in the workplace. In the cluster analysis, they grouped together employees who share similar views on particular dimensions of opinion. Based upon their findings, they developed four commitment clusters:

1. *The Engaged.* These employees fulfil both commitment conditions. They intend to stay with their company and they are sufficiently committed to and confident in it's future success to recommend to others that they join the party as well. It is estimated that engaged employees currently comprise 54% of the global workforce.
2. *The Cohabiting.* These employees think well enough of their company to recommend to others that they join but do not intend to stay themselves. As organizations move away from offering "jobs for life" to a focus on "employability" as a career strategy. Cohabiting employees currently are expected to comprise 14% of the global workforce.
3. *The Separated.* These employees think poorly of their companies, but do not intend to leave. Bound by financial ties, specialist skills, the absence of available alternatives or other circumstances they are "trapped". They would leave if they could, but they can't. They are physically tied to their companies, but mentally and emotionally "separated". These employees

currently are expected to comprise 16% of the global workforce.

4. *The Divorced.* These employees are about to become memories. They would not recommend to others that they join their company and are actively seeking to leave. They dislike it where they are and plan to move on. These employees currently comprise 16% of the global workforce.

2.5 DETERMINANTS OF ORGANISATIONAL COMMITMENT

Determinants are various factors that determine the degree of commitment in the organization. *Ashwathappa* (2001) classified these determinants as:

1. External conditions imposed on the organization which determines the organizational commitment. These include organizational strategy, authority structure, formal regulations, organizational resources, procurement of personnel, performance appraisal and reward system, organizational culture and physical work setting.
2. Group member resources including Ability, Personality and Characteristics.
3. Group structure includes Leadership, Role, Group size, Interpersonal compatibilities, Membership homogeneity and heterogeneity and Status congruence.
4. Group process, i.e. the communication pattern used by members for information exchange, group discussion processes, leader behaviour power dynamics and conflict interactions. Group processes are significant as they can create outputs greater than the sum of their inputs.

Critical appraisal of the literature has led to delineation of following parameters governing organisational commitment: (a) Power, (b) Achievement, (c) Affiliation, (d) Meaning,

(e) Growth, (f) Status, (g) Creativity, (h) Wealth, (i) Security, and (j) Autonomy.

Research studies have shown that organizations with high levels of commitment provide employees with opportunities to develop their abilities, learn new skills, acquire new knowledge and realize their creative potential. They regard their people as assets to be invested in not costs to be cut. They realize that an investment in their people is also an investment in their own future. When companies invest in their people, their people invest in them. Employees are attracted to and stay with organizations, which allow them to grow and develop as individuals. They avoid or psychologically separate from or leave organizations that do not.

2.6 MEASURING ORGANISATIONAL COMMITMENT

Employee's commitment is manifested in three ways:

1. The committed employees want to remain part of the organization but not just for job security reasons.
2. The committed employee is willing to exert extra efforts on the behalf of the organization.
3. The committed employees believe and adhere to the organizational values. Such employees are better performers and hence result in benefits to the company.

There appear to be three main measures of attitudinal commitment in the field: the Organizational Commitment Questionnaire (OCQ) created by *Porter et. al.* (1974); the British Organizational Commitment Scale (BOCS) developed by *Cook & Wall* (1980); and the Affective Commitment Scale (ACS) conceptualized by *Meyer & Allen* (1984). Each seeks to measure the three components reflected in *Buchanan's* (1974) definition of commitment.

Perusal of existing literature reflects that some human capital metrics have also been used to measure the Organisational Commitment levels. These include:

1. *Cost per Hire*—measures the average amount spent on

hiring costs for each employee. By allocating sufficient funding for hiring costs, organisations can ensure that the best employees are selected which may positively impact long-term employee commitment.

2. *Training Cost Factor*—measures the money spent on training for each regular employee receiving training. This metric can be used to monitor training costs and the organisation's return on investment. Studies have shown that proper training positively influences employee commitment.
3. *Employee Cost Factor*—measures the average remuneration paid to each regular employee. As pay is often linked to turnover, by offering competitive salaries organisations can increase the likelihood of employees being more committed and staying longer with the organisation.
4. *Benefit Factor*—measures the average cost of benefits for each regular employee. Similar to providing competitive salaries, providing good benefits will also help to ensure employees stay longer with the organisation.
5. *Career Path Ratio*—measures the percentage of employee movement within the organisation that is upward promotions. Career development for employees is a crucial factor in sustaining job satisfaction and therefore affects employee commitment. Employees who are fully engaged demonstrate increased levels of commitment.
6. *Voluntary Separation Rate*—measures the percentage of regular employees that voluntarily left the organisation. Monitoring turnover will help assess the stability, productivity and profitability of a business.

2.7. DEVELOPING ORGANISATIONAL COMMITMENT

Marcoulides & Heck (1993) found that employees from a wide range of different organisations reported that the degree to which the organisation allowed them to participate in decision-making (supposedly reflecting the extent to which the organisation valued their opinions and assistance) is directly related to levels of organisational commitment.

Creating commitment on its own however is not sufficient. People can be highly committed but still ineffective. An organization needs to be able to harness employee commitment effectively in order to ensure that it is directed towards the achievement of the organization's strategies and goals. Certain conditions need to exist for this to happen:

1. *An appropriate talent pool.* The organization must first ensure that its recruitment and selection practices succeed in securing the caliber and type of employee that will fit with the company's culture, ethos and values.
2. *Clarity of direction.* Employees must understand what is expected of them and how this relates to the bigger picture. This requires regular two-way communication, open disclosure of information concerning company strategy and performance and timely feedback regarding individual performance.
3. *Capability.* Employees must be equipped with the skills and competencies to enable them to operate effectively and enhance their contribution to the organization. This entails a focus on both formal and self-directed learning, particularly developing the team working and flexibility necessary to enable the organization to be responsive and adaptive.
4. *Effective deployment and support.* Employees must be deployed in roles that play to their strengths and provided with the autonomy and empowerment to enable them to be effective. They must also be equipped with the tools, techniques and information necessary for effective discharge of their role.

Successful companies have been found to adopt following measures to improve organisational commitment among its employees:

- Organisations demonstrate to their employees that they value them by investing in their training and continuing development and by taking seriously employee appraisal and personal development plans.

- They communicate to employees a strong business context and awareness and enable them to implement their ideas to make the organisation better.
- Encourage a continuing and open dialogue between employees and the organisation to maintain positive feelings of involvement.
- Realize that as length of service increases, it is harder maintaining engagement. Factors such as career frustration, boredom and cynicism can be overcome by offering new development opportunities and career challenges.
- Understand that professional workers are more likely to engage with their craft rather than with the organisation they work for. These workers are valuable assets, so it is worth making the extra effort to engage and therefore retain them.
- Provide equality of opportunity to all employees and deal effectively and sympathetically with 'shocks to the system' such as accidents and harassment.
- Monitor levels of employee engagement, overall and for different employee groups within the organisation. Low levels can result in increased staff absence, reduced customer satisfaction and lower intention to stay with the organisation. All of which will have impact on the customer and therefore on the 'bottom line.'
- Have clear and accessible HR policies and practices and a commitment to employee health, safety and well-being.

References

Allen, N.J. and Meyer, J.P. (1990): "Organizational Socialization Tactics: A Longitudinal Analysis of Links to Newcomers' Commitment and Role Orientation", *Academy of Management Journal*, Vol. 33, pp. 847-58.

Allen, N.J. and Meyer, J.P. (1990): "The Measurement and Antecedents of Affective, Continuance and Normative Commitment to the Organization", *Journal of Occupational Psychology*, Vol. 63, pp. 1-18.

Aswathapa, K. (2001): *Organisational Behaviour: Text and Cases*, Himalaya Publication House, New Delhi.

Becker, H. (1960): "Notes on the Concept of Commitment", *American Journal of Sociology*, Vol. 66, pp. 32-40.

Buchanan, B. (1974): "Building Organizational Commitment: The Socialization of Managers in Work Organizations", *Administrative Science Quarterly*, Vol. 19, pp. 533-46.

Collins, J.C. and Porras, J.I. (1994): *Built to Last*, New York: Harper.

Cohen, A. (1998): "An Examination of the Relationship between Work Commitment and Work Outcomes among Hospital Nurses", *Scandinavian Journal of Management*, Vol. 14(1-2), pp. 1-17.

Cook, J. and Wall, T. (1980): "New Work Attitude Measures of Trust, Organizational Commitment and Personal Need Non-fulfilment", *Journal of Occupational Psychology*, Vol. 53, pp. 39-52.

Cordery, J.L. (1991): "Attitudinal and Behavioural Effects of Autonomous Group Working: A Longitudinal Field Study", *Academy of Management Journal*, Vol. 34(2), pp. 464-76.

Davis, K. (1981): *Human Behaviour at Work—Organisational Behaviour*, New York: McGraw Hill.

Fierman, J. (1994): "Are Companies Less Family Friendly?", *Fortune*, pp. 64-67.

Finegan, J.E. (2000): "The Impact of Person and Organizational Values on Organizational Commitment", *Journal of Occupational and Organizational Psychology*, Vol. 73, pp. 149-69.

Gardner, D.L. (1992): "Career Commitment in Nursing." *Journal of Professional Nursing*, Vol. 8, pp. 155-60.

Guest, D. (1995): "Human Resource Management, Trade Unions and Industrial Relations", In J. Storey (Ed.), *Human Resource Management, A Critical Text*. London, Routledge.

Johnston, M.W., Parasuraman, A., Futrell, C.M. and Black, W.C. (1990): "A Longitudinal Assessment of the Impact of Selected Organizational Influences on Salespeople' Organizational Commitment during Early Employment", *Journal of Marketing Research*, Vol. 27, pp. 333-34.

Kobasa, S.C. (1982): "Commitment and coping in stress resistance among lawyers", *Journal of Personality and Social Psychology*, Vol. 42, pp. 707-17.

Lawler, D.J. (1979): *Organizational Behaviour: The Psychology of Effective Management*, Englewood Cliffs, New Jersey: Prentice Hall.

Legge, K. (1995): *Human Resource Management: Rhetoric and Realities*, Basingstoke: Macmillan.

Marcoulides, G.A. and Heck, R.H. (1993): "Organizational Culture and Performance: Proposing and Testing a Model", *Organization Science*, Vol. 4, pp. 209-25.

McNeese-Smith, D.K. (2001): "A Nursing Shortage: Building Organizational Commitment Among Nurses", *Journal of Healthcare Management*, Vol. 46(3), pp. 173-87.

Meyer J.P. and Allen, N.J. (1991): "A three Component Conceptualization of Organizational Commitment", *Human Resource Management Review*, pp. 61-89.

Meyer J.P., Allen, N.J. and Smith, C.A. (1993): "Commitment to Organizations and Occupations: Extension and Test of a three-component Conceptualization", *Journal of Applied Psychology*, Vol. 78(4), pp. 538-51.

Meyer, J.P. and Allen, N.J. (1984): "Testing the Side bet Theory of Organisational Commitment", *Journal of Applied Psychology*, Vol. 69(3), pp. 372-78.

Meyer, J.P. and Allen, N.J. (1997): *Commitment in the Workplace: Theory, Research, and Applications*, Thousand Oaks, San Francisco, CA: Sage Publications.

Mowday, R.T., Steers, R.M. and Porter, L.W. (1979): "The Measurement of Organizational Commitment", *Journal of Vocational Behaviour*, Vol. 14, pp. 224-47.

Mowday, R.T., Porter, L.W. and Steers, R.M. (1982): *Employee-Organization linkages: The Psychology of Commitment, Absenteeism and Turnover*, New York: Academic Press.

Porter, L.W., Steers, R.M., Mowday, R.T. and Boulian, P.V. (1974): "Organizational Commitment, Job Satisfaction and Turnover among Psychiatric Technicians", *Journal of Applied Psychology*, Vol. 59, pp. 603-09.

Ritzer, G. and Trice, H. (1969): "An Empirical Study of Howard Becker's side bet Theory", *Social Forces*, Vol. June, pp. 475-79.

Scholl, R.W. (1981): "Differentiating Organizational Commitment From Expectancy as a Motivating Force", *Academy of Management Review*, Vol. 4, pp. 589-99.

Sharma, S. and Sharma, R.K. (1978): "A Study of Job Involvement in Relation to Certain Demographic Variables among Engineers", *Indian Journal of Industrial Relation*, Vol. 14(1), pp. 141-47.

Staw, B. and Salancik, G. (1977): *New Directions in Organizational Behaviour*, Chicago: St Clair Press.

Steers, R.M. (1977): "Antecedents and Outcomes of Organizational Commitment", *Administrative Science Quarterly*, Vol. 22, pp. 46-56.

Steers, R.M. (1977): *Organizational effectiveness: A Behavioural View*, Goodyear, Santa Monica, CA.

Takao, S. (1998): "The Multidimensional Model of Organizational Commitment: An Analysis of Its Antecedents and Consequences among Japanese Systems Engineers", Institute for Economic and Industry Studies Keio University: Tokyo.

Tett, R.P. and Meyer, J.P. (1993): "Job Satisfaction, Organizational Commitment, Turnover Intention and Turnover: A Path Analysis based on Meta-analytic Findings", *Personnel Psychology*, Vol. 46, pp. 259-93.

Whitener, E.M. and Walz, P.M. (1993): "Exchange theory Determinants of Affective and Continuance Commitment and Turnover," *Journal of Vocational Behaviour*, Vol. 42, pp. 265-81.

Wiener, Y. and Vardi, Y. (1980): "Relationships between Job Organization and Career Commitments and Work Outcomes—An Integrative Approach", *Organizational Behaviour and Human Performance*, Vol. 26, pp. 81-96.

Wiener, Y. (1982): "Commitment in Organizations: A Normative View", *Academy of Management Review*, Vol. 7, pp. 418-28.

Williams, L.J. and Anderson, S.E. (1991): "Job Satisfaction and Organizational Commitment as Predictors of Organizational Citizenship and in-role Behaviours", *Journal of Management*, Vol. 17, pp. 601-17.

CHAPTER

3

Changing Dimensions of Quality of Work Life

3.1 QUALITY OF WORK LIFE

QWL is an individual's views about every dimension of his work encompassing economic and other fringe benefits. Cooperative or partnership relationships in business organizations can have a symbiotic impact that increases financial performance; competitiveness and mutually benefits all groups. Thus fostering of partnership relationships between employee organizations such as unions and management may result in increasing employee and company security and well being.

According to *Gupta* (1993), QWL signifies the relationship between individuals, their work environment and social setting. It is the behaviour and attitude that is important for society both on and off the job. Due to technological advancement, industrial productivity and economic growth, industrial society neglected certain environmental and humanistic values. QWL describes all these values. QWL programmes contribute to job satisfaction, productivity and organizational success.

Studies on QWL in companies confirm a positive association between quality of work life and business performance. In the context of human resource development, employees play an important role in transforming an organization. Motivating employees to contribute their best ability and knowledge in work has long been an active research agenda. Previous QWL research has suggested that if management wants to develop a cohesive, loyal and dedicated workforce, a clear and nurturing policy must be in place. Management often fails to provide sufficient QWL, especially in the areas of job security, perks and pay for a fear of a negative effect on a company's financial performance. Effective human resource development programs are key to organizational survival and change, providing important competitive advantages in the global environment. For organizations to synergize, it must encourage, reinforce and empower all departments (work teams).

A dominant theme of much of the QWL research is the assumption that an individual's satisfaction or dissatisfaction experiences define the quality of his/her work life. Associated with this paradigm are the ideas that objective job characteristics induce satisfaction or dissatisfaction attitudes and that the association between working conditions is moderated by an individual's abilities, values and expectations (*Seashore*, 1975). Satisfaction has often been used as a measure of the quality of work life although there are limitations to its use as such satisfaction is only one of the many aspects of QWL (*White*, 1981; *Davis & Cherns*, 1975). As with many attitudinal measures, it can be regarded as a self-fulfilling prophecy where expectations adapt to what the work realistically provides (*Davis & Cherns*, 1975). The assumption in using job satisfaction in this research was not that it would be an all encompassing measure of the quality of work life, but rather that it served as a motivator through which employees change and accommodate to their jobs and environment.

Other job-related components of satisfaction which have been reported are: participative supervision, interaction with peers, high wages, opportunity for promotion, level of interest in the job, having enough authority and information to do the job, use/development of personal skills and seeing concrete evidence of an individual's efforts (*Scanlan,* 1976; *Bar-haim,* 1984; *Headey,* 1983; *Burstein et al,* 1975).

An inspirational and talented top leadership has been identified as necessary for a successful QWL program. Organizational culture with a supportive group-based belief system and a peer-based support system wherein trust is the critical ingredient in empowerment is creating in employees "a sense of ownership of their work" and being "proud of their work and their organization." Employee empowerment acts as self-motivation that results from a fuller understanding of responsibilities.

Organizational culture does affect employees' quality of work life factors. Human relations cultural values are positively related to organizational commitment, job involvement, empowerment and job satisfaction and negatively related to intent to turnover. Thus improving quality of work life may be a more practical and long-term approach to improving employee retention and job satisfaction.

3.1.1 Concept of QWL

Dissatisfaction with organization of work in 1960's and 1970's led to the beginning of quality of working life movement (*Walton,* 1973; *Liltler & Salaman,* 1984). QWL movement was aimed to improve utilization of worker initiative and to reduce job dis-satisfaction. Job enlargement and job enrichment also improve Quality of Work Life. According to *Herzberg et al* (1959), QWL is aimed at attaining higher level of participation and motivation by improving the attractiveness of the work itself. Individual employees' perceptions, experiences, values and cognitive processes translate into judgments about the organization's treatment of its work force. Conducive organisational climate for opportunity is antecedent to outcomes at the individual, work group and organizational levels.

The term 'Quality of Work Life' was first introduced at an international conference in New York in 1972. It was used to describe the conditions that create 'humane working life' (*Rajan,*

1995). It is focused on work environment that leads to workers' satisfaction and motivation. It is concerned with replacing repetitive and boring jobs based on Taylor's principles by more interesting and human task that ultimately leads to happiness at work place. Jobs have three major components: complexity, the social environment and physical organisational climate. Variables in this factor are either positive or negative. Some enhance feelings of enthusiasm, team spirit, empowerment and job satisfaction due to positive management styles, clear roles, professional development opportunities and interaction. However, some situations are negative in that they cause distress in the workplace, especially when it involves excessive work demands.

Cooperative or partnership relationships in business organizations can have a symbiotic impact that increases financial performance, competitiveness and mutually benefits all groups. Thus, fostering of partnership relationships between employee organizations such as unions and management may result in increasing employee and company security and well being. Organizations must develop, train and enable all work teams in such a way that all work teams can focus more directly on the achievements of its purposeful and meaningful goals.

3.1.2 Defining Quality of Work Life

Different researchers have defined QWL in different terms. Some described it in terms of works performance while others highlighted the physical and psychological well-being of workers. It is also a means of instilling a sense of belongingness among workers by reducing alienation from processes and society both. By mid-1980s, the term also included a sociological approach involving group and organizational aspects.

QWL is the description of working conditions and facilities where workers have to work. It aims at giving human shape to working condition as QWL is often described as 'humanization of work place.'

It also explains the relationship between a worker and his work settings. It creates a sense of belongingness with work place. It describes work not merely in terms of technical or economic dimensions rather in terms of human dimensions.

Davis (1981) defined QWL as favorableness or unfavorableness of a job environment for people. The purpose of QWL is to develop jobs that are excellent for people as well as for production. It provides careful balance of human imperative and the technological imperative. QWL efforts are required for these reasons:

1. Employees are now becoming more aware of their needs and rights. They want empowerment in work place.
2. Taylor principles of work design are no more acceptable to new generation employees. They want creativity and innovation and prefer that environment which is conducive for growth and advancement.

Luthans (1981) defined QWL as a "process of joint decision-making, collaboration and building mental respect between management and employees. It is concerned with overall climate at work. The basic idea is to change the climate at work place so as to boost cooperation between technological human organizational interface."

Jain (1991) explained QWL as not related to work only but also as an effort to improve life outside work. It is aimed at improving working condition, work content and its related outcomes like safety, security, wages, benefits, etc. Work groups are collectives of individuals defined by organizational structure and job requirements. Each work group has its own unique set of characteristics (e.g., supervisor, norms and co-worker behaviours) which have a strong influence on climate for opportunity due to their proximity thereby determining quality of work life.

Sharma & Ghosh (1993) defined QWL in terms of work performance. Performance manifests itself not only in physical output but also in behaviour of employees in their readiness to help others, accept organizational challenges promoting team spirit, etc. Improved QWL leads to improved performance.

Bhagat (1993) describes QWL as an attitude of an individual towards work. It covers his feelings and sentiments about every thing related to work. Good quality of work life promotes creativity.

Rao (1993) suggested that "the QWL is cooperative rather than authoritarian; evolutionary and open rather than static and rigid; informal rather than role bound; impersonal rather than mechanistic; mutual respect and trust rather than hatred against each other."

Guest (1979) describes QWL as a process by which an organization attempts to unlock the creative potential of its people by involving them in decision affecting their work life.

Bowditch & Brono (1992) equate QWL to the existence of some human resource practices and conditions like worker participation, safe and healthy working environment, challenging and intrusting jobs, etc.

Quality of life encompasses qualitative and quantitative, material and non-material, objective and subjective dimensions of work. It is concerned with determining and measuring individual's quality of life (*Nussbaums & Sen*, 1990).

Zapf (1984) describes QWL as good living conditions that are related with a positive feeling of well-being. QWL is a function of different conditions of life and components of subjective well-being. Conditions of life implies visible tangible living conditions like income, housing, working condition, family relationship, social contacts, health, social and political participation. Subjective well-being is the attitude of affected persons concerning particular condition of life and life in general.

3.1.3 Determinants of Quality of Work Life

Perusal of literature on Quality of Work Life helps to identify various factors affecting the perception of the employees on the quality of work life existing in their organization. Many factors contribute in developing perception of employees about the organizational culture, thereby forming the quality of work life indicators. Some of these factors include:

- *Workplace Morale*—Staff show enthusiasm, pride in their work, team spirit and energy.

- *Workplace Distress*—Staff feel frustrated, stressed, tense and anxious and depressed about their work.
- *Supportive Leadership*—Managers are approachable, dependable and supportive, know the problems faced by staff and communicate well with them.
- *Participative Decision-making*—Staff is asked to participate in decisions and is given opportunities to express their views.
- *Role Clarity*—Expectations, work objectives, responsibilities and authority are clearly defined.
- *Professional Interaction*—Acceptance and support from others, with involvement, sharing, good communication and help when needed.
- *Appraisal and Recognition*—Quality and regular recognition and feedback on work performance.
- *Professional Growth*—Interest, encouragement, opportunity for training, career development and professional growth.
- *Goal Congruence*—Personal goals are in agreement with workplace goals which are clearly stated and easily understood.
- *Excessive Work Demands*—Staff are overloaded with constant pressure to keep working, leaving no time to relax.

In addition, a number of positive work events add to a person's feelings of empowerment and success in the workplace. The job, management styles, co-workers, equipment, resources and workloads all provide opportunities for individuals to enjoy meaningful and rewarding work lives. Variables in this factor include:

- *The Job Itself*—Work that is interesting, challenging and worthwhile has variety and involves responsibility.
- *Customer Service*—Helping clients and providing quality service.
- *Workload*—Working hard, managing a heavy workload, meeting deadlines and getting things done.
- *Work Schedule*—Good working hours that fit in with other activities.

- *Administration*—Application of rules and policy, clear operational guidelines and plans showing results.
- *Management*—Immediate managers/supervisors, who are helpful, provide feedback, recognize good work, are honest about work, willing to delegate, trusting, open and willing to listen.
- *Amenities*—Good facilities, tidy work area and a comfortable and safe work environment.
- *Equipment and Resources*—Sufficient resources, including staff and operational equipment.
- *Co-workers*—Working with people who are considerate, easy to get along with, know what they are doing, competent, likeable and who like me and who do the right thing.
- *Decision-making*—Being involved in and having a say in making decisions and solving problems.
- *Family*—Having sufficient time for family life, a balance between work and home and support for work from partner.

There are many negative deterrents also which make employees feel disempowered. These could be the inappropriate management style, excessive workload, personality clashes, lack of job security and fewer career opportunities. Some other factors include:

- *Communication*—Lack of consultation, participation and communication and adequate feedback, guidance, encouragement and backup.
- *Workload*—Too much to do in too little time.
- *Co-workers*—Working with people who are incompetent, do not pull their weight, are inconsiderate, do not listen and who lack professionalism.
- *Outside Support*—Absence of emotional and practical support from those outside work and lack of stability at home.
- *Administration*—Excessive paperwork and red tape, inconsistent application of rules and policy, lack of clarity in operational guidelines and lack of forward planning.

- *Job Insecurity*—Threat of impending redundancy or early retirement.
- *Resources*—Insufficient funds, equipment and other resources.
- *Dual careers*—Home life with a non-supportive career-oriented spouse.
- *Work and Home Life*—Demands of work on private and social life, including spouse, partner, children; having to work long hours and take work home.
- *Career Opportunities*—Uncertainty about or lack of possibilities for career advancement.
- *Personality Clashes*—Problems and conflicts with co-workers.

The following symptoms are considered significant indicators of poor perceived QWL: (1) disaffection; (2) powerlessness; (3) meaninglessness; (4) normlessness; (5) social isolation; (6) value isolation; (7) self and/or work group estrangement; (8) disciplinary and grievance difficulties; (9) blaming others; (10) sub-goal formation; (11) lack of awareness of real common problems; (12) acting contrary to data, information and company policies and actions; (13) displaying extreme displeasure with trifling circumstances; and (14) behaving differently outside the work organization.

3.1.4 Dimensions of QWL

QWL can be considered under five dimensions:

1. *Work/life balance*: Encompasses evenly distribution of work and family responsibility. There should be compatibility between demands of work and private life. Work/life balance is having control and flexibility over when, where and how to work (*Pillinger*, 2001).
2. *Employability:* It is the sum total of the potential, abilities, skills, education experience of a person which makes him fit for an employment. An organization's work settings and procedures contribute to lifelong learning process and thus enhance employability of a person.

3. *Income security and social security:* From any job results income security however less or high it is and income security gives social security. Better QWL arrangements generate good income and social security.
4. *Quality of work:* This could manifest itself through (a) career and employment security; (b) health and well-being; (c) skill development and/or (d) reconciliation of working and non-working life.
   Career and employment security means how one's present responsibilities lead to growth and advancement to make a person more capable of assuming more responsibility at a later stage.
   More stress, time squeeze and less autonomy or decreased communication makes employees prone to mental and physical hazards.
5. *Time sovereignty:* It is the right and ability of a person to allocate his life qualitatively and quantitatively among working and non-working activities throughout their life. *Schilling* (2001) suggests that "time wealth and time sovereignty should be seen together with sovereignty in the field of working life. Only those who are able to influence the contents of work in individual fields of life also have a larger scope of influence as far as the duration and timing of working hours are concerned."

Cordery (1991) argued the necessity of differentiating the importance of three dimensions of job autonomy, for improved quality of work life:

(a) Method control as defined by the amount of discretion one has over the way in which work is performed,
(b) Timing control in terms of the influence one has over scheduling of work, and
(c) Discretion in setting performance goals.

He found four interrelated dimensions that affect quality of work life, namely the extent to which the supervisor (a) provides clear attainable goals, (b) exerts control over work activities, (c) ensures that the requisite resources are available, and (d) gives timely accurate feedback on progress toward goal attainment.

Sinha (1977) suggested that foremost indicator of Quality of Work Life culture in an organisation is the possibility of fulfilment of basic needs of man and reduction of the enormous economic disparities in the haves and have not's. In order to experience better QWL, the employees are required to recognize their basic and upper level needs and to develop their potentialities to meet these needs.

According to *Chander* (1993) QWL has following dimensions :

(i) Decision-making authority
(ii) Growth and development
(iii) Job security
(iv) Organizational prestige
(v) Feeling of worthwhile accomplishment
(vi) Pay and allowances
(vii) Promotional avenues
(viii) Reorganization and appreciation

Sinha (1982) highlighted four-main dimensions of QWL:

(i) Job satisfaction
(ii) Job attractiveness
(iii) Intrinsic motivation
(iv) Control and influence

Rao (1993) suggested following dimensions of QWL:

(i) Pay benefits
(ii) Job security
(iii) Occupational stress
(iv) Worker participation
(v) Social integration
(vi) Work and total life space
(vii) Alternative work schedules:
   (a) Flexible
   (b) Staggered hours

(c) Compressed work week
(d) Job enrichment
(e) Autonomous workgroup

Kumar & Shanubhogue (1996) defined QWL as "an approach that penetrates several activities in the work place like work redesigning to provide job enrichment and enlargement, improving working conditions, flexible work schedules and theory to participative management."

The components by *Walton* (1974) as being comprehensive of the QWL concept were as follows:

(1) Compensation (salary and benefits *per se* and in relation to co-workers);
(2) Working conditions (schedule and environment);
(3) Skill development and application;
(4) Opportunity for advancement;
(5) Social integration among peers ("team spirit");
(6) Constitutionalism (participation in decision-making);
(7) Work and social life (relative balance); and
(8) Social relevance of work (perception of product and company image).

Effective human resource development programs are central and not tangential to the bottom line and overall competitiveness of the firm. Maintaining a strong employee orientated culture that provides employees with job security and satisfaction facilitates the retention of the most productive workers. The costs of hiring and retaining new employees can be substantial. Retaining workers is essential to minimize the costs and disruption inherent in employee turnover. Retention of productive workers coupled with extensive human resource development enables the firm to effectively compete in varying economic environments and requires a conducive organizational culture.

A good quality of work life allows employees the opportunity to make certain decisions about the design of their workplace, the processes to be used and the resources they need to do their jobs most effectively. In fact an employee who has performed a particular job over several years may be in a better position to make this determination. To be effective, good quality of work life can not only be used as a device by management to disengage unions or to keep unions out of the workplace, but also can instill employee commitment. Thus many successful organizations have established a policy to encourage and enable all employees to become involved in and contribute to the organization.

3.2 CONCLUSIONS

Quality of work life (QWL) consists of opportunities for active involvement in group working arrangements or problem-solving that are of mutual benefit to employees and employers (*Johnston et al*, 1978; *Mills*, 1981). It requires employee commitment to the organization and an environment in which this commitment can flourish (*Walton*, 1974). Part of the commitment to the organization is the various attitudes or value judgments of people to their jobs and to their total work environment (*Kolodny et al*, 1979; *Skinner*, 1979). Organization-wide policies, practices and procedures send implicit and explicit messages to employees about the organization's stance toward the allocation of opportunities to remain competitive. Organizations must be willing to create an environment that supports teamwork in which work teams can find new and creative ways to meet the societal and employee expectations. Organizations must renew their commitment in communicating accurate information in a timely manner so that all can do their jobs effectively. In creating a teamwork-based environment, organizations must ensure that the methods of communication they use are timely, accurate and effective in communicating to empowered work teams the information they must have in order to contribute effectively and efficiently. Organizational culture shapes the environmental stimuli and experiences to which one is exposed and to which one will react. As such, it directly and indirectly influences QWL for employees and influences individual attitudes concerning outcomes such as commitment, motivation, satisfaction, morale and power (*Harris & Mossholder*, 1996). A human relations culture emphasizes cohesion and morale through means such as training and human resource development. Organisations have to put less emphasis on formal coordination and control systems and a greater emphasis on decentralized decision-making, horizontal communications and teamwork. Cordial interpersonal relations tend toward higher levels of trust, morale and leader credibility and relatively low levels of conflict and resistance to change.

3.3 INTERRELATIONSHIP BETWEEN QUALITY OF WORK, LEADERSHIP BEHAVIOUR AND ORGANISATIONAL COMMITMENT

Organizations must develop leaders that have the appropriate philosophy, attitude, commitment and skills that can set a good example of teamwork. Leaders who can work with other leaders in a team setting are needed. But leaders that can reinforce and actively participate in the development and maintenance of their own high-quality work teams are the need of time. Leaders must value in word and in behaviour, the importance of respecting the worth and significance of the individual employee.

The key concepts captured and discussed in the existing literature include job security, better reward systems, higher pay, opportunity for growth, participative groups and increased organizational productivity among others.

Kerr et. al. (1974) reviewed the published literature involving the leader behaviour dimensions "Consideration" and "Initiating Structure," for the purpose of developing some situational propositions of leader effectiveness. Among the variables found by researchers to significantly moderate relationships between leader behaviour predictors, satisfaction and performance criteria are the following: subordinate's need for information, job level, subordinate expectations of leader behaviour, perceived organizational independence, leader's similarity of attitudes, behaviour to managerial style of higher management, leader upward influence and characteristics of the task, including pressure and provision of intrinsic satisfaction.

Teo & Waters (2002) have argued that a supportive human resource (HR) environment (i.e., an organizational environment where a high number of the employee-friendly HR practices) will reduce the occupational stressors of role overload and responsibility directly, will reduce levels of vocational strain and interpersonal strain directly and will decrease these forms of strain indirectly through its positive influence on levels of organizational commitment.

Lok (1999) examined the influence of organizational culture, sub-culture and leadership style and job satisfaction on organizational commitment. He indicated that the leadership style variable, consideration, exerted a relatively strong influence on commitment when compared with other variables included in his study. Job involvement is an affective reaction to the job that is related to but is both conceptually and empirically distinct from job satisfaction, as well as forms of work commitment such as career commitment and organizational commitment.

Rosin & *Korabik* (1995) demonstrated that when managers felt that their expectations of the job had not been met, their level of commitment to the organization was reduced, which, in turn, predicted intention to leave.

For contemporary organizations seeking to maximize organizational success, the challenge is how to achieve a complementary pairing between the organization's disposition toward change and the nature of the change demands in the environment. Organizations must effectively communicate at all times the goals of its organization to all employees. It is vital that organizations not only communicate what the goals are, but why they are important and the role of individuals and work teams in the accomplishment of those goals.

The most important factor determining job quality as measured by autonomy, meaningfulness opportunities for learning, advancement and job security to create a good quality of work life is employee involvement. Employee involvement is a variety of techniques that are used to enable employees to participate in the decision-making processes that affect their working environment. Integrity and trust are important aspects of successful participative initiatives. The purpose of involving employees in the decision-making processes relates primarily to morale, productivity and employee satisfaction.

3.4 RATIONALE FOR THE PRESENT STUDY

Researchers have realized that it is a futile quest for universal leadership principles that apply equivalently across all cultures as there are bound to be variations in leadership styles, practices and preferences. Combination of technological advances, larger multicultural samples, enhanced clarification of dimensions of culture and better understanding and measurement of cognitive processes across cultures will allow us to better understand the role societal culture plays in the enactment and interpretation of the leadership behaviour.

Leaders may move across different industries and organizations during their career span, yet they may exhibit similar leadership behavioural patterns which may get developed over a period of time. The contemporary leader is expected to make moderate use of visionary, transactional and empowering behaviours while avoiding autocratic behaviours. Exploring the role of leadership styles in converting knowledge into competitive advantages is important to our understanding of leaders and organizations.

Over the past decade the area of organizational commitment has received considerable attention from both researchers and managers. Of particular interest are the links between this and other constructs such as trust, task performance and turnover. Despite the widespread acknowledgement of the importance and value of organizational commitment, there has been limited research that has specifically addressed the relationship between leader behaviour and employee commitment, particularly in the consumer durable sector. The present study examines the nature of the relationships between organizational commitment and two dimensions of leader behaviour—supportive behaviours and extinction behaviours. There is, however, a considerable body of literature that examines relationships between supervisor behaviour, particularly the level of support provided by supervisors and a range of desired organizational outcomes. It is argued that since employees do not differentiate between supervisors, managers and leaders in any practical sense, supervisor behaviours can be equated to leader behaviours.

Present study seeks to examine the relationship between perceptions of leader behaviour in the work environment, Quality of Work Life and levels of Organizational Commitment among employees in a large segment of Indian economy, i.e. white goods industry.

Improving employee retention is a difficult challenge to managers since the bureaucratic cultural norm of most organisations with its hierarchical structures, roles, regulations, with heavy emphasis on measurement of outcomes and costs may not be the culture most conducive to enhancing job satisfaction and commitment. Accordingly, this study investigates the relationships between Leadership Behaviour and perceived QWL besides several important job-related variables for organizational commitment.

Kao & Sek-Hong (1993) argued that the high levels of trust, loyalty and altruism ingrained in Oriental cultures mean that Asian employees often display high levels of commitment to their organization. This needs to be cross-examined in Indian context. The study assumes even greater importance as the white goods (consumer durable) industry is dominated with Japanese, Korean and Taiwanese origin companies.

References

Bar-Haim, A. (1984). "The Desire for Workers' Participation: Conflicting Forces in the Workplace", *Relations Industrielles*, Vol. 39(2), pp. 301-12.

Bennis, W. and Nanus, B. (1985): *Leaders: The Strategies for Taking Charge*, New York: Harper and Row.

Bhagat, M. (1993): "Technology and Quality of Work Life." *The Indian Journal of Labour Economics*, Vol. 36(4), pp. 782-84.

Blake, R.R. and Mouton, J.S. (1982): "A Comparative Analysis of Situationalism and 9,9 Management by Principle", *Organizational Dynamics*, Vol. 10 (4), pp. 20-43.

Bowditch, J.L. and Buono, A.F. (1992): *Element do Comportamento Organizational*, Sao Paulo: Pioneira.

Burstein, M., Tienhaara, N., Hewson, P. and Warrander, B. (1975): *Canadian Work Values: Findings of a Work Ethic Survey and a Job Satisfaction Survey*, Ottawa: Manpower and Immigration.

Chander, S. (1993): "Quality of Work Life in A University: An Empirical Investigation", *Management and Labour Studies*, Vol. 18(2), pp. 97-107.

Davis, L. and Cherns, A. (eds) (1975): *"The Quality of Working Life"*, Vol. 1, Free Press, New York.

Dubinsky, A.J. and Yammarino, F.J. (1994): "Closeness of Supervision and Salesperson Work Outcomes: An Alternate Perspective." *Journal of Business Research*, Vol. 29 (3), pp. 225-37.

Gatton, F. (1860): *Hereditary Genius*, Imprint by Meridian Books, Cleveland, OH 1962.

Guest, R. (1979): "Quality of Worklife: Learning from Experiences", *Harvard Business Review*, July/August, pp. 76-87.

Gupta, T.K. (1993): "Quality of Work Life." *The Indian Journal of Labour Economics*, Vol. 36(4), pp. 770-76.

Harris, S.G. and Mossholder, K.W. (1996): "The Affective Implications of Perceived Congruence with Culture Dimensions During Organizational Transformation." *Journal of Management*, Vol. 22(4), pp. 527-47.

Headey, B. (1983): "Quality of Life Studies: Their Implications for Social and Market Researchers", *European Research*, April, pp. 56-67.

Hertzberg, F.B, Mausner, B. and Snyderman, B.B. (1959): *The Motivation To Work*, New York: John Wiley and Sons.

Jain, S. (1991): *Quality of Work Life*, Deep and Deep Publications, New Delhi.

Johnston, C.P., Mark, A. and Jacquelin, R. (1978): *Quality of Working Life: The Idea and Its Application*, Ottawa: Labour Canada.

Kao, H. and Sek-Hong, N. (1993): "Organisational Commitment: From Trust to Altruism at Work." *Psychology and Developing Societies*, Vol. 5, pp. 43-60.

Kerr, S. and Schriesheim, C.A. (1974): "Toward a Contingency Theory of Leadership based upon the Consideration and Initiating Structure Literature", *Organizational Behaviour and Human Performance*, Vol. 12 (1), pp. 62-82.

Kolodny, H.F., Johnston, C.P. and Jeffery, W. (1979): "Job Design and Socio-technical Systems", in *Quality of Working Life Series*, Ottawa: Labour Canada.

Kumar, H. and Shanubhogue, A. (1996): "Quality of Work Life—An Empirical Approach", *Manpower Journal*, Vol. 32(3), pp. 17-23.

Littler, C. and Salaman, G. (1984): *Class at Work: The Design, Allocation and Control of Jobs*, London: Batsford.

Lok, P. (1999): "The Influence of Organisational Culture, Subculture, Leadership Style and Job Satisfaction on Organisation Commitment", *Leadership and Organisation Development*, Vol. 20(7), pp. 365-73.

Luthans, F. (1981): *Organizational Behaviour*, McGraw- Hill International Book Company, New York.

Mills, T. (1981): *"What is the Quality of Working Life?"*, Ottawa: Labour Canada.

Nussbaum, M.C. and Sen, A. (Eds.) (1990): *The Quality of Work life*. Oxford University Press, pp. 11-21.

Pillinger, J. (2001): *"Work—Life Balance concern", available on* http://www.tue.org.uk/*work_life/tue4002_fo.cfm cited* dated July 30, 2005.

Rao, M.G. (1993): "Quality of Work Life and Quality Circle", *Human Behaviour At Work*, Vol. 1, pp. 43-54.

Rosin, H. and Korabi, K. (1995): "Organizational Experiences and Propensity to Leave: A Multivariate Investigation of Men and Women Managers", *Journal of Vocational Behaviour*, Vol. 46, pp. 1-16.

Scanlan, B.R. (1976): "Determinants of Job Satisfaction and Productivity", *Personnel Journal*, Vol. 55, pp. 12-14.

Schilling, G. (2001): "Gutes Leben mit weniger Arbeit? Perspetiven Fiir mehr Lebensqualitat", in Weniger Arbeit—Arbeit fur alle, U. Becker (Ed.), Marburg (Germany). Abstract in English Version.

Schriesheim, C.A. and Kerr, S. (1977): "Theories and Measures of Leadership: A Critical Appraisal of Current and Future Directions." In *Leadership: The Cutting Edge.* Eds. Hunt. J.G. and Larson, L.L. Carbondale, IL: Southern Illinois University Press.

Seashore, S.E. (1975): "Defining and Measuring the Quality of Working Life" in the *Quality of Working Life Vol. 1: Problems, Prospects and State of the Art,* Louis E. Davis, Albert B. Chems and Associates, New York: The Free Press.

Sharma, A. and Ghosh, S. (1993): "Quality of Work Life and Productivity", *The Indian Journal of Labour Economics,* Vol. 36(4), pp. 785-88.

Sinha, J.B.P. (1977): "Styles of Leadership and their Effect on Group Productivity", *Indian Journal of Industrial Relation,* Vol. 13(2), pp. 209-23.

Sinha, P. (1982): "Quality of Working Life and Quality of Life", *Indian Journal of Industrial Relations,* Vol. 17(3), pp. 373-94.

Skinner, W. (1979): "The Impact of Changing Technology on the Working Environment" in *Work in America: The Decade Ahead,* Clark Kerr and Jerome R. Rosow ed., New York: Van Nostrand Reinhold Company.

Teo, C. and Waters, L. (2002): "The Role of Human Resource Practices in Reducing Occupational Stress and Strain", *International Journal of Stress Management,* Vol. 9(3), pp. 207-26.

Vroom, V.H. (1976): "Leadership", In *Handbook of Industrial and Organizational Psychology.* Ed. M.D. Dunnette. Chicago: Rand-McNally.

Walton, R.E. (1973): "Quality of Work Life: What Is It?", *Sloan Management Review,* Vol. 15(1), pp. 11-21.

Walton, R.E. (1974): "Improving the Quality of Work Life", *Harvard Business Review,* Vol. 52(3), May-June, pp. 12, 16, 155.

Walton, R.E. (1985): "From Control to Commitment in the Workplace", *Harvard Business Review,* Vol. 63(2), pp. 77-84.

Weber, M. (1946): "The Sociology of Charismatic Authority." In Mills, H.H and Mills, C.W. Editors, *From Max Weber: Essays in Sociology,* Oxford University Press, New York.

White, T.A. (1981): "The Relative Importance of Work as a Factor in Life Satisfaction", *Relations Industrielles,* Vol. 36(l), pp. 179-91.

Zapf, W. (1984): Individuelle Wohlfahrt. Lebenshedingungen und wahrgenommene Lebensqualitat' in Labensqualitat in der Bundesrepublik. Objektive Lebensbedingungen und subjectives Wohlbefinden, W. Glatzer and W. Zapf (Eds.), Main Publ. Frankfurt (Germany).

CHAPTER

4

Contemporary Thoughts on Leadership Behaviour

4.1 INTRODUCTION

The purpose of contemporary leadership is to create vision and value congruence across the organization. Leadership must exhibit those qualities of personality and training, which make the guidance and control of others successful. With this aim, the present study has been undertaken to understand the impact of leadership behaviour on quality of work life and the job commitment among the subordinates in the consumer durable industry. It has to be recognized that different groups of employees are managed differently and may require different leadership styles.

Leaders have to focus on social capital and building more productive relationships that enhance networking, collaboration and resource exchange. Today's organizations and its employees exhibit different work ethics, dissimilar ways of solving problems or even contrasting values. Integrating all these changes requires greater transparency, communication, accountability and skills that have to be continuously nurtured. Human connections are essential to organizational performance.

Several leadership activators are key to the success of any organization. These include mutual respect, trust, open communication, flexibility and commitment. These ingredients are crucial because they lay the groundwork for taking risks, embracing conflict, striving for excellence and holding people accountable. This may hold the key to organizational commitment and productivity.

Business in India has been witnessing a significant transformation fuelled by liberalization and privatization. Heightened competition, squeezing profits, increased customer awareness about their rights, increased spending powers, access to information has made the tasks of today's business leaders more challenging. The key to success is the close cooperation of the employees as a single entity and meeting the expectations of the customers.

The present chapter and succeeding two chapters aim at delineating the trends in the research on three aspects, viz., leadership behaviour, organizational commitment and quality of work life. Hence a critique on the existing literature has been presented under these three components besides reporting the inter-relationship between them.

4.2 A CRITIQUE ON EXISTING LITERATURE ON LEADERSHIP BEHAVIOUR

Leadership involves the ability to inspire and influence the thinking, attitudes and behaviour of other people (*Adler*, 1991; *Bass*, 1985; *Bass and Stogdill*, 1989; *Bennis and Nanus*, 1985; *Kotter*, 1988). Diverse theories of leadership can be found in the organizational literature. These theories can be distinguished by several historically distinct approaches that focus on traits, behaviours, situational contingencies or transformational leadership.

Two fundamentally different approaches to theory, research and to the practice of leadership point in opposite and mutually contradictory directions. Because both cannot be valid, a controversy has arisen as to whether leadership should be conceived of as being contingent upon the situation or whether there is one most effective style for all situations. In the first case, the leader changes behaviour to fit the situation. In the second, the leader changes the situation to bring it into line with sound principles of behaviour as these are emerging in the behavioural sciences.

Blake and Nouton (1982) have examined the roots of this controversy and the assumptions embedded within the conceptual structure supporting each side of it. Eight interrelated kinds of evidence have been presented that lead to the conclusion that one best style is a sounder basis for the exercise of effective leadership than to the fit approach. This clarification makes it possible to strengthen leadership in its many applications within industry and government, mental health settings and the academic world by bringing leadership practices into alignment with sound leadership theory.

Skansi (2000) analysed the relation of the managerial efficiency and leadership styles. The dominant leadership style in HEP (Hrvatska Elektroprivreda) was found to be consultation. There was found to be a significant interdependence between leadership styles of HEP's managers and the degree of management work efficiency. The closer the leadership style is to participation, the higher was the managerial efficiency. No significant difference between lower and middle management in HEP was found regarding the relation between leadership styles and efficiency. Thus, managers at both levels of management got better grades for their efficiency if they belong to a consultation and participation leadership style.

Elkin and Keller (2003) have presented a conceptual framework and review of the empirical literature on leadership in research and development (R&D) organizations. Findings of studies reviewed suggest that transformational project leaders who communicate an inspirational vision and provide intellectual stimulation and leaders who develop a high-quality leader-member exchange (LMX) relationship with project members are associated with project success. Boundary-spanning activity and championing by the leader are also found to be important factors for project success. The review also suggested that a number of moderators and contextual variables such as project group membership and rate of technological change makes leadership in R&D organizations different from that in operating organizations.

Liu et. al. (2003) opine that leadership plays a critical role in effective management of employees. By drawing on strategic human resource development and leadership literatures, these researchers have provided a typology of employment mode-leadership style fit that matches leadership styles with the requirement of different employee groups. Different groups of employees are managed differently and may require different leadership styles. Based on contingency approach to leadership, researchers have explored leadership style most consistent with the underlying objectives and psychological obligations of different groups of employees.

Palmon and Illies (2004) have opined that employees in many jobs encounter novel and ill-defined problems. Finding creative solutions to these problems may be the critical factor that allows their organization to maintain a competitive advantage. Solving problems creatively requires extensive and effortful cognitive processing. This requirement is magnified further by the complex, ambiguous situations in which most organizational problems occur. Employees must define and construct a problem, search and retrieve problem-relevant information and generate and evaluate a diverse set of alternative solutions. Creativity necessitates that all these activities are completed effectively. It is unlikely that creative outcomes will be realized without a large degree of support from organizations and organizational leaders. To provide this support leader must understand the cognitive requirements of creative problem-solving. The researchers identified cognitive processes underlying creative problem-solving and suggested avenues through which organizational leaders can facilitate these processes in an effort to enhance the creative problem solving of their employees.

4.2.1 Studies on Leadership Behaviour in Indian Context

Hingar (1984) undertook study to find out the various factors affecting leadership styles in the Rajasthan State Electricity Board (RSEB)—A Public Sector Undertaking. The sample (100) comprised Executive and Assistant Engineers to whom Leader Behaviour Descriptive Questionnaire (LBDQ) was administered. For data analysis the techniques of factor analysis and the varimax rotation were used as a result of which six factors emerged which affect the leadership style. These factors corresponded to initiating and consideration variables.

Dhar and Mishra (2001) opine that leadership being the ability to influence a group may manifest its effectiveness in several ways, ranging from financial performance to employee morale and commitment. A number of theories have evolved by integrating contemporary socio-economic and cultural changes occurring in the business environment. The authors feel that constitution of effectiveness itself may be changing and it needs to be looked into for more clarity.

Madhok (1995) studied motivational patterns and leadership styles of managers and subordinate interpersonal perceptions. She concluded that: (1) high task-low relationship style was related to activation of the autonomy need as was related in the higher scores on importance of that need category. (2) Low task-high relationship style related to importance of the security need. (3) Low task-low relationship style was related to satisfaction of esteem and activation of actualization needs. (4) Bureaucratic style was related to the deprivation of the autonomy need.

Bowman (2000) has suggested that there are six change-leadership styles—each with a different set of assumptions and goals—which when paired with the complementary organizational environment will promote the optimum degree of organizational innovation. How an organization absorbs change can either serve as a strategic asset or place an organization at a distinct competitive disadvantage.

Conner (1998) has contended that what is required to manage torrential change today is a menu of change-leadership styles. Based upon two decades of research, he isolated six distinct leadership styles related to change: Anti-Change, Rational, Panacea, Bolt-on, Integrated and Continuous. Each leadership style "represents a unique set of perceptions, attitudes and behaviours regarding how organizational disruption should be addressed."

Willemsen (2001) investigated whether the gender-typing of the organizational context influences leadership behaviour of male and female managers. Shop assistants in masculine- to feminine-typed departments described their manager in terms of task-oriented, people-oriented and transformational leadership styles. No gender differences in leadership styles were found. The gender-typing of departments did not affect perceived leadership styles. Another contextual variable, the site of the department store influenced leader behaviour.

Eagly and Johnson (1990) reported that female managers are considerably more democratic than male managers.

4.2.2 Studies on Leadership Styles

It has been hypothesized that certain leadership styles are better suited than others to enhancing productivity within the work force (*Hersey et. al.*, 1996). Styles of leadership may also need to be flexible in order to respond to changes that may occur in the work environment, changes that can occur with particular rapidity in high-technology fields. Under Western management theories, the leadership style is usually situational, contingent on the environment. This quality of contingency—what works in one organizational setting may not work in another—suggests a corollary: that within a given culture, the more stable and uniform its presiding values, the less necessary it is that a leadership style be situational.

The recent trend in management theory and management practice is one leading towards employee participation and empowerment. The accompanying management style is referred to by different authors as transformational, visionary, charismatic, or inspirational leadership (e.g. *Bryman*, 1992; *Conger and Kanungo*, 1994; *Hartog et. al.*, 1994; *House and Howell*, 1992). Transformational leaders "articulate a vision, use lateral or non-traditional thinking, encourage individual development, give regular feedback, use participative decision-making and promote a cooperative and trusting work environment" (*Carless*, 1998).

Wang (2001) studied the impact of Taiwanese leadership styles on the productivity of Taiwanese business organizations. Both adaptive and non-adaptive leaders have 6 measures of productivity: absenteeism, turnover rate, quality of work, reject rates, profitability and units produced. The results indicated that greater the level of adaptability more productive the organization is likely to be. Although not all of the computed correlations were statistically significant, they were all in the predicted directions. In particular, the findings for units produced and reject rates were consistently statistically significant. The study was also an examination of the usefulness of the Leadership Effectiveness and Adaptability Description (LEAD) questionnaire (*Hersey and Blanchard,* 1988), which appeared to be an accurate predictor of adaptability. Statistical Analysis also revealed that successful companies were more likely to have a greater percentage of adaptive leaders than unsuccessful companies.

Hersey et. al. (1996) indicated that the most effective leaders are those capable of using different leadership styles in response to the demands of the situation and to the fluctuating maturity levels of their subordinates. It seems that flexibility in leadership style is a necessity if a high level of leadership effectiveness is desired and required by the situation.

The non-adaptive or inflexible style of leadership is associated with those who manage using a paternalistic philosophy that the leaders feel is appropriate in all or almost all situations. These managers think of their subordinates as "children" and of themselves as "parents" (*Anderson,* 1992). This approach is in keeping with Confucian concepts that are often integral to Chinese business management practices.

The second approach is the adaptive style of leadership. This refers to the leader who takes into account the task to be done, the situation in which the task is to be accomplished and the readiness of their employees to accomplish the task. "Readiness" refers to the psychological and task competencies of those involved in a task (*Hersey et. al.,* 1996).

The situational leadership model as quantified by *Hersey et. al.* (1996) and *Hambleton and Gumpert* (1982) suggests that leadership styles change as a function both of a leader's maturity and of an organization's (and its work force's) maturity, now referred to as "readiness" (*Hersey et. al.,* 1996). Although readiness is conceptually equivalent to maturity, readiness is considered as a less emotionally charged word than maturity, which has certain connotations, some of which may be considered pejorative.

According to *Greenberg* (1996), employee-centered (considerate) and task-oriented (initiating structure) leadership styles are not the opposite ends of a continuum as are the autocratic and participation styles. A leader who is oriented toward the considerate style, for instance, does not necessarily become less concerned with production. Because these orientations are independent of one another, managers may use both orientations to varying degrees. In fact, when one orientation exists alone the other may be bypassed and this may result in decreased overall organizational productivity.

It appears that successful leaders are those who are able to balance their leadership-style approach between the consideration and the structure-initiation models (*Greenberg*, 1996). When flexibility and adaptability were measured to compare a manager's perceptions of his or her own leadership style with the level of use of personal computers by subordinates, there was a positive relationship found between a leader's perceptions of his or her own leadership ability and the use of computers by employees (*Stone*, 1990).

Choosing a leader with an appropriate leadership style is critical for a firm's success. Thus, it is important to understand which leadership styles are most effective. *Fey et. al.* (2001) investigated the leadership characteristics most commonly used to describe Russian leaders. Respondents from 90 firms identified task-orientated, relations-orientated, authoritarian and democratic as the four most commonly chosen descriptors. These descriptors were then used to construct a model (a 2 x 2 matrix) which identified four different leadership styles (statesman, clergyman, politician and military-man). Middle managers from 101 firms in Russia then evaluated the effectiveness of these four leadership styles. Responses revealed that the statesman style (task-oriented democrat) and the clergyman style (relations-oriented democrat) were considered most effective.

Lowin and Craig (1968) conducted study to evaluate the effect of various leadership styles on subordinate performance. To evaluate an experiment was conducted in which performance was manipulated and style observed in a realistic setting. Very strong evidence was obtained that performance shapes the following leadership styles: closeness of supervision, initiating structure and consideration for subordinate.

Collins and Porras (1994) reinforced the idea that finding the right leadership style is key to organizational effectiveness. In extensive research on organizations that they labeled as long-term, successful companies found there was no evidence to suggest that leadership is the distinguishing variable between successful and less successful companies. They opined that company success is associated with leaders who are appropriate to the organization and the organization shares in the responsibility of ensuring that leadership succession plans are in place.

According to *Yukl* (1994) situational leadership style is more appropriate in organizations in such areas as research and development, communications, project management, health care and education.

Manz and Sims (1991) describe four broad leadership archetypes: strongman, transactor, visionary hero and Super Leader. The strongman relies on authority and coercion to make subordinates perform the tasks. The authors opine that although authoritarianism is considered a relic of past managerial practice many contemporary leaders still employ this style. The transactor uses rewards and sanctions to motivate employees. This approach assumes that employees rationally evaluate the exchange of rewards and performance. The third type, visionary hero, uses inspiration and vision to motivate employees. The Super Leader encourages subordinates to become self-leaders. Super Leaders accomplish this by encouraging individuals to set their own goals, monitor their own behaviours and develop intrinsic rewards.

As the firm transitions to the simple bureaucracy, transactional leadership behaviours become more salient (*Gibbons,* 1992) while visionary leadership behaviours often become detrimental (*Argenti,* 1976). Although the visionary leader from the simple structure may· remain in power, the necessity for vision begins to recede. The increased centralization and autocratic leadership found in the simple bureaucracy precludes Super Leader behaviours. Given the increasing reliance on teamwork and the fluidity of authority and power, the most suitable leadership style in this configuration is Super Leadership.

Grinnell (2003) studied leadership patterns in small bureaucratic organizations. The seminal research took a more holistic view than past research as majority of other studies paid inordinate attention to visionary leadership while neglecting other styles. By studying four leadership styles simultaneously, the researcher highlighted that relating the macro-approach to leadership could be an important progression in the evolution of situational/contingency approaches.

Situational/contingency models of leadership over-emphasize micro/behavioural elements (e.g., subordinate task readiness, leader-subordinate relations, subordinate maturity) while neglecting macro/structural variables. A problem with such an approach is that it fails to acknowledge that upper executives must be concerned with external as well as internal integration (*Hunt, Baliga and Peterson*, 1989). This is particularly so in smaller enterprises where leaders combine the tasks of building organizational competencies and managing the environment. Nevertheless, in recent years there has been an increase in both conceptual (*Shamir and Howell*, 1999) and empirical (*Pillai and Meindl*, 1998) research adopting a macro-framework.

Puffer (1990) assessed the impact of decision style (intuitive versus technical), decision outcome (successful versus unsuccessful) and organizational role of the observer (managers *versus* non-managers) on attributions of charismatic leadership. Results showed that all three variables have a significant influence on the attribution process, but that it is important to distinguish between different components of charismatic leadership.

4.2.3 Studies on Transformational Leadership

Bryant (2003) suggests that leaders are central to the process of managing knowledge effectively. Managing knowledge includes three key processes: creating, sharing, and exploiting knowledge. Leaders are central to each of these processes at multiple levels of the firm. Examining the role of leadership in converting knowledge into competitive advantages is important to our understanding of leaders and organizations. Transformational leadership may be more effective at creating and sharing knowledge at the individual and group levels, while transactional leadership is more effective at exploiting knowledge at the organizational level.

Leaders play a central role in the process of managing organizational knowledge. Leaders provide vision, motivation, systems and structures at all levels of the organization that facilitate the conversion of knowledge into competitive advantages. Managing knowledge requires a conscious effort on the part of leaders at all levels of the organization to manage three key knowledge processes: creating, sharing and exploiting knowledge. Transformational leadership theory and transactional leadership theory provide a foundation for understanding how leaders impact the cultivation of knowledge (*Bass*, 1985; *Conger and Kanungo*, 1998; *House*, 1977; *House and Aditya*, 1997).

Strategy scholars have begun to outline a knowledge-based view of the firm, which suggests that managing organizational knowledge effectively can provide firms with a source of sustainable competitive advantage (*Boisot*, 1998; *Glazer*, 1998; *Grant*, 1996; *Teece*, 1998). These theorists argue that intangible knowledge-based resources, rather than physical and financial resources, provide the key source of a firm's competitive advantage. Effectively leading organizational knowledge processes is essential to achieving and sustaining a competitive advantage.

Transformational and charismatic leadership theories provide a useful tool for understanding how leaders impact the management of organizational knowledge. Though there are differences between the transformational and charismatic leadership theories, scholars are now viewing them as sharing much in common and referring to this body of work as the "new leadership" theory (*Hunt and Conger*, 1999) or "neo-charismatic" leadership theory (*Fiol et. al.*, 1999).

Transformational leaders are active leaders that have four distinguishing characteristics: charisma, inspiration, intellectual stimulation and individualized consideration (*Bass*, 1985; *Conger*, 1999). Charisma is the extent of pride, faith and respect leaders encourage their workers to have in themselves, their leaders and their organizations. Inspiration is the ability to motivate followers largely through communication of high expectations. Intellectual stimulation is the frequency with which leaders encourage employees to be innovative in their problem-solving and solutions. Individualized consideration is the degree of personal attention and encouragement of self-development a leader imparts to the employees (*Bass,* 1985; 1990). Transformational leaders devote significant energy to leading and respect abilities of their workers.

Transactional leaders resemble traditional managers, emphasizing dependence. Transformational leaders are visionaries, identifying the mission and values of the organization and pulling not pushing subordinates along the path to their goal.

The transformational leadership style was introduced by *Burns* (1978) and extensively researched by *Bass* and his associates (1985). The charismatic leadership style shares much in common with Bass's transformational leadership construct and has been developed largely by *House* (1977), *House* and associates (1991), *Conger* (1999) and *Conger and Kanungo* (1998). *Sashkin* (1988) has done related work on visionary leadership that highlights the visionary nature of top leaders.

Recent leadership studies in a wide variety of organizations have examined the impact of transformational and charismatic leaders on subjects in a wide variety of settings, including corporations, schools and military units (*Conger and Kanungo,* 1998; *House and Aditya,* 1997; *Fiol et. al.,* 1999; *Podsakoff, McKenzie and Bommer,* 1996; *Lowe et. al.,* 1996; *Keller,* 1992). Across all these studies, researchers found that transformational and charismatic leadership styles "result in a high-level of follower motivation and commitment and well-above-average organizational performance, especially under conditions of crisis or uncertainty" (*House and Aditya,* 1997; *Lowe et. al.,* 1996). With the advent of the internet and the growth of virtual work teams, researchers have begun to examine the impact of transformational leadership on knowledge creation in these computer-mediated groups (*Sosik,* 1997).

Bass (1985) suggested that under certain conditions employees could rise above their own self-interests and give extra effort in order to achieve the organization's mission. He argued that transformational leaders are able to elicit this extraordinary performance. Transformational leaders can be defined both by their effect on followers and their behaviours that seem to motivate exceptional performance (*Conger and Kanungo,* 1998).

Several leadership scholars have argued that Bass's model is incomplete because it does not properly account for organizational context factors that will significantly impact the effectiveness of the transformational leader (*Conger and Kanungo,* 1998; *Conger,* 1999; *Yukl and Howell,* 1999). These authors add sensitivity to the environment as a key dimension of the charismatic leader. This element is important because charismatic leaders are generally quite shrewd at evaluating the climate of the team and the organization and modifying their plans accordingly.

Several elements of transformational leadership theory fit well with managing knowledge. Employees are more productive when they have the freedom to create new ideas, share those ideas with co-workers and test out their new ideas (*Sosik,* 1997). Transformational leaders create an atmosphere conducive to knowledge creation, sharing and exploitation. In particular, by using charisma, encouraging intellectual development and by paying individual attention to workers, transformational leaders motivate their workers to create and share knowledge. Transformational leaders are able to attract talented individuals by clearly articulating a challenging vision and strategic goals for the organization (*Conger and Kanungo,* 1998). Having bright and talented people is necessary but not sufficient to effectively facilitate the creating, sharing and exploiting of knowledge. Transformational leaders inspire workers on to higher levels of innovation and effectiveness.

Bass (1985) contrasts transformational leaders with transactional leaders and *Conger and Kanungo* (1998) contrast charismatic leaders with non-charismatic leaders. While transformational leaders inspire exceptional performance, transactional or non-charismatic leaders aspire to achieve solid and consistent performance that meets agreed upon goals. Transactional leaders give rewards and punishments to encourage performance, making the leader/worker relationship essentially an economic transaction. Transactional leaders have three primary characteristics. First, transactional leaders work with their team members to develop clear, specific goals and ensure that workers get the reward promised for meeting the goals. Second, they exchange rewards and promises of rewards for worker effort. Finally, transactional leaders are responsive to the immediate self-interests of workers if their needs can be met while getting the work done.

Transactional leadership encourages specific exchanges and a close connection between goals and rewards. Consequently, workers are not motivated to give anything beyond what is clearly specified in their contract. This is especially troubling for knowledge workers for whom it is much more difficult to specify complete job descriptions in advance. Workers may also choose to utilize their excess brain capacity by consulting or starting their own business if they are not challenged and rewarded for extra effort in the firm. Leaders exhibit characteristics of both transformational and transactional leadership styles. Individual leaders tend to emphasize one of these styles more than the other. Both types of leaders are required to effectively manage knowledge (*Conger,* 1999).

Van Eton and Burke (1992) have demonstrated that differences in managers' personality preferences are related to divergent leadership orientations that along with subsequent variation in associated behaviour can result in very specific patterns of communication with subordinates. Other research based on this same basic framework has yielded interesting results with respect to personality factors and transformational leadership styles among champions of technological innovation (*Howell and Higgins,* 1990), organization development and change practitioners (*Church, Waclawski and Burke,* 1996), and implicit theories of leadership in military institutions (*Atwater and Yammarino,* 1993). Some authors (*Kuhnert and Lewis,* 1987; *Kuhnert and Russell,* 1990) have gone so far as to suggest that certain critical personality differences in leaders may actually result in the formation of either transformational or transactional leadership styles and that these behavioural differences observed in various types of leaders may reflect different stages or levels of maturity in terms of personal development and goal orientation.

There has been a tremendous impetus within the last decade to define the role of leader as opposed to manager in any organization. A review of the literature reveals that this vision of the "effective leader" crosses the boundaries of many professions. A contemporary theory of leadership is the transformational leader. According to *Sullivan and Decker* (1997), the transformational leader is not interested in the *status quo*, rather with "effecting revolutionary change in organizations and human service." The transformational leader generates the commitment and passion of staff for the mission and values of the organization. The leader has to identify the future of the organization and pulls, rather than pushes, constituents along the path to carry out the mission. The transformational leader, according to *Medley and Larochelle* (1995), is "an individual who is concerned with long-term second order change and associated processes that relate to the higher order needs of individuals."

Berson and Avolio (2004) examined how the leadership style of top and middle-level managers in a large telecommunications organization was related to their effectiveness in conveying strategic organizational goals. Using quantitative and qualitative methods, they found that transformational leaders perceived organizational goals as prospector-oriented and were rated as more effective communicators by their direct reports. They examined research questions regarding the methods by which transformational leaders disseminate organizational goals. An exploratory analysis indicated that managers who reported to transformational leaders tended to have higher agreement on the strategic goals of the organization. Leaders who were effective communicators had direct reports who were more familiar with the goals of the organization.

Berson et. al. (2001) examined the relationship between leadership style and the content of vision statements of the firms. The transformational leadership style of 141 leaders positively predicted the inspirational "strength" of their vision statements. Organizational size was related to vision strength and moderated the relationship between passive leadership style and vision strength.

Putti and Tong (1992) observed initiation of structure, integration, role assumption and tolerance of freedom as their dominate leadership styles among civic service Asians. They also found positive and significant correlations between leadership styles and subordinates satisfaction.

Bourantas (1988) presented the results of an empirical study of the relation between the leadership styles, need satisfaction and the organizational commitment of Greek managers. The findings show that there is a negative relationship between need satisfaction and organizational commitment. This relationship is stronger for the higher-order than for the lower-order needs. Furthermore, the results provide some empirical evidence regarding the relationship between the superior's leadership style and the subordinate's organizational commitment. The findings show that in most cases studied, the commitment of the Greek managers was higher when the superior adopted a consultative leadership style. This style was also the one preferred by the majority of the respondents.

Brownell (1983) studied the effects of leadership style and budgetary participation on performance and job satisfaction. The first two variables have been given much attention in the organizational behaviour and management accounting literatures, respectively, while little consideration has been given to both jointly. The two variables interact in their effects on the criterion variables. Under certain leadership conditions, budgetary participation was found to have strong positive effects on performance and job satisfaction. Under other conditions, the reverse was true.

Casimir (2001) introduced the concept of combinative aspects of leadership style, which addresses elements of leadership style such as the ordering and temporal spacing of leadership behaviours. The perceptions of leadership are influenced by the manner in which leadership behaviours are combined. The task-oriented leadership should not be provided without socio-emotional leadership and that socio-emotionally-oriented leadership should generally be provided immediately before task-oriented leadership.

Chong et. al. (1997) examined followers' perceptions of the leadership style of leaders who were culturally similar or different to themselves. Participants were members of two ethnic groups who were employed in one of four New Zealand organizations. Findings indicated that leader and follower ethnicity interact to affect follower satisfaction. Additionally, leadership prototypes held by members of the two ethnic groups appeared to have culturally-based differences. Researchers highlight the complexity of cross-cultural leadership situations and the need to consider the effects of both leader and follower ethnicity on leader-follower relationships.

Dubinsky et. al. (1994) reported results of a study that explored both the level and nature of closeness of sales supervision by the manager of his subordinate. Operationalization was based on the degree of active involvement sales managers have with their salespeople expressed in terms of differing leadership styles. Findings reveal that highly active involvement with salespeople generally has a more favorable impact on work outcomes of sales subordinates than inactive or moderately active involvement.

4.2.4 Emerging Trends in the Behavioural Research on Leadership

The leadership literature has focused on the effects of leaders whereas much less attention has been given to the followers' role in shaping their leader's style. *Dvir* and *Shamir* (2003) tested follower developmental characteristics as predictors of transformational leadership. The sample included 54 military units and their leaders, in which there were 90 direct followers and 724 indirect followers. Results at the group level of analysis indicated that followers' initial developmental level, as expressed by the initial level of their self-actualization needs, internalization of the organization's moral values, collectivistic orientation, critical-independent approach, active engagement in the task and self-efficacy positively predicted transformational leadership among indirect followers, whereas these relationships were negative among direct followers.

Eagly et. al. (2003) found that female leaders were more transformational than male leaders and also engaged in more of the contingent reward behaviours that are a component of transactional leadership. Male leaders were generally more likely to manifest the other aspects of transactional leadership (active and passive management by exception) and *laissez-faire* leadership. Although these differences between male and female leaders were small, the research has established that all of the aspects of leadership style on which women exceeded men relate positively to leaders' effectiveness whereas all of the aspects on which men exceeded women have negative or null relations to effectiveness.

Existing research on charismatic leadership focuses primarily on the traits and behaviours of charismatic leaders and the effects of charismatic leaders on their followers. One issue that has been neglected is the disposition of the followers who form charismatic relationships with their leaders. To investigate this topic, *Ehrhart and Klein* (2001) conducted a laboratory study in which participants' values and personality dimensions were used to predict participants' preferences for charismatic leadership *v.* two other leadership styles: relationship-oriented and task-oriented leadership. The results showed that values and personality were useful in predicting leadership preferences.

Fernandez and Vecchio (1997) suggested that supervisory monitoring and consideration may interact with job level such that monitoring has a positive impact for lower level employees, while consideration has a more positive impact for higher level employees. The interaction suggests that some of the intuitively-appealing aspects of the situational theory may be correct, but that couching these processes in terms of reaciness/maturity and the Ohio State dimensions of initiation structure and consideration is incorrect.

Green and Nebeker (1977) predicted that when the situation was unfavourable the relationship-motivated leaders behaved in a more interpersonally oriented and less task-oriented manner than did the task-motivated leaders. On the other hand, when the situation was favorable the task-motivated leaders emphasized interpersonal behaviour more and task behaviour less than the relationship-motivated leaders. Leader LPC by situation interactions indicate that both leader personality and the situation are important determinants in leader behaviour and that LPC and situational favourability may be helpful in understanding this interaction.

Hill (1973) measured subordinates' perceptions of their leaders' ability to use different leadership styles. Subjects were 124 middle and first level supervisors from accounting and R and D departments in the United Kingdom. The results indicated that subjects did not believe that their supervisors would either use the same style (irrespective of what style) or randomly employ styles to deal with four typical but hypothetical problems. These results persisted when respondents were sub-divided on the basis of both organizational level and functional area.

Howell and Frost (1989) examined the interactive influence of three different leadership styles and two levels of group productivity norms on individuals' adjustment and performance on a decision-making task. Participants working under the charismatic leader, regardless of the directionality of group productivity norms had high task performance, task adjustment and adjustment to the leader and to the group. Participants working under the structuring leader and in the high productivity norm group reported higher task satisfaction and lower role conflict than participants working under the structuring leader and in the low productivity norm group. Individuals with a considerate leader and in a high productivity norm group had significantly higher task satisfaction than those with a considerate leader and in a low productivity norm group.

Jago and Vroom (1977) investigated the relationship between the hierarchical level of managerial personnel and individual differences in their leadership styles, specifically the degree to which they are disposed to the use of participative *versus* autocratic decision-making strategies. Analysis of self-report data collected from four different levels of managers suggested a greater propensity for use of participative methods at higher organizational levels. Subordinate descriptions of their immediate superiors further support this relationship.

A wide range of factors has been found to affect organizational innovation. Of these, top managers' leadership style has been identified as being one of the most important. *Jung et. al.* (2003) support a direct and positive link between a style of leadership that has been labeled as "transformational" and organizational innovation. They also indicated that transformational leadership has significant and positive relations with both empowerment and an innovation-supporting organizational climate. The former is found to have a significant but negative relation with organizational innovation, while the latter has a significant and positive relationship.

Kahai et. al. (2003) conducted laboratory experiment to study the effects of leadership style (transactional *v.* transformational), anonymity (identified *v.* anonymous interaction) and rewards (individual *v.* group) on creativity-relevant group processes and outcomes in two decision-making tasks supported by an electronic meeting system (EMS). Evidence for social loafing was observed, i.e., anonymity led to lower participation and cooperation in the group rewards condition relative to the individual rewards condition. Social loafing was confined to the transactional leadership condition. Corresponding to the social loafing effect, anonymity led to lower group efficacy and satisfaction with the task and higher originality of solutions in the group rewards condition relative to the individual rewards condition. Transactional leadership was associated with greater group efficacy and solution originality than transformational leadership. Anonymity moderated the effects of leadership on group efficacy and satisfaction with the task; transactional leadership was associated with higher group efficacy and satisfaction with the task in the identified condition only.

Lindell (1991) discussed the need for top managers to change their style in small entrepreneurial firms during a business life cycle. He reported that managers find it hard to move from an innovative style when the company is young to task-oriented behaviour in the firm's mature stage. He attributed it to the link between management style and the corporate system, structure and values. The corporate context itself must change if managers are to be able to change their own styles effectively and smoothly. Based on contingency approaches to leadership he explored leadership style most consistent with the underlying objectives and psychological obligations underlying different groups of employees.

McColl-Kennedy and Anderson (2002) examined whether the emotions of frustration and optimism mediate, fully or partially, the relationship between leadership style and subordinate performance in the context of structural equation modeling. The findings show that transformational leadership has a significant direct influence on frustration and optimism, with the negative influence of frustration having a stronger effect on performance than the positive influence of optimism. Frustration and optimism were found to have a direct influence on performance and the emotions, frustration and optimism, fully mediate the relationship between transformational leadership and performance. Thus, the effect of transformational leadership style on performance is significant but indirect.

Decision styles defined by the primary and secondary considerations in choice making and the implementation tactics preferred by managers were used by *Nutt* (1986) to explain the ways in which managers with a given style take action. He highlighted the unique approaches taken by managers with each style in their decisions concerning leadership, team building, strategic management, control and related issues that managers grapple with to fashion a desired future.

Scontrino (1972) tried to compare the effectiveness of different leadership styles. He used twelve groups with five subjects per group. Six groups were told that their leader would be participative. Three of these groups received a participative leader; three received an authoritarian leader. Six groups were told that their leader would be authoritarian. Three of these groups received an authoritarian leader; three received a participative leader. All groups solved Maier's New Truck Dilemma and completed four attitude scales. Participative leadership resulted in attitudes that were more positive and less variable than the attitudes resulting from authoritarian leadership regardless of whether expectations were fulfilled or violated.

Shea and Howell (1999) examined the interactive effects of two different leadership styles (charismatic and non-charismatic) and three types of task feedback (internal, external and no feedback) on individuals' self-efficacy and performance quality over four trials of a manufacturing task. The subjects manufactured electrical wiring harnesses under the direction of either a charismatic or non-charismatic leader (an experimental confederate). Participants exposed to the charismatic leader had similar task performance regardless of task feedback condition, while participants exposed to the non-charismatic leader differed in their task performance depending on whether or not they received task feedback. Self-efficacy mediated the effect of task feedback and its interaction with charismatic leadership on performance.

Skogstad and Einarsen (1999) scrutinized the existence of a change-centered leadership style in a sample consisting of four organizations. Exploratory factor analysis yielded substantial support for a distinct change-centered dimension. Significant positive correlations were found in the sample as a whole between a change-centered leadership style and job satisfaction, organizational commitment and evaluations of the leader's competence. The notion that such correlations would be strongest in the developmental culture was confirmed only in the case of organizational commitment.

Sosik et. al. (2002) indicated that complexity of desired charismatic identity was positively related to self-monitoring. Self-monitoring was negatively related to ratings of pro-social impression management and positively related to ratings of self-serving impression management. Pro-social impression management related positively to charismatic leadership, which predicted managerial and unit performance.

Tracey and Hinkin (1996) showed that transformational leadership has a direct impact on perceptions of subordinate satisfaction with the leader and leader effectiveness, as well as an indirect effect on these variables through its impact on openness of communication, mission clarity and role clarity.

Vecchio and Boatwright (2002) confirmed that employees with higher levels of education and greater levels of job tenure expressed less preference for leader structuring, while females (relative to males) expressed greater preference for leader considerateness. These results suggest that an understanding of employee expectations for leader behaviours may be of value in optimizing the level and nature of leader involvement with subordinates.

Dasborough and Ashkanasy (2002) presented a model of emotions and attributions of intentionality within the leader-member relationship. The model is predicated on two central ideas. The first is that leadership is intrinsically an emotional process where leaders display emotion and attempt to evoke emotion in their members. The second is that leadership is a process of social interaction and is therefore appropriately defined in terms of social and psychological theories such as the attribution theory. Members' attributions about their leader's intentions influence how the members evaluate, interpret and eventually label the leader's influence attempts on transformational leadership. These attributions are determined by and themselves influence the members' emotions.

Parrish (2001) examined the influence of leadership behaviour on perceived organizational commitment and job autonomy. This study revealed that there was a significant and positive relationship between both components of leadership behaviour, consideration and initiating structure and perceived affective commitment in library supervisors. Consideration was also found to be significantly and positively related to perceptions of work methods, work scheduling and work criteria autonomy. When gender was controlled, it did not have a moderating effect on the relationship between either dimension of leadership behaviour and any dimension of perceived organizational commitment.

Yu (2000) investigated conductor leadership behaviour as a force for choral ensemble success. The findings of this study revealed that (a) the consideration dimension of leadership behaviour (CLS) group had higher member satisfaction with the CLS conductor's efforts than did the initiating structure dimension of leadership behaviour (SLS) with the SLS conductor's efforts. The CLS group appeared high in self-motivation, cohesiveness and morale in comparison with the SLS group.

References

Adler, N.J. (1991): *International Dimensions of Organizational Behaviour*, Boston, MA: Kent.

Anderson, T.D. (1992): *Transforming Leadership*, Amherst, MA: Human Resource Development Press.

Argenti, J. (1976): *Corporate Collapse: The Causes and Symptoms*, New York: John Wiley and Sons.

Atwater, L.E. and Yammarino, F.J. (1993): "Personal Attributes as Predictors of Superiors' and Subordinates' Perceptions of Military Academy Leadership." *Human Relations*, Vol. 46, pp. 645-668.

Bass, B.M. and Stogdill, R.M. (1989): *The Handbook of Leadership*, New York: The Free Press.

Bass, B.M. (1985): *Leadership and Performance Beyond Expectations*, New York: The Free Press.

Bass, B.M. (1990): *Bass and Stogdill's Handbook of Leadership: Theory, Research and Managerial Applications*, New York: Free Press.

Bass, B.M., Avolio, B.J. and Atwater, L. (1996): The Transformational and Transactional Leadership of Men and Women." *Applied Psychology: An International Review*, Vol. 45, pp. 5-34.

Belkaoui, A. (1990): "Leadership Style, Dimensions of Superior's Upward Influence and Participative Budgeting." *Scandinavian Journal of Management*, Vol. 6 (3), pp. 217-30.

Bennis, W. and Nanus, B. (1985): *Leaders*, New York: Harper and Row.

Berson, Y. and Avolio, B.J. (2004): "Transformational Leadership and the Dissemination of Organizational Goals: A Case Study of a Telecommunication Firm." *The Leadership Quarterly*, Vol. 15 (5), pp. 625-46.

Berson, Y. and Shamir, B. (2001): "The relationship between vision strength, leadership style and context." *The Leadership Quarterly*, Vol. 12(1), pp. 53-73.

Blake, R.R. and Mouton, J.S. (1982): "A Comparative Analysis of Situationalism and 9, 9 Management by Principle." *Organizational Dynamics*, Vol. 10 (4), pp. 20-43.

Boisot, M.H. (1998): *Knowledge Assets: Securing Competitive Advantage in the Information Economy*, New York: Oxford University Press.

Bourantas, D. (1988): "Leadership Styles, Need Satisfaction and the Organizational Commitment of Greek Managers." *Scandinavian Journal of Management*, Vol. 4 (3-4), pp. 121-134.

Bowman, R. Jr. (2000): "Examining Six Different Leadership Styles In Relation to Constrained Change at Winona State University." *Education*, 22 March.

Brownell, P. (1983): "Leadership Style, Budgetary Participation and Managerial Behaviour." *Accounting, Organizations and Society*, Vol. 8 (4), pp. 307-321.

Bryant, S.E. (2003): "The Role of Transformational and Transactional Leadership in Creating, Sharing and Exploiting Organizational Knowledge." *Journal of Leadership and Organizational Studies*, 22 March.

Bryman, A. (1992): *Charisma and Leadership in Organizations*, London: Sage.

Burns, J.M. (1978): *Leadership*, New York: Harper and Row.

Carless, S.A. (1998): "Gender Differences in Transformational Leadership: An Examination of Superior, Leader and Subordinate Perspectives." *Sex Roles*, Vol. 39, pp. 887-902.

Carlson, H.C. (1981): "Improving Quality of Work Life." *Management Handbook Operating Guidelines, Techniques and Practices*, New York: Ronald Press.

Casimir, G. (2001): "Combinative Aspects of Leadership Style: The Ordering and Temporal Spacing of Leadership Behaviours." *The Leadership Quarterly*, Vol. 12 (3), pp. 245-78.

Chong, L.M.A. and Thomas, D.C. (1997): "Leadership Perceptions in Cross-cultural Context: Pakeha and Pacific Islanders in Newzeland." *The Leadership Quarterly*, Vol. 8 (3), pp. 275-93.

Church, A.H. and Waclawski, J. (1996): "The Effects of Personality Orientation and Executive Behaviour on Subordinate Perceptions of Workgroup Enablement." *International Journal of Organizational Analysis*, Vol. 4, pp. 20-51.

Collins, J.C. and Porras, J.I. (1994): *Built to Last*, New York: Harper.

Conger, J.A. and Kanungo, R.N. (1994): "Charismatic Leadership in Organizations: Perceived behavioural attributes and their measurement." *Journal of Organizational Behaviour*, Vol. 15, pp. 439-52.

Conger, J.A. and Kanungo, R.N. (1998): *Charismatic Leadership in Organizations*, Thousand Oaks, CA: Sage.

Conger, J.A. (1999): "Charismatic and Transformational Leadership in Organizations: An Insider's Perspective on these Developing Streams of Research." *Leadership Quarterly*, Vol. 10, pp. 145-69.

Conner, D.R. (1998): *Leading at the Edge of Chaos*, New York: John Wiley.

Crouch, A. and Yetton, P. (1987): "Manager Behaviour, Leadership Style, and Subordinate Performance: An Empirical Extension of the Vroom-Yetton conflict rule1." *Organizational Behaviour and Human Decision Processes*, Vol. 39 (3), pp. 384-96.

Dasborough, M.T. and Ashkanasy, N.M. (2002): "Emotion and Attribution of Intentionality in Leader–member Relationships." *The Leadership Quarterly*, Vol. 13 (5), pp. 615-34.

Dhar, U. and Mishra, M. (2001): "Leadership Effectiveness." *Journal of Management Research*, Vol. 1(4), pp. 254-66.

Dickson, M.W. and Hartog, D.N.D. (2003): "Research on Leadership in a Cross-cultural Context: Making Progress and Raising New Questions." *The Leadership Quarterly*, Vol. 14(6), pp. 729-68.

Doherty, A.J. (1997): "The Effect of Leader Characteristics on the Perceived Transformational/Transactional Leadership and Impact of Interuniversity Athletic Administrators." *Journal of Sport Management*, Vol. 11, pp. 275-85.

Druskat, V.U. (1994): "Gender and Leadership Style: Transformational and Transactional Leadership in the Roman Catholic Church." *Leadership Quarterly*, Vol. 5 (2), pp. 99-119.

Dubinsky, A.J. and Yammarino, F.J. (1994): "Closeness of Supervision and Salesperson Work Outcomes: An Alternate Perspective." *Journal of Business Research*, Vol. 29(3), pp. 225-37.

Dvir, T. and Shamir, B. (2003): "Follower Developmental Characteristics as Predicting Transformational Leadership: A Longitudinal Field Study." *The Leadership Quarterly*, Vol. 14 (3), pp. 327-44.

Eagly, A.H. and Johnson, B.T. (1990): "Gender and Leadership Style: A Meta-Analysis." *Psychological Bulletin*, Vol. 108 (2), pp. 233-56.

Eagly, A.H., Johannesen, M.C. and Schmidt, P. (2003): "Transformational, Transactional and Laissez-Faire Leadership Styles: A Meta-Analysis Comparing Women and Men." *Psychological Bulletin*, Vol. 129(4), pp. 569-91.

Ehrhart, M.G. and Klein, K.J. (2001): "Predicting Followers' Preferences for Charismatic Leadership: The Influence of Follower Values and Personality." *The Leadership Quarterly*, Vol. 12 (2), pp. 153-79.

Ekvall, G. and Arvonen, J. (1991): "Change-centered Leadership: An Extension of the Two-dimensional Model." *Scandinavian Journal of Management*, Vol. 7 (1), pp. 17-26.

Elangovan, A.R. and Xie, J.L. (1999): "Effects of Perceived Power of Supervisor on Subordinate Stress and Motivation: The Moderating Role of Subordinate Characteristics." *Journal of Organizational Behaviour*, Vol. 20(3), pp. 359-73.

Elkins, T. and Keller, R.T. (2003): "Leadership in Research and Development Organizations: A Literature Review and Conceptual Framework." *The Leadership Quarterly*, Vol. 14(4-5), pp. 587-606.

Fernandez, C. and Vecchio, R.P. (1997): "Situational Leadership Theory Revisited: a test of an Across-jobs Perspective." *Leadership Quarterly*, Vol. 8, pp. 67-84.

Fey, C.F. and Adaeva, M. (2001): "Developing a Model of Leadership Styles: What Works best in Russia?" *International Business Review*, Vol. 10(6), pp. 615-43.

Fiedler, F. E. (1966): "The Effect of Leadership and Cultural Heterogeneity on Group Performance: A Test of the Contingency Model." *Journal of Experimental Social Psychology*, Vol. 2 (3), pp. 237-64.

Fiedler, F.E. (1967): *A Contingency Model of Leadership Effectiveness*, New York: McGraw-Hill.

Fiol, M.C., Harris, D. and House, R. (1999): "Charismatic Leadership: Strategies for Effecting Social Change." *Leadership Quarterly*, Vol. 10, pp. 449-82.

George, N. and Von Der Embse, T.J. (1971): "Six Propositions for Managerial Leadership: Diagnostic Tools for Definition and Focus." *Business Horizons*, Vol. 14 (6), pp. 33-43.

Gibbons, P.T. (1992): "Impacts of Organizational Evolution on Leadership Roles and Behaviours." *Human Relations*, Vol. 45, pp. 1-18.

Graen, G.K., Alvares, K., Orris, J.G. and Martella, J.A. (1972): "Contingency Model of Leadership Effectiveness: Antecedent and Evidential Results." *Psychological Bulletin*, Vol. 74, pp. 285-296.

Graham, S., Wedman, J.F. and Garvin-Kester, B. (1994): "Manager Coaching Skills: What makes a Good Coach?" *Performance Improvement Quarterly*, Vol. 7 (2), pp. 81-94.

Green, S.G. and Nebeker, D.M. (1977): "The Effects of Situational Factors and Leadership Style on Leader Behaviour." *Organizational Behaviour and Human Performance*, Vol. 19 (2), pp. 368-77.

Greenberg, J. (1996): *Managing Behaviour in Organizations*, Upper Saddle River, New Jersy: Prentice-Hall.

Hambleton, R.K. and Gumpert, R. (1982): "The Validity of Hersey and Blanchard's Theory of Leader Effectiveness." *Group and Organizational Studies*, Vol. 7 (2), pp. 225-42.

Hartog, D., Muijen, V.J. and Koopman, P. (1994): "Transactional *versus* Transformational Leadership: An Analysis of the MLQ in Dutch Organizations." *Gedrag en Organisatie*, Vol. 7, pp. 155-66.

Hersey, P. and Blanchard, K. (1988): *LEAD Questionnaires*. Escondido, CA: Center for Leadership Studies Press.

Hersey, P., Blanchard, K. and Johnson, D.E. (1996): *Management of Organizational Behaviour: Utilizing Human Resources* (7th ed.), Englewood Cliffs, New Jersy: Prentice-Hall.

Hill, W.A. (1973): "Leadership Style: Rigid or Flexible?" *Organizational Behaviour and Human Performance*, Vol. 9 (1), pp. 35-47.

Hingar, A. (1984): "Psychometric Verification of Leadership Styles." *Indian Management*, September.

House, R.J. and Aditya, R.N. (1997): "The Social Scientific Study of Leadership: Quo vadis?" *Journal of Management*, Vol. 23, pp. 409-73.

House, R.J. and Howell, J.M. (1992): "Personality and Charismatic Leadership." *Leadership Quarterly*, Vol. 3, pp. 81-108.

House, R.J. (1977): "A 1976 Theory of Charismatic Leadership." In: Hunt, J.G. and Larson, L.L. (Eds.). *Leadership: The Cutting Edge*. Carbondale: Southern Illinois University Press.

House, R.J. (1984): "Power in Organizations: A Social Psychological Perspective." Unpublished paper, *Faculty of Management*, University of Toronto.

House, R.J., Spangler, W.D. and Woycke, J. (1991): "Personality and Charisma in the U.S. Presidency: A Psychological Theory of Leader Effectiveness." *Administrative Science Quarterly*, Vol. 36, pp. 364-96.

Howell, J.M. and Frost, P.J. (1989): "A Laboratory Study of Charismatic Leadership." *Organizational Behaviour and Human Decision Processes*, Vol. 43 (2), pp. 243-269.

Howell, J.M. and Higgins, C.A. (1990): "Champions of Technological Innovation." *Administrative Science Quarterly*, Vol. 35, pp. 317-41.

Hunt, J.G., Baliga, B.R. and Peterson, M.F. (1989): "Strategic Apex Leadership Scripts and an Organizational Life Sycle Approach to Leadership and Excellence." *Journal of Management Development*, Vol. 7, pp. 61-83.

Jago, A.G. and Vroom, V.H. (1977): "Hierarchical Level and Leadership Style." *Organizational Behaviour and Human Performance*, Vol. 18 (1), pp. 131-45.

Jung, D.I. and Chow, C. (2003): "The Role of Transformational Leadership in Enhancing Organizational Innovation: Hypotheses and some Preliminary Findings." *The Leadership Quarterly*, Vol. 14(4-5), pp. 525-44.

Kahai, S.S. and Sosik, J.J. (2003): "Effects of Leadership Style, Anonymity and Rewards on Creativity-relevant Processes and Outcomes in an Electronic Meeting System Context." *The Leadership Quarterly*, Vol. 14(4-5), pp. 499-524.

Keller, R.T. (1992): "Transformational Leadership and the Performance of Research and Development Project Groups." *Journal of Management*, Vol. 18, pp. 489-501.

Kotter, J.P. (1988): *The Leadership Factor*, New York: The Free Press.

Kuhnert, K.W. and Russell, C.J. (1990): "Using Constructive Developmental Theory and Biodata to Bridge the Gap between Personnel Selection and Leadership." *Journal of Management*, Vol. 16, pp. 595-607.

Kuhnert, R. and Lewis, G. (1987): "Transactional and Transformational Leadership: A Constructive/Developmental Analysis." *Academy of Management Review*, Vol. 12 (4), pp. 648-57.

Lindell, M. (1991): "How Managers should change their Style in a Business Life Cycle." *European Management Journal*, Vol. 9 (3), pp. 271-79.

Liu, W., Lepak, D.P., Takeuchi, R. and Sims, H.P. (2003): "Matching Leadership Styles with Employment Modes: Strategic Human Resource Management Perspective." *Human Resource Management Review*, Vol. 13(1), pp. 127-52.

Lowin, A. and Craig, J.R. (1968): "The influence of level of Performance on Managerial Style: An Experimental Object—Lesson in the Ambiguity of Correlational Data." *Organizational Behaviour and Human Performance*, Vol. 3 (4), pp. 440-58.

Manz, C.C. and Sims, H.P. (1991): "Super Leadership: Beyond the myth of Heroic Leadership." *Organization Dynamics*, Vol. 19, pp. 18-35.

Medley, F. and Larochelle, D.R. (1995): "Transformational Leadership and Job Satisfaction." *Nursing Management*, Vol. 26 (9), pp. 64 JJ-LL.

Nutt, P.C. (1986): "Decision Style and its Impact on Managers and Management." *Technological Forecasting and Social Change*, Vol. 29 (4), pp. 341-66.

Palmon, R.R. and Illies, J.J. (2004): "Leadership and Creativity: Understanding Leadership from a Creative Problem-solving Perspective." *The Leadership Quarterly*, Vol. 15(1), pp. 55-77.

Parrish, L. (2001), "Can State Incentives Compacts Work?" *Accountability: The Newsletter of the Business Incentives Clearinghouse*, Vol. 3(1).

Pearce, C.L. and Conger, J.A. (2003): *Shared leadership: Reframing the hows and whys of leadership*, Thousand Oaks, CA: Sage.

Puffer, S.M. (1990): "Attributions of Charismatic Leadership: The Impact of Decision Style, Outcome and Observer Characteristics." *The Leadership Quarterly*, Vol. 1(3), pp. 177-92.

Putti, J.M. and Tong, A.C. (1992): "Effects of Leader Behaviour on Subordinate Satisfaction in a Civil Service Asian Context." *Public Personnel Management*, Vol. 21(1), pp. 53-63.

Schein, E.H. (1991): *Organizational Culture and Leadership*, San Francisco: Jossey-Bass.

Scontrino, M.P. (1972): "The Effects of Fulfilling and Violating Group Members' Expectations about Leadership Style." *Organizational Behaviour and Human Performance*, Vol. 8 (1), pp. 118-38.

Shea, C.M. and Howell, J.M. (1999): "Charismatic Leadership and Task Feedback: A Laboratory Study of their effects on self-efficacy and task Performance." *The Leadership Quarterly*, Vol. 10 (3), pp. 375-96.

Skansi, D. (2000): "Relationship of Managerial Efficiency and Leadership Styles—Empirical Study in Hrvatska Elektroprivreda D.D." *Management*, Vol. 5(2), pp. 51-67.

Skogstad, A. and Einarsen, S. (1999): "The Importance of a Change-centered Leadership Style in Four Organizational Cultures." *Scandinavian Journal of Management*, Vol. 15 (3), pp. 289-306.

Sosik, J.J. and Avolio, B.J. (2002): "Beneath the Mask: Examining the Relationship of Self-presentation Attributes and Impression Management to Charismatic Leadership." *The Leadership Quarterly*, Vol. 13(3), pp. 217-42.

Sosik, J.J. (1997): "Effects of Transformational Leadership and Anonymity on Idea Generation in Computer-mediated Groups." *Group and Organization Management*, Vol. 22, pp. 460-79.

Stone, R.A. (1990): "Leadership Style and Managers' Attitudes toward using Personal Computers: A Field Study." *Psychological Reports*, Vol. 67(3), pp. 915-22.

Sullivan, E. and Decker, P. (1997): *Effective Leadership and Management in Nursing* (4th ed.), Addison Wesley Longman, Inc.Cincinnati, Ohio, pp. 408-10.

Teece, D.J. (1998): "Capturing Value from Knowledge Assets: The New Economy, Markets for know-how and Intangible Assets." *California Management Review*, Vol. 40, pp. 55-79.

Tracey, J.B. and Hinkin, T.R. (1996): "How Transformational Leaders Lead in the Hospitality Industry." *International Journal of Hospitality Management*, Vol. 15 (2), pp. 165-76.

Tracy, L. (1993): "Conflict and Divided Loyalty: A Fundamental Leadership Dilemma. Mid-American." *Journal of Business*, Vol. 8, pp. 21-28.

Ulrich, D., Brockbank, W., Yeung, A.K. and Lake, D.G. (1995): "Human Resource Competencies: An Empirical Assessment." *Human Resource Management*, Vol. 34, pp. 473-95.

Van Eton, A.M. and Burke, W.W. (1992): "The Transformation/Transactional Leadership Model: A Study of Critical Components." In Clark, K.E., Clark, M.B. and Campbell, D.P. (Eds), *Impact of Leadership*, pp. 149-67. Greensboro, NC: Center for Creative Leadership.

Vecchio, R.P. and Boatwright, K.J. (2002): "Preferences for Idealized Styles of Supervision." *The Leadership Quarterly*, Vol. 13(4), pp. 327-42.

Wang, T.H. (2001): "Situational Leadership Style as a Predictor of Success and Productivity among Taiwanese Business Organizations." *The Journal of Psychology*, 1 July.

Willemsen, T.M. (2001): "Gender, Context and Leadership Styles: A Field Study." *Journal of Occupational and Organizational Psychology*, 12 Jan.

Wright, P., Dunford, B. and Snell, S.A. (2001): "Human Resources and the Resource-based view of the firm." *Journal of Management*, Vol. 27, pp. 701-21.

Yu, H. (2000): "Transformational Leadership and HongKong Teachers' Commitment to Change." Unpublished Ph.D. Dissertation, University of Toronto, Canada.

Yukl, G. and Howell, J.M. (1999): "Organizational and Contextual Influences on the Emergence and Effectiveness of Charismatic Leadership." *Leadership Quarterly*, Vol. 10, pp. 257-83.

Yukl, G.A. (1994): *Leadership in Organizations* (3rd ed.), Englewood Cliffs, New Jersy: Prentice-Hall.

Zanna (Ed.), *Advances in Experimental Social Psychology*, Vol. 25, pp. 115-91. San Diego, CA: Academic Press.

CHAPTER

5

Recent Developments in Organisational Commitment

5.1 A CRITIQUE ON EXISTING LITERATURE ON ORGANISATIONAL COMMITMENT

Commitment is thought to be generated through a process of social exchange whereby being involved in an organization also comes to involve other interests of the employee in such a way that his or her behaviour is constrained to some extent. These can include cultural expectations which involve a penalty for their violation (for instance, production workers are normally expected to work the extra hours or time schedules) and the organization's bureaucratic arrangements such as pensions and promotion structures. The terms 'professional', 'occupational' and 'career commitment' have been used somewhat interchangeably in the literature.

Commitment to organizational ideology has attracted much rekindled attention for intriguing and compelling reasons (*Schein*, 1991; *Tracy*, 1993). Personnel pull together for the common purpose in a strong ideological organization where the unique attractiveness of its rich culture bonds members tightly and commits them individually and organizationally to identify with its rules, rewards and values (*Katz & Kahn*, 1978).

Commitment has been a subject of interest for some time. The past decades have seen a broadening of the domain within which commitment is studied. *Becker* (1992) suggested that there are different foci of commitment. Individuals can feel committed to the organization, top management, supervisors or the work group. Some of the earliest work within the organizational behaviour literature (*Porter et al*, 1974; *Mowday, Steers, & Porter*, 1979) examined employees' commitment to their employers, commonly referred to as organizational commitment.

Mueller & Lawler (1999) specified three key conditions which will result in commitment to a particular unit: a unit's 'distance' from an employee, whether proximate units produce positive emotions and whether this positive emotion is perceived to be caused by that unit. *Hunt & Morgan* (1994) suggested that commitment to a sub-group can also facilitate a more global commitment to the organization generally, which implies the existence of nested identities within an organization and nested levels of commitment.

5.1.1 Developing the Conceptual Framework of Organisational Commitment

There are two different approaches to define *Organizational commitment*. In the first approach, organizational commitment is referred to as a behaviour; the individual is viewed as committed to an organization if he/she is bound by past actions of "sunk costs" (fringe benefits, salary) as a function of age or tenure. Thus an individual becomes committed to an organization because it has become too costly for him/her to leave (*Blau & Boal*, 1987).

In the second approach, organizational commitment is referred to as an attitude. Organizational commitment has also been viewed as an attitude with three components: (a) Belief in and acceptance of organization's goals and values, (b) Willingness to exert effort on behalf of the organization; and (c) Strong desire to maintain organizational membership (*Porter et. al.*, 1974; *Mowday, Steers & Porter*, 1979, 1982; *Johnston & Snizek*, 1991).

Castells (1996) sees the new networked organization as requiring the two major components of organizational commitment—discretionary effort and employment continuance. Much higher levels of employee involvement are needed so that employees do not keep their tacit knowledge solely for their own benefit and there must be stability of employment 'because only then does it become rational for the individual to transfer his/her knowledge to the company and for the company to diffuse explicit knowledge among its workers' (*Castells*, 1996). Knowledge workers may thus seem ideal recipients of prescriptive commitment-raising HRM policies. Thus, high-technology driven should ensure high levels of organisational commitment.

Meyer & Allen (1991) described three forms of organizational commitment: commitment as an affective attachment to the organization; commitment as a perceived cost associated with leaving the organization; and commitment as an obligation to remain in the organization. These three forms are termed as affective (i.e. individuals stay in the organization because they want to), continuance (i.e. individuals stay in the organization because they need to) and normative commitment (i.e. individuals stay in the organization because they feel they should), respectively.

Within this componential framework, commitment is regarded as a positive employee response to progressive employment practices, such as team working, training provision or employee share schemes. Studies show the affective dimension of commitment to be related to generally positive employee perceptions of the organization and management; for instance, perceived organizational support (*Eisenberger et al*, 1990; *Rhoades & Eisenberger*, 2002); management trust (*Gopinath & Becker*, 2000; *Pearce*, 2003); procedural fairness or fair treatment (*Folger & Konovsky*, 1989; *Podsakoff et al*, 1996); and particularly to 'climate' factors such as being kept informed, equal opportunities and family-friendly practice (*Guest*, 2002).

Affective commitment is expected to result in elevated job performance. However, while research evidence shows that affective commitment leads to greater willingness to stay with an organization, lower absenteeism, greater effort, productivity and greater organizational citizenship behaviour (*Meyer, Allen & Smith,* 1993; *Meyer & Allen,* 1997), the identification of which particular employment practices result in heightened affective commitment and thus performance outcomes, is beset with difficulties.

Reichers (1985) proposes a multiple constituency's model of organizational commitment which accepts the possibility of multiple foci of commitment (such as work-team, project group, union, supervisor, colleagues and customers) which may be reinforcing or competing. There is after all no reason to believe that these multiple loyalties will always be complementary. The 'discovery' that launched the whole human relations movement in the late 1920s was that commitment to the norms of the workgroup could be more immediate and influencing on behaviour than the values of the wider organization.

Organizational identification is distinct from organizational commitment (*Ashforth & Mael,* 1989; *Mael & Tetrick,* 1992) as the latter implies an internalisation of values. Employees will most strongly identify with the unit with the greatest salience for them and this in turn will result in affective commitment directed to that unit.

According to *Gaertner* (1999), it is even possible that all of these determinants do not predict *both* job satisfaction and organisational commitment. For example, from a theoretical point of view, supervisory support and promotional chances could be directly related to organisational commitment over and above job satisfaction, while other structural determinants could be related to job satisfaction alone. It is also important to point out that compared to organisational commitment, job satisfaction varies more directly and instantaneously with changing working conditions (*Mowday et al,* 1982). Moreover, if managers would conceptualise major work characteristics (i.e. staffing, training, assigning work, appraising performance, allocating rewards, etc.) within a human resource framework, it might enhance employees' awareness in human resource departments of their responsibilities regarding work groups (*Campion et al,* 1993). This encourages decentralisation of power in subordinates' hands that would be more suitable to work as leaders, responsible for their team functioning in well-adapted working conditions.

The various views on organisational commitment seem to reflect three general components: affective attachment to the organisation (affective commitment), perceived costs associated with leaving the organisation (continuance commitment) and feelings of obligation to the organisation (normative commitment) (*Allen & Meyer*, 1990). Although each of these components increases the likelihood that the employee will choose to remain within the organisation, the nature of these psychological ties differs from one another.

Recent research supports a three-dimensional construct of professional commitment that is similar to the one for organisational commitment. According to *Meyer et al* (1993), the nature of the person's involvement in the occupation might differ depending on which form of commitment is predominant. A person who is affectively committed may keep up with developments in the occupation (e.g. by subscribing to trade journals or attending conferences) or join and participate in relevant associations. Individuals who have a strong continuance commitment may, in contrast, be less inclined to involve themselves in occupational activities besides those required to continue membership (*Meyer et al*, 1993).

Finegan (2000) studied the influence of personal and organisational values on AC, NC and CC. She found that AC is highest when there is congruence between individual's personal values and those of the organisation in which they worked. This was not the case for NC, where there was a closer relationship between an individual's personal value system and NC, with the organisational culture playing little or no part in the relationship. Continuance commitment scores in her study were not predicted by person-organisation value fit.

Thus it may be reasonable to assume that an employee's AC is influenced by the fit between an organisations value system and that of the employee. If however the organisation is facing rapid change with a requirement for reactivity which alters job characteristic and work-unit values, the "fit" may become a mismatch which might predict a fall in AC scores. As organisational values appear not to influence NC or AC directly one might suggest that internal organisational changes may not impact these facets of commitment.

Professional commitment is argued to be an even stronger determinant of ones' turnover than commitment to the organisation and work (*Mueller et al*, 1992). Lacking professional commitment has been found to be associated with intention to leave the profession in several studies (*Bedeian et al*, 1991; *Cohen*, 1998) and also with intention to leave the organisation (*Cohen*, 1998). Research in employee turnover has generated several models of determinants and processes underlying voluntary turnover. In the most recent models, job satisfaction and organisational commitment proved to have empirical relationships with voluntary turnover even in meta-analyses (*Gaertner*, 1999). Among determinants, leadership is viewed as an important predictor of job satisfaction and commitment, beside the other work setting characteristics.

Meyer & Herscovitch (2001) recognized that employees can develop multiple work-relevant commitments and that commitment itself is a multi-dimensional construct. There remains considerable disagreement both within and across work commitment literatures (e.g., organizational, occupational, union) about what commitment is, its dimensionality, how it develops and how it affects behaviour. Commitment should have a "core essence" regardless of the context in which it is studied and that it should therefore be possible to develop a general model of workplace commitment.

Vandenberghe et. al. (2004) showed that organizational commitment (a) had an indirect effect on turnover through intent to quit, (b) partially mediated the effect of commitment to the supervisor on intent to quit, and (c) completely mediated the effect of commitment to the work group on intent to quit. They determined that (a) commitment to the supervisor had a direct effect on job performance, and (b) organizational commitment had an indirect effect on job performance through commitment to the supervisor.

Cheng et. al. (2004) presented a long-term commitment model that can support the long existing change process of a strategic alliance in construction. The model embraces components that help to stimulate the level of employee and management commitment in order to satisfy the stakeholders.

They suggested the measure of satisfaction under project, business and corporate levels so that the performance of individual organizations and the alliance can be traced according to these levels. Employee and management satisfaction resulting from the favourable performance of the organizations and the alliance will reinforce their commitment further. This interdependence process occurring between commitment and satisfaction supports a growing and never-ending survival of the strategic alliance.

Hackett et. al. (2001) investigated the conceptual distinctiveness and causal relationship between organizational commitment (OC), occupational commitment (OcC), job involvement (JI), work involvement (WI) and intentions to withdraw from the organization and from the occupation. The process involved exploratory and confirmatory factor analyses which supported the distinctiveness of the constructs. Results suggest that WI affects both OC and OcC indirectly through its effect on JI. JI affects intention to leave the organization indirectly through its effect on OC and affects intention to leave the occupation indirectly through its effect on OcC. Analyses also suggest that OC and OcC have direct and indirect effects on both forms of withdrawal intentions.

Meyer et. al. (2002) conducted meta-analyses to assess (a) relations among affective, continuance and normative commitment to the organization and (b) relations between the three forms of commitment and variables identified as their antecedents, correlates and consequences in *Meyer & Allen's* (1991) Three-Component Model. They found that the three forms of commitment are related yet distinguishable from one another as well as from job satisfaction, job involvement and occupational commitment. Affective and continuance commitment generally correlated as expected with their hypothesized antecedent variables; no unique antecedents of normative commitment were identified. All three forms of commitment related negatively to withdrawal cognition and turnover. Affective commitment had the strongest and most favourable correlations with organization-relevant (attendance, performance and organizational citizenship behaviour) and employee-relevant (stress and work-family conflict) outcomes.

Normative commitment was also associated with desirable outcomes albeit not as strongly. Continuance commitment was unrelated or related negatively to these outcomes.

5.1.2 International Studies on Organisational Commitment

Jaramillo et. al. (2005) opined that relationship between organizational commitment and job performance is positive and stronger for sales employees than for non-sales employees. Stronger correlations between organizational commitment and job performance are found for collectivist compared to individualistic cultures.

Tellefsen & Thomas (2005) explored the potential for business service customers to form separate bonds of commitment with the service firm and the service representative. They examined the role of the individual and identified six potential antecedents to each type of commitment. They proposed that both types of commitment will influence the degree of relational exchange between the customer and the service firm.

Cheng & Stockdale (2003) examined the construct validity of Meyer and Allen's (1991) three-component model of organizational commitment in a Chinese context and compared levels of OC between the Chinese sample and previously published data from Canada and South Korea. The proposed antecedents of each of the three principal OC dimensions tended to associate most strongly with their respective scales. Affective commitment and normative commitment significantly predicted job satisfaction and all three components predicted turnover intention, although associations between continuance commitment and these outcomes were moderated by normative commitment. The normative and affective commitment was significantly higher in the Chinese sample than in previously published samples from Canada and South Korea. Continuance commitment in the Chinese sample was lower than the Canadian and Korean samples.

Chen & Francesco (2003) examined the relationship between the three components of organizational commitment and performance. Results showed that affective commitment (AC) related positively to in-role performance and OCB, while continuance commitment (CC) was not associated with in-role performance but negatively correlated with OCB. In addition, normative commitment (NC) moderated the relationship between AC and in-role performance as well as OCB. The linear relationship between AC and in-role performance/OCB was stronger for those with lower NC.

Wright & Bonett (2002) investigated the correlation between attitudinal commitment and job performance for 3,630 employees obtained from 27 independent studies across various levels of employee tenure. Controlling for employee age and other nuisance variables the authors found that tenure had a very strong non-linear moderating effect on the commitment–performance correlation, with correlations tending to decrease exponentially with increasing tenure. Their findings do not appear to be the result of differences across studies in terms of the type of performance measure (supervisory *v.* self), type of tenure (job *v.* organizational) or commitment measure.

Riketta & Dick (2005) opined that the workgroup and the organization as a whole are common foci of employee attachment (i.e., identification and commitment). They reviewed theorizing and empirical research on the relative impact of attachment to these foci on work attitudes and behaviour. Confirming predictions derived from a wide range of previous models a meta-analysis revealed that (a) on average workgroup attachment is stronger than organizational attachment, and (b) each form of attachment is most strongly related to potential outcome variables of the same focus.

Verquer et. al. (2003) have presented a meta-analytic review of 21 studies on relations of person-organization fit with job satisfaction, organizational commitment and intent to turnover. Four specific moderators were investigated: the type of fit measure, method of calculating fit, dimensions of fit and use of an established measure of person-organization fit. Mean effect sizes for the outcome variables ranged from—.18 for intent to turnover to .28 for organizational commitment. Subjective fit measures, the use of correlations to calculate fit, value congruence as the fit dimension and the use of an established measure of person-organization fit increased effect sizes.

Cohen & Freund (2005) examined the relationship between multiple commitments (affective organizational commitment, continuance organizational commitment, occupational commitment and job involvement) and withdrawal cognitions with three different time intervals between the two. The findings showed that commitment forms were related to withdrawal cognitions even when withdrawal cognitions measured earlier than or at the same time as commitment forms were controlled for. The results also showed that the timing of the measurement of the research variables had a strong effect on the findings. More specifically, the prediction of withdrawal is better, the shorter the interval between its measurement and the measurement of multiple commitments. The findings also showed that commitment and withdrawal are both dynamic concepts. The effect of timing on the accuracy of the prediction can be a result of more immediate changes in commitment forms across time or more immediate changes in withdrawal cognitions over time.

Dawley et. al. (2005) explored the multi-dimensionality of organizational commitment of volunteer chamber of commerce board members using the *Meyer & Allen* (1997) scale. The effect of organizational commitment on desirable board member roles was also tested. Theory was developed by uniting past research in both organizational commitment and employee motivation. A proposed scale was tested using Confirmatory Factor Analysis with data gathered from 616 respondents at 116 chambers of commerce in 36 states. Structural Equations Modeling was then used to examine the effects of organizational commitment on several critical roles the board member is hoped to perform. These results indicated that normative, affective and continuance commitment based on low alternatives are the three distinct constructs applicable to volunteer employees. Moreover, these components were found to have positive effect on board member's roles.

Kim et. al. (2005) examined the relationship between employee service orientation (customer focus, organizational support and service under pressure) and employees' job satisfaction, organizational commitment and employees' intention of leaving. The empirical results indicated that the customer focus of employees was negatively associated with employees' job satisfaction but positively associated with their organizational commitment. Second, organizational support was positively associated with job satisfaction. Third, job satisfaction was positively associated with organizational commitment but negatively associated with employees' intention of leaving. Finally, organizational commitment was negatively associated with intention of leaving.

Stinglhamber et al (2002) tested the generalizability of *Meyer & Allen's* (1991) three-component model of commitment to five foci. First, measures of affective, continuance and normative commitment to the organization, the occupation, the supervisor, the work group and customers were developed and tested using confirmatory factor analysis. Results provided strong support for the three-component model both within and across foci. They showed that "high sacrifice" and "low alternatives" were distinguishable sub-components within the continuance organizational commitment scale. Second, commitments directed to foci other than the organization contribute unique variance in intent to quit the organization above and beyond organizational commitment. Finally, logistic regression analysis used to examine the relationships between commitment components and actual turnover measured 18 months after among the alumni sample revealed that affective organizational commitment and high sacrifice were the single significant predictors of turnover.

Kondratuk et. al. (2004) assessed the relationship between career mobility history and a recent internal or external job change on organizational commitment using (*Allen & Meyer,* 1990) three-dimensional model. External career mobility history (i.e., number of external job moves over one's career) was negatively related to normative commitment but not to affective and continuance commitment. Affective and continuance commitment were significantly lower for external movers prior to a move when compared to non-movers over the same period. In contrast, only continuance commitment was significantly lower for internal movers prior to a move when compared to non-movers over the same period. Affective commitment increased significantly after the move for both internal and external movers.

5.1.3 A Critique on Studies on Organisational Commitment in Indian Perspective

Verma (1986) found that the degree of managerial respect affected the Organisational Commitment of the employee. The employee who received more managerial respect showed more managerial commitment whereas the employee who received less managerial respect showed lesser organisational commitment. Officers were found to have more organisational commitment than clerks. The interaction effect between two variables: managerial respect and status was found to be insignificant though they have affected the organisational commitment.

Sharma & Chauhan (1991) assessed the level of motivation and morale of public sector managers and also found determinants thereof. They used 'organisational commitment' as a measure of motivation. Highly motivated employees or those with high morale feel more committed to their organisation than those who are less motivated.

Khan & Mishra (2002) estimated the canonical correlation between need satisfaction and organisational commitment. A sample of 150 rail engine driver was administered the Indian adaptation of Porter's Need Satisfaction Scale (*Khan and Mishra*, 2001) and organisational commitment Scale (*Allen & Meyer*, 1993). The need satisfaction scale measured five needs-compensation, social/common, autonomy/egoism, esteem and self-accomplishment. The organisational commitment scale measured three dimensions of organisational commitment—Affective, normative and continuance. Needs of social attachment and esteem were significantly correlated with affective and normative commitment. The canonical correlation between the five needs and three dimensions of organisational commitment was significant.

Sinha et. al. (2002) investigated the relationship between organisational commitment, self-efficacy and perceived psychological barriers to technological change. The sample consisted of 167 male managers. It was found that organisational commitment was positively related to age, length of service in present cadre and self-efficacy. It was negatively related to psychological barriers to technological change.

Psychological barriers to technological change were positively related to age, length of service in recent cadre and negatively related to self-efficacy. There was a negative correlation between self-efficacy and age as well as between self-efficacy and length of service in present cadre.

Lok (1999) examined the influence of organizational culture, sub-culture and leadership style and job satisfaction on organizational commitment. He indicated that the leadership style variable, consideration, exerted a relatively strong influence on commitment when compared with other variables included in this study.

Subramaniam & Mia (2003) examined the effect of the interaction between managers' quest for innovation and budget emphasis (an integral part of MAS) on their organisational commitment. The results indicate that the adoption of low budget emphasis led to high organisational commitment when managers' quest for innovation was high, but not when managers' quest for innovation was low. The results also indicated that marketing managers held higher quest for innovation than production managers. The post-survey interviews provided further insight into how a more customer- and competitor-focused sub-culture of marketing managers and a more technical and efficiency-focused sub-culture of production managers may promote the difference in their WRV for innovation and affect their attitudes towards budget emphasis.

5.1.4 Relationship between Organisational Commitment and Leadership Styles

Several studies have attempted to investigate the relationship between leadership and organisational commitment. Relation between participatory leadership and organisational commitment were reported by *Jermier & Berks* (1979) and *Rhodes & Steers* (1981). Both of the studies examined and found a positive relationship between organisational commitment and participatory leadership.

Morris & Sherman (1981) studied the relationship of leadership styles among other variables as correlates of organisational commitment. The result indicated that leadership behaviour may constitute an important and under-researched component in the commitment process. It was not surprising that high structure/high consideration behaviour mix on the part of leaders tended to be associated with high level of commitment among subordinates within the sample.

Bruning & Snyder (1983) studied the relationship between leader communication and organisational commitment and found a large positive correlation between the two. They reported that a leader who provides more accurate and timely communication to subordinates enhances the work environment and thereby is likely to increase employee's commitment to the organisation.

Jermier & Berks (1979) found that participatory leadership was most effective at influencing the communication levels of police officers working in unpredictable environments.

Mathieu & Zajac (1990) in their review and meta-analysis of antecedent correlates and consequences of organisational commitment reported correlation between organisational commitment, leader initiating structure and leader consideration. Most studies asserted leader behaviour with one of the several forms of the Leader Behaviour Description Questionnaire. The results of the meta-analysis showed medium positive correlates for each behaviour.

According to *Scandura & Williams* (2004) leaders may need to serve as mentors to activate transformational leadership and promote positive work attitudes and career expectations of followers. To test this premise, incremental effects of transformational leadership and mentoring over each other were examined using (*N*=275) employed MBAs. Respondents with supervisory mentors reported receiving higher levels of career mentoring than respondents with non-supervisory mentors. Supervisory career mentoring (SCM) and transformational leadership had incremental effects over each other for job satisfaction. SCM had mediating effects over transformational leadership for organizational commitment and career expectations. Career mentoring by non-supervisory mentors was not associated with career expectations but there were incremental effects with idealized influence and inspirational motivation for job satisfaction and organizational commitment.

Whittington et. al. (2004) conducted field study of 209 leader-follower dyads from 12 different organizations to test the moderating effects of job enrichment and goal difficulty on the relationship between transformational leadership and three follower outcomes: performance, affective organizational commitment and organizational citizenship behaviour. Moderated regression analyses were conducted to test for direct and moderated relationships. Transformational leadership and job enrichment each had significant main effects. They found that job enrichment substituted the effects of transformational leadership on affective commitment, whereas goal setting enhanced relationships between transformational leadership and both affective commitment and performance.

Rhodes & Steers (1981) found a higher correlation between participatory leadership and organisational commitment in worker-owned as compared with conventional organisations.

Banai et. al. (2004) examined the influence of managerial and personal control upon work-related alienation and organizational commitment in the Eastern-European nation of Hungary. The research identified the extent to which Western management theory and practices are relevant to transitional economic nations such as Hungary. Researchers chose leadership and job characteristics as managerial control mechanisms and locus of control as a personal mechanism of control. These categories of control variables have well-established associations to attitudes and behaviours in the Western management literature but limited evidence has been generated in developing countries. A survey among 395 Hungarian workers in five companies found that leadership; job characteristics and individual locus of control explained work-related alienation but did not explain organizational commitment.

5.1.5 Role of Firm's Human Resource Practices on Developing Organisational Commitment among Employees

HR practices play an indirect role in organizational effectiveness, i.e. by enhancing organizational commitment (*Meyer & Smith,* 2000; *Whitener,* 2001), perceptions of procedural fairness or justice (*Meyer & Allen*, 2000), organizational citizenship behaviours (*Podsakoff, MacKenzie, Paine & Bachrach*, 2000) and turnover intentions (*Vandenberg et. al.*, 1999).

Research has focused on individual differences as antecedents of commitment, revealing that factors such as age and organisational tenure are positively correlated with commitment (*Mathieu & Zajac*, 1990; *Angle & Perry*, 1981). Research has also revealed an inverse relationship between commitment and turnover intention (*Porter et. al.*, 1974) in addition to showing a positive relationship between commitment and regular employee attendance (*Steers*, 1977).

Pare & Tremblay (2004) investigated the role of high-involvement human resources practices, organizational commitment and citizenship behaviours on turnover intentions among a sample of highly skilled professionals. Five significant findings emerged: first, structural equation modeling analyses revealed that non-monetary recognition and competency development, fair rewards and information sharing practices are negatively related to turnover intentions. Second, both forms of organizational commitment together with citizenship behaviours are negatively associated with turnover intentions. Third, extensive investment in competence development is strongly and positively associated with the development of perception of continuance commitment among IT professionals. Fourth, procedural justice mediated the influence of HR practices on organizational commitment behaviours and turnover intentions. Fifth, four out of five high involvement HR practices have a direct negative influence on turnover intentions among IT specialists.

Research on organizational justice suggests that when an organization treats its employees fairly employees are likely to reciprocate by adopting behaviours beneficial to the organization (*Organ*, 1988). Some scholars have proposed that the use of fair procedures and systems may enhance employee commitment because fairness suggests that employees are respected members of the organization (*Lind & Tyler*, 1988). The group value model (*Tyler & Lind*, 1992) specifies that individuals greatly value long-term relations with the group to which they belong. Fair procedures enhance the feeling of being treated as a full member of the organization which, in turn, reinforces the emotional bond to the group and/or the organization. In the same vein, a positive relationship has been found between perception of procedural justice and affective commitment (*Folger & Konovsky*, 1989; *McFarlin & Sweeney*, 1992; *Kerman & Hanges*, 2002).

Several empirical studies confirm the predominant role of organizational commitment in the turnover process among highly skilled professionals (*Igbaria & Greenhaus*, 1992; *Igbaria & Guimaraes*, 1999) and several conceptualizations for this construct have been advanced (*Meyer & Herscovitch*, 2001). Several studies of turnover intentions among professionals have considered the first and most studied dimension of the construct: affective commitment (*Igbaria & Greenhaus*, 1992; *Igbaria & Guimaraes*, 1999).

Characteristics of the organization, especially leadership and organization's age are the strongest predictors of commitment and satisfaction are best predicted by job task characteristics such as role ambiguity and skill variety (*Glisson & Durick*, 1988). However, an important job task characteristic, feedback has not been considered enough as a predictor of attitudes in human service work. Feedback is defined as performance-related information available to individuals in work settings. The amount and type of feedback information that is available is referred to as the feedback environment (*Herold & Parsons*, 1985).

A field experiment conducted by *Tziner & Latham* (1989) revealed increased work satisfaction and organizational commitment when a goal-setting and feedback programme was introduced but it is not possible to draw the conclusion that this effect emanates from feedback only. There is some evidence that feedback affects commitment but the outcomes vary depending on work context. *Steers* (1977) found that feedback was related to commitment among scientists and engineers but not among hospital employees.

Organizational commitment has been found to be affected by role ambiguity among human service workers (*Glisson & Durick*, 1988; *Welsch & LaVan*, 1981). Organisational commitment is built on the notion that members of a firm develop attachments to the firm apart from a purely instrumental worth. Organisational commitment has been associated with a process whereby members of a firm identify with the goals and values of the firm and desire to maintain their relationship with the firm.

It is a multi-dimensional concept that has been interpreted in a variety of different ways (*Allen & Meyer,* 1990; *Meyer & Allen,* 1997). The main contenders appear to be affective or attitudinal (*Buchanan,* 1974; *Mowday et. al.,* 1982; *Porter et. al.,* 1974), normative (*Allen & Meyer,* 1990; *Wiener & Vardi,* 1980), behavioural (*Staw & Salancik,* 1977) and calculative (*Becker,* 1960; *Ritzer & Trice,* 1969).

Probably the most popular method of examining the concept is through an individual's attitudes and feelings towards his or her employing organization. *Legge* (1995) states that, "virtually all the research conducted on organizational commitment, *per se,* has used the attitudinal conceptualization". This conceptualization suggests that committed employees have a strong belief in and acceptance of the organization's goals and values, show a willingness to exert considerable effort on behalf of the organization and have a strong desire to maintain membership with the organization.

Whitener (2001) explored the relationships among human resource practices, trust-in-management and organizational commitment. Individual-level analyses from a sample of 1689 employees from 180 credit unions indicate that trust-in-management partially mediates the relationship between perceived organizational support and organizational commitment. Cross-level analyses using hierarchical linear modeling indicate that human resource practices affect the relationship between perceived organizational support and organizational commitment or trust-in-management.

5.1.6 Emerging Trends in Research on Organisational Commitment

Kuvaas (2003) examined the relationship between the preferences and perceptions of employees regarding an ongoing share ownership plan on the one hand and the employees' affective organizational commitment on the other. The preference for ownership and the perceived fairness of the employee ownership plan were significant predictors of affective commitment. The employee ownership has intrinsic motivating effects on employees by way of a mediating mechanism whereby the effects of ownership on organizational commitment depend on how employees evaluate and perceive formal ownership plans.

Tellefsen (2002) examined commitment in business-to-business (B2B) relationships from the purchasing manager's perspective. He proposed that purchasing managers will form stronger bonds with suppliers who are better able to satisfy both the buying firm's organizational needs as well as the purchasing manager's personal needs. Purchasing managers will be more influenced by personal rather than organizational need fulfilment.

Wasti (2002) investigated organizational commitment in Turkey, a predominantly collectivist society. A model of antecedents and consequences of organizational commitment was tested, where commitment was conceptualized as composed of two dimensions, affective and continuance. Affective commitment was hypothesized to develop from positive work experiences and to predict desirable outcomes. Continuance commitment was argued to be culture-bound. He proposed that in a collectivist culture like Turkey, the normative nature of the employment relationship would generate expectations for loyalty to the organization and the perceived costs of violating these expectations would be reflected in increased continuance commitment. It was expected that the endorsement of generalized norms for loyalty to one's organization and informal recruitment would lead to higher levels of continuance commitment.

The investigation involved two phases. The results not only confirmed the cross-cultural generalizability of the antecedents and consequences of affective commitment but also indicated that loyalty norms and in group approval increased continuance commitment. The influence of norms and the in-group was stronger for allocentrics. For allocentrics, continuance commitment was related to more positive job outcomes. The results underline the importance of normative concerns in understanding employee attachment in collectivist contexts and also point to a need for a better measurement of calculative commitment.

Lau & Chong (2002) suggested that organizational interest is best served if a high budget emphasis evaluative style is used in a high participatory environment, whilst a low budget emphasis evaluative style is used in a low participatory environment. Highly committed managers are likely to strive for organizational goals and interests whereas lowly committed managers are likely to strive for personal goals and interests. These conflicting attitudes are likely to affect the relationships among budget emphasis, budgetary participation and managers' behaviour. Highly committed managers striving for organizational goals may react favourably to the compatible combinations of high (low) budget emphasis and high (low) budgetary participation. In contrast, lowly committed managers striving for personal goals may prefer other combinations of budget emphasis and budgetary participation.

Beck & Wilson (2001) suggested that some forms of work commitment develop prior to actual experience of the focus of the commitment (e.g., normative commitment and work ethic). For affective and continuance commitment it has been hypothesized that *experience* is essential. In most instances, this experience is gained after entry into the work force and specifically, into an organization. Therefore, understanding how these types of commitment develop and highlighting the factors related to tenure that cause changes in commitment will not only fill a gap in the empirical work and strengthen commitment theory but will help managers to optimize the commitment of their employees.

Wong et. al. (2001) argued that in countries exhibiting cultures which values loyalty organizations will benefit in the long-run if they cultivate employees' organizational commitment in those countries. Data from two samples from the PRC and Hong Kong were analyzed to understand the role of organizational commitment in affecting other attitudinal antecedents (i.e., job satisfaction and turnover intention) to turnover. Results indicated that organizational commitment among Chinese employees has a much stronger effect on job satisfaction and turnover intention than results from studies conducted in the West.

Organizational commitment has long been considered a key predictor of Organizational Commitment Behaviour CB

(*Meyer, Stanly, Herscovitch & Topolnytsky,* 2002). According to *Mowday, Porter and Steers* (1982) those who are committed to the organization "are willing to give something of them in order to contribute to the organization's well-being". Employees who are highly committed to their organization often perceive their work roles more extensively and such an enlargement of role definition tends to increase employees' motivation to exhibit OCB behaviours (*Lee,* 2001; *Morrison,* 1994; *Tepper & Taylor,* 2003). In accordance with this view, previous studies show that affective commitment is positively related to extra-role behaviours while continuance commitment is either negatively or not significantly associated with OCB (*Allen & Smith,* 1987; *Meyer & Allen,* 1991; *Mayer & Schoorman,* 1992; *Chen et. al.,* 1998; *Meyer et. al.,* 1998; *Lee,* 2001; *Riketta,* 2002; *Meyer et. al.,* 2002). A plausible explanation for these findings is that employees that exhibit a high level of continuance commitment are more likely to develop a transactional relationship (as opposed to a relational relationship) with their employer. Indeed, according to the psychological contract theory (*Rousseau,* 1995), employees who perceive their relation with their employer as primarily instrumental are more likely to restrict their professional obligations to those activities they are paid for (i.e. intra-role behaviours). In contrast, a relational contract encompasses a higher level of affectivity that predisposes workers to adopt a much broader view of their relationship with their employer and thus encourages extra-role behaviours.

The concept of organizational commitment has recently impacted the participative budgeting and employee performance streams of accounting research. Specifically, a series of studies by *Nouri, Nouri* and *Parker* have shown that an individual's level of organizational commitment negatively impacts budgetary slack and positively impacts employee performance (*Nouri,* 1994; *Nouri & Parker,* 1996, *Nouri & Parker,* 1998).

Quirin et. al. (2001) attempted to address this issue by investigating the relationship between an individual's perception of equity and organizational commitment. Using a cross-organizational design, measures of perceptions of pay and workload equity, organizational commitment and self-rated performance were gathered from a sample of 105 employees from 15 organizations. Research revealed that a significant portion of an individual's organizational commitment can be explained by his/her perception of pay equity and workload equity. Additional analysis reveals that perception of equity has a significant and direct effect on performance but this effect is fully-mediated by organizational commitment.

Leadership quality is a core element of management. It is not only strongly related to the amount of employee commitment but it is also logically linked to organisational performance and customer satisfaction (*Rogg et. al.*, 2001). He feels that the future employability should be considered in order to prevent premature loss of capabilities, knowledge and commitment.

Sociological perspectives have a longer tradition of extending the parameters beyond the confines of the workplace and identifying additional external foci of employee commitment, for example to occupation or profession. An external occupational community can function as a psychological group in just the same way as the organization: i.e. as a collection of people who share the same social identification but with whom the individual does not necessarily have to interact personally. *Alvesson* (2000) suggests, in a discussion of IT professionals, that the possibility of a professional identity makes it likely that ties to the organization may be weaker as belonging to the latter is less essential for one's self-identity.

The organizational commitment can be mediated or filtered through a stronger sense of commitment to other more salient groups of which the employee is a member. *Capelli* (1999; 2000) argues that the economic turbulence at the end of the 1990s has resulted in a shift towards this indirect form of commitment as employers broke the long-term commitment understanding they had previously held with their employees. Downsizing, flatter organizations and corporate relocations negatively affected employment continuity and internal promotion prospects causing firms to construct a new contract with employees no longer based on long-term commitment but on offering employees the means and opportunities to develop their own skills in ways that enhance their professional and occupational careers external to the organization if need be.

Organizations do not expect employees to stay with them for life-long employment but aim to become 'employers of choice' by offering professional development and training.

This changing psychological contract can be seen as a 'new deal' in which high commitment and trust can only be generated through a negotiated process of reciprocity. The importance of reciprocity in these arguments suggests that rather than employees' sense of commitment reflecting a steady state or equilibrium there is a constant process of re-evaluation on their part based on such variables as perceived reciprocity and the salience of other groups within and outside the organization for feelings of loyalty. If the employee stays late, works beyond contract and remains with the organization, this may be for attitudinal reasons or alternatively it may be for what *Becker* (1960) termed 'side bets', a calculation of what might be lost if these behaviours were not adhered to (enhanced career potential, chances of promotion, pension scheme, holiday entitlement, company savings plan or share option).

While support exists to suggest that normative element is a separate dimension of commitment, normative measures have generally correlated highly with those of affective commitment (*Meyer & Allen,* 1997). Affective commitment—or emotional attachment, identification and involvement with the organization—has been found to be the predictor of employee turnover. Two recent meta-analyses conducted by *Griffeth, Hom, & Gaertner* (2000) and *Meyer et. al.* (2002) confirm that affective commitment is well established as an important antecedent of withdrawal behaviours; a finding which has also been validated with populations of information technology professionals (*Igbaria & Greenhaus,* 1992; *Igbaria & Guimaraes,* 1999). Scholars have also found a negative relationship between continuance commitment and turnover intentions (e.g. *Jaros, Jermier, Koehler & Sincich,* 1993; *Chen et. al.,* 1998). This finding indicates that employees that display a high level of continuance commitment remain in their organization either because they must or because they simply cannot do otherwise.

According to side-bet theory (*Becker,* 1960), continuance commitment is more likely to develop when employees recognize that they have acquired specialized know-how or expertise, have accumulated numerous achievements or accomplishments and have a profitable retirement pension plan, to name a few examples. According to the same theory, when employees recognize that availability of comparable alternatives is limited elsewhere, they will be more predisposed to stay in their current organization in order to avoid losing their relative advantages or privileges.

Two complementary conceptual frameworks have been developed for organisational commitment. First, the high involvement model proposed by *Lawler* (1986), which is seen as the primary engine behind the evolution of contemporary strategic HR management (*McMahan, Bell & Virick,* 1998), suggests that four organizational processes may influence work-related attitudes and behaviours, namely, empowerment, competence development, information sharing and reward. Second, the high performance work system model proposed by *Bailey* (1993) postulates that workers will exhibit discretionary efforts if and only if they have the opportunity to participate, they possess the necessary skills to make their effort meaningful and they are given appropriate incentives to deploy such discretionary efforts.

HR practices that enhance these three components are likely to heighten the perception of organizational commitment (both affective and continuance), perception of procedural justice and OCB-helping behaviours and decrease intentions of resigning among employees because individuals tend to respond positively to top-management commitment and support (*Eisenberger & LaMastro,* 1990).

While the positive link between HR practices and affective commitment has received extensive support, the role of HR practices in the reinforcement of continuance commitment has been less clearly established. *Meyer & Allen* (1997) and more recently *McElroy* (2001) have suggested that HR practices positively influence continuance commitment. More recently, *Meyer & Smith* (2000) found no significant relationship between HR practices and continuance commitment. Despite the latter result, they predicted a positive link between HR practices and continuance commitment. Consider employee empowerment. Employees who are empowered in their job might not only view the organization as caring and supportive and thus experience a stronger affective commitment; but might also believe that to lose the benefits associated with a high level of empowerment would be costly therefore experiencing greater continuance commitment.

Meyer & Herscovich (2001) suggested that employees who develop strong affective commitment become less sensitive to signals or constraints that may demarcate their behaviour. This affective commitment thus predisposes individuals to adopt a fairly broad range of discretionary or intentional behaviours. Similarly, researchers (e.g. *Morrison*, 1994) have demonstrated that a strong affective commitment motivate individuals to construe their work role as extending beyond tasks formally prescribed, which in turn encourages them to adopt extra role behaviours.

According to *Becker* (1975) when a substantial investment is allocated to developing skills specific to an organization, the employees' chances of finding a job elsewhere are reduced because the knowledge acquired is difficult to export. The strong association between this HR practice and continuance commitment leads us to believe that the development of this form of commitment may be better explained by the perception of a lack of alternatives on the job market than by the feeling that knowledge is lost as presumed earlier.

Rhoades et. al. (2001) found that the link between procedural justice and affective commitment was mediated by perceived organizational support. *Gould-Williams* (2003) recently observed that the association between procedural justice and organizational commitment was conditioned by the perception of trust. As a whole, these findings suggest that procedural fairness may play a determining role in shaping employees' affective commitment but only when employees perceive their organization to be supportive of or committed to them in a trusting relationship and environment.

Some authors have argued that organizational commitment represents a more stable construct than job satisfaction (*Mowday et. al.*, 1982). Recent studies conducted by *Gould-Williams* (2003) show that while organizational commitment and job satisfaction are both considered antecedents of behavioural outcomes only organizational commitment has a significant influence on the dependent variables. Some scholars (*Organ*, 1990; *Moorman*, 1991) have suggested that job satisfaction largely reflects employees' perceptions of organizational justice or fairness.

According to *Pousette & Jacobsson* (1999) positive and negative feedback were related to role ambiguity. Positive feedback was found to reduce role ambiguity, while negative feedback contributed to role ambiguity. As expected, role ambiguity was strongly related to job satisfaction and organizational commitment. However, there was no support for a direct relationship between the feedback factors and job satisfaction or organizational commitment. Instead the relationships between feedback and work attitudes were mediated by role ambiguity.

Hasenfeld (1983) feels that when staff feel positively toward their work, have a sense of control over it and feel able to express themselves through it they are more likely to impart these attitudes to their clients who constitute the most important component of the job. When staff members feel alienated from their work they are also likely to feel alienated from their clients and to regard relationships with them as unrewarding.

5.1.7 Studies on Measures of Organisational Commitment

There appear to be three main measures of attitudinal commitment in the field: the Organizational Commitment Questionnaire (OCQ) created by *Porter et. al.* (1974); the British Organizational Commitment Scale (BOCS) developed by *Cook & Wall* (1980); and the Affective Commitment Scale (ACS) conceptualized by *Meyer & Allen* (1984). Each seeks to measure the three components reflected in *Buchanan's* (1974) definition of commitment.

Commitment is also a multi-faceted construct. It has been defined as a job attitude or belief that reflects 'the relative strength of an individual's identification and involvement in a particular organisation' (*Steers*, 1977).

Ulrich (1998) suggested that commitment is gained by engaging employees' emotional energy, avoiding burnout and stress through high involvement work practices based on high levels of employee autonomy and self-regulation (job control).

Ulrich acknowledges that structural variables have an impact on commitment but does not include them in his model. Similarly, there is a growing body of research that highlights that competence can be influenced by structural factors, specifically job control (*Burr & Cordery,* 2001; *Parker & Wall,* 1998).

King (1995) presented a multiphase model of organizational ideology in a major thermoplastics manufacturing firm. This framework shows that there is a stepwise progression from loyalty to value congruence to perceived commitment in fortifying ideological attraction to organization. It also presents the concurrent validity of progressive phases related to perceived quality of work organization. Despite the progressive prepotency and valence of the levels and phases in prognosticating employee attraction to organization and commitment, the model demonstrates the different patterns and paths via phases for individuals.

According to social exchange theory (*Blau,* 1964), organizations are considered loci of mutual social and long-term transactions between employees and employers (*Wayne, Shore & Linden,* 1997). These social exchange relationships characteristically trigger unspecified future obligations (*Konovsky,* 2000). Moreover, social exchange relationships are strongly influenced by the level of mutual confidence in compliance with fairly long-term obligations by either party. Procedural justice is then considered one of the main factors of trust (*Konovsky & Pugh,* 1994; *Folger & Konovsky,* 1989) and as an important input in exchange relations with employees (*Masterson, Lewis, Goldman & Taylor,* 2000). A social exchange relationship founded on fair procedures is therefore more likely to promote a contractual relationship that gives the employees the freedom to adopt discretionary behaviours.

Management practice itself seems to be unclear about its own conceptual underpinnings and utilizes a confused mixture of both. Both direct models tend to be either static models in which individual traits once discovered are taken as given or equilibrium models in which the mind-set of the employee moves from a state of un-committedness via the application of high commitment work practices and culture change to a new state of committedness.

5.2 SUMMARY

Organizations are undergoing constant and substantial change due to many internal and external forces. These changes are impacting on the inter- and intra-organizational career mobility of managers and employees. As organizations transform and mutate, the employment relationship for employees necessarily transforms as well. This transformation of the work relationship and responsibility has been treated in some detail by those researching the issue of psychological contract and particularly psychological contract violation (*Freese & Schalk,* 1996; *Herriot, & Pemberton,* 1995; *Turnley & Feldman,* 1999).

Research has indicated that organisational change which necessitates employees redefining their work contract (psychologically) may have a series of negative impacts. This is particularly true if the employee feels the transformation involves the violation of the previously held psychological contract. Negative outcomes may typically include loss of trust, lower job satisfaction (*Robinson & Rousseau,* 1994), perceptions of inequity (*Morrison & Robinsion,* 1997) and fewer organisations enhancing discretionary behaviours (*Robinson & Morrison,* 1995) or just sheer disappointment in management for not reaching employee expectations (*Buckley, Monks & Sinnott,* 1998). *Lord & Hartley* (1998) demonstrated that job insecurity which comes from a perceived pressure to become involved in change is linked with reduced organisational commitment.

Organizational commitment is considered at the heart of human resource management and is a "central feature that distinguishes HRM from traditional personnel management" (*Guest,* 1995). The importance of employee commitment has been further highlighted in the work of *Storey* (1995), *Tyson* (1995) and *Legge* (1995). Commitment is an internalized employee belief often associated with Human Resource Management practices and high-trust organizational culture.

An organization that invests in its human capital and grants employees sufficient resources and opportunities to improve their skills (competence development), sets up systems allowing immediate supervisors to recognize individual contributions (recognition) and accepts greater power-sharing in the definition, coordination and conduct of work (empowerment) has a greater likelihood of developing a higher level of affective commitment among its highly-skilled professionals. Such practices mâke the professionals feel important, responsible and free to optimally channel their creativity and competencies. They also signal that the organization is supportive of the employees and is seeking to establish or maintain a social exchange relationship with them.

References

Allen, N.J. and Meyer, J.P. (1990): "Organizational Socialization Tactics: A Longitudinal Analysis of Links to Newcomers' Commitment and Role Orientation," *Academy of Management Journal*, Vol. 33, pp. 847-58.

Alvesson, M. (2000): "Social Identity and the Problem of Loyalty in Knowledge intensive Companies." *Journal of Management Studies*, Vol. 37 (8), pp. 101-23.

Angle, H.L. and Perry, J.L. (1981): "An Empirical Assessment of Organisational Commitment and Organisational Effectiveness." *Administrative Science Quarterly*, Vol. 21, pp. 1-14.

Ashforth, B. and Mael, F. (1989): "Social Identity Theory and the Organization." *Academy of Management Review*, Vol. 14 (1), pp. 20-39.

Bailey, T. (1993): Discretionary Efforts and the Organisation of Work Employee Participation and Work Reforms Since Hawthrone." Unpublished Paper.

Banai, M., Reisel, W.D. and Probst, T.M. (2004): "A Managerial and Personal Control Model: Predictions of Work Alienation and Organizational Commitment in Hungary." *Journal of International Management*, Vol. 10 (3), pp. 375-92.

Beck, K. and Wilson, C. (2001): "Have We Studied, Should We Study and Can We Study the Development of Commitment? Methodological Issues and the Developmental Study of Work-related Commitment." *Human Resource Management Review*, Vol. 11 (3), pp. 257-78.

Becker, H. (1960): "Notes on the Concept of Commitment." *American Journal of Sociology*, Vol. 66, pp. 32-40.

Becker, H. (1992): "FOCI and Bases of Commitment: Are These Distinctions Worth Making?" *Academy of Management Journal*, Vol. 35, pp. 232-44.

Bedeian, A.G., Kemery, E.R. and Pizzolatto, A.B. (1991): "Career Commitment and Expected Utility of Present Job As Predictors of Turnover Intentions and Turnover Behaviour." *Journal of Vocational Behaviour*, Vol. 39, pp. 331-43.

Blau, G.J. and Boal, K.B. (1987): "Conceptualizing How Job Involvement and Organizational Commitment Affect Turnover and Absenteeism," *Academy of Management Review*, Vol. 12(2), pp. 288-300.

Blau, G.J. (1989): "Testing the Generalisability of A Career Commitment Measures and its Impact on Employee Turnover." *Journal of Vocational Behaviour*, Vol. 35, pp. 88-103.

Bourantas, D. (1988): "Leadership Styles, Need Satisfaction and the Organizational Commitment of Greek Managers." *Scandinavian Journal of Management*, Vol. 4 (3-4), pp. 121-34.

Bozeman, D.P. and Perrewe, P.L. (2001): "The Effects of Item Content Overlap on Organizational Commitment Questionnaire—Turnover Cognitions Relationship." *Journal of Applied Psychology*, Vol. 86(1), pp. 161-73.

Bruning, N.S. and Snyder, R.A. (1983): "Sex and Positions as Predictors of Organisational Commitment." *Academy of Management Journal*, Vol. 26, pp. 485-91.

Buchanan, B. (1974): "Building Organizational Commitment: The Socialization of Managers in Work Organizations." *Administrative Science Quarterly*, Vol. 19, pp. 533-46.

Burr, R. and Cordery, J.L. (2001): "Self-management Efficacy as a Mediator of the Relation Between Job Design and Employee Motivation." *Human Performance*, Vol. 14 (1), pp. 27-44.

Campion, M.A., Medsker, G.J. and Higgs, A.C. (1993): "Relations Between Work Group Characteristics and Effectiveness: Implications For Designing Effective Work Groups." *Personnel Psychology*, Vol. 46, pp. 823-50.

Capelli, P. (1999): "The New Deal At Work: Managing the Market-driven Workforce, Boston." *Harvard Business School Press*.

Capelli, P. (2000): "Managing Without Commitment." *Organizational Dynamics*, Vol. 28 (4), pp. 11-24.

Castells, M. (1996): *The Rise of the Networked Society*, Oxford: Blackwell.

Chen, X.P., Hui, C. and Sego, D.J. (1998): "The Role of Organizational Citizenship Behaviour in Turnover: Conceptualization and Preliminary Tests of Key Hypotheses." *Journal of Applied Psychology*, Vol. 83 (6), pp. 922-31.

Chen, Z.X. and Francesco, A.M. (2003): "The Relationship Between the Three Components of Commitment and Employee Performance in China." *Journal of Vocational Behaviour*, Vol. 62(3), pp. 490-510.

Cheng, E., Li, H., Love, P. and Irani, P. (2004): "Strategic Alliances: A Model For Establishing Long-term Commitment to inter-organizational Relations in Construction." *Building and Environment*, Vol. 39(4), pp. 459-68.

Cheng, Y. and Stockdale, M.S. (2003): "The Validity of the Three-component Model of Organizational Commitment in a Chinese Context." *Journal of Vocational Behaviour*, Vol. 62(3), pp. 465-89.

Cohen, A. and Freund, A. (2005): "A Longitudinal Analysis of the Relationship Between Multiple Commitments and Withdrawal Cognitions." *Scandinavian Journal of Management*, Article in Press.

Cohen, A. (1998): "An Examination of the Relationship Between Work Commitment and Work Outcomes Among Hospital Nurses." *Scandinavian Journal of Management*, Vol. 14(1-2), pp. 1-17.

Cook, J. and Wall, T. (1980): "New Work Attitude Measures of Trust, Organizational Commitment and Personal Need Non-fulfilment." *Journal of Occupational Psychology*, Vol. 53, pp. 39-52.

Dawley, D.D., Stephens, R.D. and Stephens, D.B. (2005): "Dimensionality of Organizational Commitment in Volunteer Workers: Chamber of Commerce Board Members and Role Fulfilment." *Journal of Vocational Behaviour*, Article in Press.

Eisenberger, R., Fasalo, P. and Davis-lamastro, V. (1990): "Perceived Organizational Support and Employee Diligence, Commitment and Innovation." *Journal of Applied Psychology*, Vol. 75, pp. 51-59.

Eisenberger, R., Huntington, R., Hutchison, S. and Sowa, D. (1986): "Perceived Organizational Support." *Journal of Applied Psychology*, Vol. 71, pp. 500-07.

Ferres, N., Travaglione, A and Firns, I. (2004): "Attitudinal Differences Between Generation-x and Older Employees." *International Journal of Organizational Behaviour*, Vol. 6 (3), pp. 320-33.

Finegan, J.E. (2000): "The Impact of Person and Organizational Values on Organizational Commitment." *Journal of Occupational and Organizational Psychology*, Vol. 73, pp. 149-69.

Folger, R. and Konovsky, M.A. (1989): "Effect of Procedural and Distributive Justice on Reactions to Pay Raise Decisions." *Academy of Management Journal*, Vol. 32(1), pp. 115-30.

Freese, C. and Schalk, R. (1996): "Implications of Differences in Psychological Contracts For Human Resource Management." *European Journal of Work and Organizational Psychology*, Vol. 5, pp. 501-09.

Fox, A. (1974): Beyond Contract: Work Power and Trust Relations, London: Faber and Faber.

Gaertner, S. (1999): "Structural Determinants of Job Satisfaction and Organizational Commitment in Turnover Models." *Human Resource Management Review*, Vol. 9(4), pp. 479-93.

Glisson, C. and Durick, M. (1988): "Predictors of Job Satisfaction and Organizational Commitment in Human Service Organizations." *Administrative Science Quarterly*, Vol. 33 (1), pp. 61-81.

Gopinath, C. and Becker, T.E. (2000): "Communication, Procedural Justice and Employee Attitudes: Relationships Under Conditions of Divestiture." *Journal of Management*, Vol. 26, pp. 63-83.

Gould-Williams, J. (2003): "The Importance of HR Practices and Workplace Trust in Achieving Superior Performance: A Study of Public-sector Organizations." *International Journal of Human Resource Management*, Vol. 14(1), pp. 28-54.

Griffeth, R.W., Hom, P.W. and Gaertner, S. (2000): "A Meta-analysis of Antecedents and Correlates of Employee Turnover: Update, Moderator Tests and Research Implications For the Next Millennium." *Journal of Management*, Vol. 26(3), pp. 463-88.

Guest, D. (1995): "Human Resource Management, Trade Unions and Industrial Relations." In J. Storey (Ed.), *Human Resource Management: A Critical Text*. London: Routledge.

Guest, D. (2002): "Human Resource Management, Corporate Performance and Employee Well-being: Building the Worker into HRM." *Journal of Industrial Relations*, Vol. 44(3), pp. 335-58.

Hackett, R.D., Lapierre, L.M. and Hausdorf, P.A. (2001): "Understanding the Links Between Work Commitment Constructs." *Journal of Vocational Behaviour*, Vol. 58 (3), pp. 392-413.

Hasenfeld, Y. (1983): *Human Service Organizations*, Englewood Cliffs, New Jersy: Prentice Hall.

Herold, D.M. and Parsons, C.K. (1985): "Assessing the Feedback Environment in Work Organizations, Development of the Job Feedback Survey." *Journal of Applied Psychology*, Vol. 70, pp. 290-305.

Herriot, P. and Pemberton, C. (1995): *New Deals: The Revolution in Managerial Careers*, Chichester: Wiley.

Hunt, S. and Morgan, R. (1994): "Organizational Commitment: One of Many Commitments or Key Mediating Construct?' *Academy of Management Journal*, Vol. 37 (6), pp. 1568-88.

Igbaria, M., and Greenhaus, J.H. (1992): "Determinants of Mis Employees' Turnover Intentions: A Structural Equation Model." *Communication of the Acm*, Vol. 35(2), pp. 35-49.

Igbaria, M., and Guimaraes, T. (1999): "Exploring Differences in Employee Turnover Intentions and its Determinants Among Telecommuters and Non-telecommuters." *Journal of Mis*, Vol. 16 (1), pp. 147-64.

Jaramillo, F., Mulki, J.P. and Marshal, G.W. (2005): "A Meta-analysis of the Relationship Between Organizational Commitment and Salesperson Job Performance: 25 Years of Research." *Journal of Business Research*, Vol. 58 (6), pp. 705-14.

Jaros, S., Jermier, J., Koehler, J. and Sincich, T. (1993): "Effects of Continuance, Affective and Moral Commitment on the Withdrawal Process: An Evaluation of Eight Structural Equations Models." *Academy of Management Journal*, Vol. 36, pp. 951-95.

Jermier, J.M. and Berks, L.J. (1979): "Leader Behaviour in a Police Command Bureaucracy: A Closer Look At the Quasi-military Model." *Administrative Science Quarterly*, Vol. 24, pp. 1-23.

Johnston, G.P. and Snizek, W.E. (1991): "Combining Head and Heart in Complex Organizations: A Test of Etzioni's Dual Compliance Structure Hypothesis." *Human Relations*, Vol. 44, pp. 1255-72.

Katz, D. and Kahn, R.L. (1978): *Social Psychology of Organization*, (2nd Edition). New York: John Wiley and Sons.

Kerman, M. and Hanges, P. (2002): "Survivor Reactions To Reorganization: Antecedents and Consequences of Procedural, Interpersonal and Informational Justice." *Journal of Applied Psychology*, Vol. 87(5), pp. 916-28.

Khan, S.M. and Mishra, P.C. (2002): "Need Satisfaction and Organisational Commitment—Canonical Correlation Analysis." *Journal of Community Guidance and Research*, Vol. 19(2), pp. 199-208.

Kim, W.G., Leong, J.K. and Lee, Y.K. (2005): "Effect of Service Orientation on Job Satisfaction, Organizational Commitment and Intention of Leaving in a Casual Dining Chain Restaurant." *International Journal of Hospitality Management*, Article in Press.

King, A.S. (1995): "Multiphase Progression of Organizational Ideology and Commitment." *Mid-atlantic Journal of Business*, 1 June.

Kondratuk, T.B., Hausdorf, P.A., Korabik, K. and Rosin, H.M. (2004): "Linking Career Mobility With Corporate Loyalty: How Does Job Change Relate To Organizational Commitment?" *Journal of Vocational Behaviour*, Vol. 65 (2), pp. 332-49.

Konovsky, M. (2000): "Understanding Procedural Justice and its Impact on Business Organizations." *Journal of Management*, Vol. 26(3), pp. 489-511.

Konovsky, M.A. and Pugh, S.D. (1994): "Citizenship and Social Exchange." *Academy of Journal Management*, Vol. 37, pp. 656-69.

Kuvaas, B. (2003): "Employee Ownership and Affective Organizational Commitment: Employees' Perceptions of Fairness and Their Preference For Company Shares Over Cash." *Scandinavian Journal of Management*, Vol. 19 (2), pp. 193-212.

Lau, C.M. and Chong, J. (2002): "The Effects of Budget Emphasis, Participation and Organizational Commitment on Job Satisfaction: Evidence From the Financial Services Sector." *Advances in Accounting Behavioural Research*, Vol. 5, pp. 183-211.

Lawler, E.E. (1986): *High-involvement Management*. San Francisco, CA: Jossey-Bass Publishers.

Legge, K. (1995): *Human Resource Management: Rhetorics and Realities*, Basingstoke: Macmillan.

Lind, E.A. and Tyler, T.R. (1988): *The Social Psychology of Procedural Justice*, New York: Plenum Press.

Lok, P. (1999): "The Influence of Organisational Culture, Sub-culture, Leadership Style and Job Satisfaction on Organisation Commitment." *Leadership and Organisation Development*, Vol. 20(7), pp. 365-73.

Lord, A. and Hartley, J. (1998): "Organizational Commitment and Job in Security in a Changing Public Service Organization". *European Journal of Work and Organizational Psychology*, Vol. 7(3), pp. 341-54.

Luthans, F. (1981): *Organizational Behaviour*, McGraw-Hill International Book Company.

Mael, F.A. and Tetrick, L.E. (1992): "Identifying Organizational Identification." *Educational and Psychological Measurement*, Vol. 52 (4), pp. 813-25.

Masterson, S., Lewis, K., Goldman, B. and Taylor, M. (2000): "Integrating Justice and Social Exchange: The Differing Effects of Fair Procedures and Treatment on Work Relationship." *Academy of Management Journal*, Vol. 43, pp. 738-48.

Mathieu, J.F. and Zajac, D.M. (1990): "A Review and Meta-analysis of the Antecedent, Correlates and Consequences of Organisational Commitment." *Psychological Bulletin*, Vol. 108(2), pp. 171-94.

Mayer, R.C. and Schoorman, F.D. (1992): "Predicting Participation and Production Outcomes Through A Two-dimensional Model of Organizational Commitment." *Academy of Management Journal*, Vol. 35, pp. 671-84.

Mccoll-Kennedy, J.R. and Anderson, R.D. (2002): "Impact of Leadership Style and Emotions on Subordinate Performance." *The Leadership Quarterly*, Vol. 13 (5), pp. 545-59.

Mcelroy, J.C. (2001): "Managing Workplace Commitment By Putting People First." *Human Resource Management Review*, Vol. 11, pp. 327-35.

Mcfarlin, D.B. and Sweeney, P.D. (1992): "Distributive and Procedural Justice As Predictors of Satisfaction With Personal and Organizational Outcomes." *Academy of Management Journal*, Vol. 35, pp. 626-37.

Mcmahan, G.C., Bell, M. and Virick, M. (1998): "Strategic Human Resource Management: Employee Involvement, Diversity and International Issues." *Human Resource Management Review*, Vol. 8(3), pp. 193-214.

Mesmer-magnus, J.R. and Viswesvaran, C. (2005): "Convergence Between Measures of Work-to-family and Family-to-work Conflict: A Meta-Analytic Examination." *Journal of Vocational Behaviour*, Article in Press.

Meyer, J.P., Allen, N.J. and Smith, C.A. (1993): "Commitment To Organizations and Occupations: Extension and Test of a Three-component Conceptualization." *Journal of Applied Psychology*, Vol. 78(4), pp. 538-51.

Meyer, J.P. and Allen, N.J. (1984): "Testing the Side-Bet Theory of Organisational Commitment." *Journal of Applied Psychology*, Vol. 69(3), pp. 372-78.

Meyer, J.P. and Allen, N.J. (1991): "A Three Component Conceptualization of Organizational Commitment." *Human Resource Management Review*, pp. 61-89.

Meyer, J.P. and Allen, N.J. (1997): *Commitment in the Workplace*, San Francisco, Ca: Sage Publications.

Meyer, J.P. and Smith, C.A. (2000): "HRM Practices and Organizational Commitment: Test of A Mediation Model." *Canadian Journal of Administrative Sciences*, Vol. 17(4), pp. 319-31.

Meyer, J.P., and Herscovitch, L. (2001): "Commitment in the Workplace: Toward A General Model." *Human Resource Management Review*, Vol. 11 (3), pp. 299-326.

Meyer, J.P., Allen, N.J., and Topolnytsky, L. (1998): "Commitment in the Changing World of Work." *Canadian Psychology*, Vol. 39, pp. 83-93.

Meyer, J.P., Stanley, D.J., Herscovitch, L. and Topolnytsky, L. (2002): "Affective, Continuance and Normative Commitment To the Organization: A Meta-analysis of Antecedents, Correlates and Consequences." *Journal of Vocational Behaviour*, Vol. 61 (1), pp. 20-52.

Moorman, R.H. (1991): "Relationship Between Organisational Justice and Organisation Citizenship Behaviours: Do Fairness Perceptions Influence Employee Citizenship?" *Journal of Applied Psychology*, Vol. 76, pp. 845-55.

Morris, J.H. and Sherman, J.D. (1981): "Generalizability of An Organisational Commitment Model." *Academic Management Journal*, Vol. 24(3), pp. 512-26.

Morrison, E.W. and Robinson, S.L. (1997): "When Employees Feel Betrayed: A Model of How Psychological Contract Violation Develops". *Academy of Management Review*, Vol. 22, pp. 226-56.

Morrison, E.W. (1994): "Role Definitions and Organizational Citizenship Behaviour: The Importance of the Employee's Perspective." *Academy of Management Journal*, Vol. 37, pp. 1543-67.

Mowday, R.T., Porter, L.W. and Steers, R.M. (1982): *Employee-organization Linkages: The Psychology of Commitment, Absenteeism and Turnover*, New York: Academic Press.

Mowday, R.T., Steers, R.M. and Porter, L.W. (1979): "The Measurement of Organizational Commitment." *Journal of Vocational Behaviour*, Vol. 14, pp. 224-47.

Mueller, C.W. and Lawler, E.D. (1999): "Commitment to Nested Organizational Units: Some Basic Principles and Preliminary Findings." *Social Psychology Quarterly*, Vol. 62(4), pp. 325-47.

Muller, C.W. and Wallace, J.I.P. (1992): "Employee Commitment Resolving Issues." *In : Work and Occupations*, Vol. 19(3), pp. 211-37.

Norris-watts, C. and Levy, P.E. (2004): The Mediating Role of Affective Commitment in the Relation of the Feedback Environment to Work Outcomes." *Journal of Vocational Behaviour*, Vol. 65(3), pp. 351-65.

Nouri, H. and Parker, R.J. (1998): "The Relationship Between Budget Participation and Job Performance: The Roles of Budget Adequacy and Organizational Commitment." *Accounting, Organizations and Society*, Vol. 23, pp. 467-83.

Nouri, H. and Parker, R.J. (1996): "The Effect of Organizational Commitment on the Relation Between Budgetary Participation and Budgetary Slack." *Behavioural Research in Accounting,* Vol. 8, pp. 74-90.

Nouri, H. (1994): "Using Organizational Commitment and Job Involvement to Predict Budgetary Slack: A Research Note." *Accounting Organisations and Society,* Vol. 19(3), pp. 289-95.

O'connor, P.R. and Clarke, V.A. (1990): "Determinants of Teacher Stress." *Australian Journal of Education,* Vol. 34, pp. 41-51.

Olorunniwo, F. and Udo, G. (2002): "The Impact of Management and Employees on Cellular Manufacturing Implementation." *International Journal of Production Economics,* Vol. 76(1), pp. 27-38.

Organ, D.W. (1988): *Organizational Citizenship Behaviour: The Good Soldier Syndrome,* Lexington, Ma: Lexington Books.

Organ, D.W. (1990): "The Motivational Basis of Organizational Citizenship Behaviour." in Staw, B.M. and Cummings, L.L. (Eds.), *Research in Organizational Behaviour,* pp. 43-72. Greenwich, Ct: Jai Press.

Pare, G. and Tremblay, M. (2004): "The Influence of High-involvement Human Resources Practices, Procedural Justice, Organizational Commitment and Citizenship Behaviours on Information Technology Professionals' Turnover Intentions." Hec Montreal.

Parker, S. and Wall, T. (1998): *Job and Work Design: Organising Work to Promote Well-being and Effectiveness,* Sage Publications inc., Thousand Oaks, California.

Peters, T., and Waterman, R. (1982): In Search of Excellence: Lessons From America's Best-run Companies, New York: Harper and Row.

Podsakoff, P.M., Mckenzie, S.B. and Bommer, W.H. (1996): "Transformational Leader Behaviours and Substitutes for Leadership As Determinants of Employee Satisfaction, Commitment, Trust and Organizational Citizenship Behaviours." *Journal of Management,* Vol. 22, pp. 259-98.

Porter, L., Steers, R., Mowday, R. and Boulian, P. (1974): "Organizational Commitment, Job Satisfaction and Turnover Among Psychiatric Technicians." *Journal of Applied Psychology,* Vol. 59, pp. 603-09.

Pousette, A. and Jacobsson, J. (1999): "Consequences of Feedback Environment in Human Service Organizations." *Goteborg Psychological Reports,* Vol. 29(7).

Powell, D.M. and Meyer, J.P. (2004): "Side-bet Theory and the Three-Component Model of Organizational Commitment." *Journal of Vocational Behaviour,* Vol. 65 (1), pp. 157-77.

Quirin, J.J., Donnelly, D.P. and O'bryan, D. (2001): "Antecedents of Organizational Commitment: The Role of Perception of Equity." *Advances in Accounting Behavioural Research,* Vol. 4, pp. 261-80.

Reichers, A.E. (1985): "A Review and Reconceptualization of Organizational Commitment." *Academy of Management Review,* Vol. 10, pp. 465-76.

Rhoades, L. and Eisenberger, R. (2002): "Perceived Organisational Support: A Review of the Literature." *Journal of Applied Psychology,* Vol. 87(4), pp. 698-714.

Rhoades, L., Eisenberger, R. and Armeli, S. (2001): "Affective Commitment To the Organization: The Contribution of Perceived Organizational Support." *Journal of Applied Psychology,* Vol. 86 (5), pp. 825-36.

Rhodes, S.R. and Steers, R.M. (1981): "Conventional *v.* Worker-owned Organisations." *Human Relations*, Vol. 34, pp. 1013-35.

Riketta, M. and Dick, R.V. (2005): "Foci of Attachment in Organizations: A Meta-analytic Comparison of the Strength and Correlates of Workgroup *versus* Organizational Identification and Commitment." *Journal of Vocational Behaviour,* Article in Press.

Riketta, M. (2002): "Attitudinal Organizational Commitment and Job Performance: A Meta Analysis." *Journal of Organizational Behaviour,* Vol. 23, pp. 257-66.

Ritzer, G. and Trice, H. (1969): "An Empirical Study of Howard Becker's Side-Bet Theory." *Social Forces,* Vol. June, pp. 475-79.

Robinson, S.L. and Morrison, E.W. (1995): "Psychological Contracts and Ocb: the Effect of Unfulfilled Obligations on Civic Virtue Behaviour." *Journal of Organizational Behaviour,* Vol. 16, pp. 289-98.

Robinson, S.L. and Rousseau, D.M. (1994): "Violating the Psychological Contract: Not the Exception But the Norm." *Journal of Organisational Behaviour,* Vol. 15, pp. 245-59.

Rogg, K.l., Schmidt, D.B. and Shuil, C. (2001): "Human Resource Practices, Organizational Climate and Customer Satisfaction." *Journal of Management,* Vol. 27, pp. 431-49.

Rousseau, D.M. (1995): *A Psychological Contract in Organizations,* Thousand Oaks, CA: Sage.

Scandura, T.A. and Williams, E.A. (2004): "Mentoring and Transformational Leadership: The Role of Supervisory Career Mentoring." *Journal of Vocational Behaviour,* Vol. 65 (3), pp. 448-68.

Sharma, R.B. and Chauhan, P. (1991): "Organisational Commitment of Public Sector Managers." *Productivity,* Vol. 32(2), pp. 203-13.

Sinha, S.P., Talwar, Toran and Rajpal (2002): "Correlational Study of Organisational Commitment, Self Efficacy and Psychological Barriers to Technological Change." *Psychologia: An International Journal of Psychology in the Orient,* Vol. 45(3), pp. 176-83.

Staw, B. and Salancik, G. (1977): *New Directions in Organizational Behaviour,* Chicago: St Clair Press.

Steers, R.M. (1977): "Antecedents and Outcomes of Organizational Commitment," *Administrative Science Quarterly,* Vol. 22, pp. 46-56.

Steers, R.M. (1977): *Organizational Effectiveness: A Behavioural View,* Goodyear, Santa Monica, Ca.

Stinglhamber, F., Bentein, K. and Vandenberghe, C. (2002): "Extension of the Three-component Model of Commitment To Five Foci: Development of Measures and Substantive Test." *European Journal of Psycological Assessment,* Vol. 18 (2), pp. 123-38.

Storey, J. (1995): *Human Resource Management: A Critical Text,* London: Routledge.

Subramaniam, N. and Mia, L. (2003): "A Note on Work-related Values, Budget Emphasis and Managers' Organisational Commitment." *Management Accounting Research,* Vol. 14(4), pp. 389-408.

Tellefsen, T. and Thomas, G.P. (2005): "The Antecedents and Consequences of Organisational and Personal Commitment in Business Service Relationships : The Role of Organizational and Personal Needs", *Industrial Marketing Management,* Vol. 34(1) in Press.

Tellefsen, T. (2002): "Commitment in Business-To-Business Relationship. The Role of Organizational and Personal Needs", *Industrial Marketing Management*, Vol. 31(8), 645-52.

Tepper, B.J. and Taylor, E.C. (2003): "Relationships Among Supervisors' and Subordinates' Procedural Justice Perceptions and Organizational Citizenship Behaviours." *Academy of Management Journal*, Vol. 46(1), pp. 97-105.

Thomas, T. and Thomas, G.P. (2005): "The Antecedents and Consequences of Organizational and Personal Commitment in Business Service Relationships." *Industrial Marketing Management*, Vol. 34 (1), pp. 23-37.

Thomas, T. (2002): "Commitment in Business-to-Business Relationships—The Role of Organizational and Personal Needs." *Industrial Marketing Management*, Vol. 31 (8), pp. 645-52.

Turnley, W.H. and Feldman, D.C. (1999): "The Impact of Psychological Contract Violations on Exit, Voice, Loyalty and Neglect". *Human Relations*, Vol. 52 (7), pp. 895-922.

Tyler, T.R. and Lind, E.A. (1992): "A Relational Model of Authority in Groups." in Zanna, M.P. (Ed.), *Advances in Experimental Social Psychology*, Vol. 25, pp. 115-91. San Diego, Ca: Academic Press.

Tyson, S. (1995): *Human Resource Strategy*, London: Pitman.

Tziner, A. and Latham, G. (1989): "The Effects of Appraisal Instrument, Feedback and Goal Setting on Worker Satisfaction and Commitment." *Journal of Organizational Behaviour*, Vol. 10, pp. 145-53.

Ulrich, D. (1998): "Intellectual Capital Equals Competence X Commitment." *Sloan Management Review*, Vol 39, pp. 15-26.

Van Dick, R. (2001): "Identification and Self-categorization Processes in Organizational Contexts: Linking Theory and Research From Social and Organizational Psychology." *International Journal of Management Reviews*, Vol. 3, pp. 265-83.

Vandenberg, R.J., Richarson, H.A. and Eastman, L.J. (1999): "The Impact of High-involvement Work Process on Organizational Effectiveness." *Group and Organization Management*, Vol. 24(3), pp. 300-39.

Vandenberghe, C., Bentein, K. and Stinglhamber, F. (2004): "Affective Commitment To the Organization, Supervisor and Work Group: Antecedents and Outcomes." *Journal of Vocational Behaviour*, Vol. 64(1), pp. 47-71.

Verma, O.P. (1986): "Organisational Commitment As A Function of Managerial Respect." *Asian Journal of Psychology and Education*, Vol. 17(1), pp. 1-6.

Verquer, M.I., Beehr, T.A. and Wagner, S.H. (2003): "A Meta-analysis of Relations Between Person–Organization Fit and Work Attitudes." *Journal of Vocational Behaviour*, Vol. 63(3), pp. 473-89.

Wasti, S.A. (2002): "Affective and Continuance Commitment to the Organization: Test of An Integrated Model in the Turkish Context." *International Journal of Intercultural Relations*, Vol. 26 (5), pp. 525-50.

Wayne, S.J., Shore, L.M. and Linden, R.C. (1997): "Perceived Organizational Support and Leader-member Exchange: A Social Exchange Perspective." *Academy of Management Journal*, Vol. 40 (1), pp. 82-111.

Wayne, S.J., Shore, L.M., Bommer, W.H. and Tetrick, L.E. (2002): "The Role of Fair Treatment and Rewards in Perceptions of Organizational Support and Leader-member Exchange." *Journal of Applied Psychology,* Vol. 87 (3), pp. 590-98.

Welsch, H.P. and Lavan, H. (1981): "Inter-relationships Between Organizational Commitment and Job Characteristics, Job Satisfaction, Professional Behaviour and Organizational Climate." *Human Relations,* Vol. 34 (12), pp. 1079-89.

Whitener, E.M. (2001): "Do 'High Commitment' Human Resource Practices Affect Employee Commitment? A Cross-level Analysis Using Hierarchical Linear Modeling." *Journal of Management,* Vol. 27 (5), pp. 515-64.

Whittington, J.L., Goodwin, V.L. and Murray, B. (2004): "Transformational Leadership, Goal difficulty and Job Design: Independent and Interactive Effects on Employee Outcomes." *The Leadership Quarterly,* Vol. 15 (5), pp. 593-606.

Wiener, Y. and Vardi, Y. (1980): "Relationships Between Job Organization and Career Commitments and Work Outcomes—An Integrative Approach." Organizational Behaviour and Human Performance, Vol. 26, pp. 81-96.

Wong, C.S., Wong, Y., Hui, C. and Law, K.S. (2001): "The Significant Role of Chinese Employees' Organizational Commitment: Implications for Managing Employees in Chinese Societies." *Journal of World Business,* Vol. 36(3), pp. 326-40.

Wright, T.A. and Bonett, D.G. (2002): "The Moderating Effects of Employee Tenure on the Relation Between Organizational Commitment and Job Performance: A Meta-Analysis." *Journal of Applied Psychology,* Vol. 87(6), pp. 1183-90.

CHAPTER

6

Researches in Quality of Work Life

6.1 CRITIQUES ON STUDIES ON QUALITY OF WORK LIFE

QWL initiatives by an organisation are major factors on employee retention and productivity, providing an excellent return on investment. A business organisation which offers better QWL may be considered an inspirational employer. Image of the better QWL in a company leads to better quality people aspiring to join the organization thereby improving effectiveness and efficiency of the organization. Mission of QWL is to create and maintain highest possible quality work environment for current and future employees so as to achieve both individual and organizational excellence. Organizational action plans and proposed interventions should be designed to result in a more egalitarian culture and climate in the organization. Review of existing literature reveals a positive relationship between better QWL and improved performance. The review of existing studies that assess employees' perceptions of the implementation of quality improvement practices and organizational climate provide direction and focus for action plans and interventions proposed to improve workforce and customer satisfaction. Organizational factors such as size, nature of business, public *v.* private sector and employee demographic factors such as years in organization and hierarchical level do influence the employee assessment of QWL and have been extensively studied.

QWL efforts are systematic attempts by an organization to give workers greater opportunities to affect their jobs and their contribution to the organization's overall effectiveness. Proactive managers and HR departments find ways to empower employees so that they draw on their "brains and wits," usually by getting the employees more involved in the decision-making process as well as by offering conducive working environment. Employee satisfaction and involvement can be accomplished in a variety of ways. Research has shown that if your employees are happy and satisfied in the workplace they will usually be more motivated, more productive and have positive self-esteem and improved morale.

Today's organizations face challenges in terms of offering improved quality products and/or services, flexibility, speed and innovation. These challenges can be met by implementing strategies that lead to improved organizational work climate and culture. Employees must feel they are being treated fairly with respect to promotions, awards, training and job assignments. Employees may perceive more equity as the organization becomes flatter or less hierarchical and as traditional supervisory and non-supervisory roles change to those where collaboration and teamwork are the norm.

Many of today's workers are experiencing great difficulty trying to juggle both work and family responsibilities. Because so many employees are single parents or members of dual-income families, often there is no one available at home during working hours to care for the family. Therefore, a number of companies have begun to institute work and family programs as part of a "totally integrated employee benefits system" in an effort to help employees cope with these problems (*Morrison,* 1990).

In order to expend resources to improve the quality of employee work life, companies must believe in the value of such investments. *Barney* (1991) propounded a resource-based theory of the firm wherein he premises that human resource activities can be a source of competitive advantage that produces improved financial performance (*Wright et. al.*, 2001). Evidence from studies such as *Huselid* (1995) and *Fulmer et. al.* (2005) are generally consistent with this proposition. Positive relationships have been found among sound management practices, quality of work life, customer service quality and satisfaction and organizational productivity and growth (*Burke*, 1995).

The objectives of attaining greater employee and customer satisfaction, higher productivity and increased market share and profitability have been met in various organizations with the implementation of quality management and QWL programs (*Burke et. al.*, 1995). Successful companies are marked with self-managing work teams, flexibility in job assignments, performance incentives, external contracting and a greater concern about company culture, environment and commitment of employees.

6.1.1 Conceptual Framework of Quality of Work Life

The term "quality of work life" (QWL) was first introduced in 1972 during an international labour relations conference (*Hian and Einstein*, 1990). QWL received more attention after United Auto Workers and General Motors initiated a QWL program for work reforms.

According to *Carlson* (1981) QWL can be said to be both a goal and an ongoing process for achieving it. As a goal it is a commitment to any organisation for work improvement, the creation of more involving, satisfying and effective jobs and work environment for people at all levels of organisation. As a process QWL calls for efforts to realize this goal through the active involvement of people through out the organisation.

Robbins (1989) has defined QWL as "a process by which an organization responds to employee needs by developing mechanisms to allow them to share fully in making the decisions that design their lives at work" QWL has been well recognized as a multi-dimensional construct and it may not be universal or eternal.

QWL is considered as a set of the favourable conditions and environments of the workplace that support and promote employee satisfaction by providing them with rewards, job security and growth opportunities. The basic objectives of an effective QWL program are improved working conditions (mainly from an employee's perspective) and greater organizational effectiveness (mainly from an employer's perspective). It is expected that better OWL may lead to reduced absenteeism, lower turnover and improved job satisfaction. QWL is considered to develop talent, ensure loyalty and motivate the employees thereby enhancing organisation's competence.

Nadler and Lawler (1982) gave a working definition of QWL concept. "QWL is a way of thinking about people, work and organisation." Thus the focus of the QWL is not only on how people can do work better but also on how work may cause people to do better. It is a concern that is different from other productivity or organisational enhancement efforts because of its focus on the outcomes for the individual.

Graser (1976) opined that the term QWL has come to mean more than job security, good working conditions, adequate and fair compensation and more than even equal employment opportunity and job enlargement. The QWL requires an organisational climate and structure that really encourage, facilitates, rewards, questions, challenges or suggests way to improve the existing *modus operandi* in any way. It also requires respectful and appropriate response to such inputs.

6.1.2 Factors Determining Quality of Work Life

Quality of Work Life (QWL) consists of opportunities for active involvement in group working arrangements or problem solving that are of mutual benefit to employees and employers. It requires employee commitment to the organization and an environment in which this commitment can flourish (*Walton,* 1985). As a part of the commitment to the organization are the various attitudes or value judgments of people to their jobs and to their total work environment.

Fritz (1993) found that organizational barriers (e.g., inadequate resources, ineffective performance appraisal, reward and recognition systems, minimal or nonexistent accountability, reactive *v.* proactive management styles, etc.) are likely to impede performance. Specific obstacles to organizational excellence must be identified and validated by objective research and diminished or removed if the organization wants to be effective in providing the highest quality of services and products to its customers.

Graham et. al. (1994) contend that there should be more focus on empowered work groups and a movement away from the traditional, rigid and hierarchical system of management in organizations. The authors suggest that as supervisors assume the role of "coach," employee involvement and performance will improve. Good coaches communicate clear performance objectives, provide immediate feedback, assist in developing self-improvement plans, recognize and reward high performance and build warm positive relationships with subordinates.

Jackson (1983) found that employee involvement in participative decision-making schemes decreased the stressors of role conflict and role ambiguity. Jackson's findings suggest that HR practices can be used to decrease levels of occupational stress by altering the work environment and reducing the number and degree of certain job stressors.

David (1981) feels that those responsible for designing work systems have considerable influence over the quality of working life of those employed both in operating and managing the system. Whilst research evidence is available regarding the impact of changes to jobs and work organization, this research has tended to be based on changes made for remedial reasons where existing arrangements have been seen as the source of problems such as high labour turnover, low productivity etc. The changes reported have often been limited in extent since assumptions regarding aspects such as the operations technology remain unchallenged. Those responsible for the initial design of work systems have an opportunity to consider means for developing a "fit" between the needs of employees and the objectives of the organisation throughout the design process. He considered those aspects of work systems which relate particularly to the motivation of employees and contrasted with those responsible for the design of the work systems. He placed emphasis upon integrating the needs of individual employees into the initial design.

Quality of Work life is "the degree to which members of a work organization are able to satisfy important personal needs through their experiences in the organization" (*Suttle,* 1977). Thus, the quality of work life of an individual is defined by the individual's affective reactions to both objective and experienced characteristics of the work organization.

Mali (1981) opined that the quest for searching for what motivates people resulted in the filtering out the concept of QWL from a variety of studies conducted in industrial and organisational psychology and related disciplines. Improvements in QWL are becoming a catch slogan of today's employers and employees.

According to *Cherns* (1978), QWL is the area of 'humanization of work place', 'work place democracy', 'work restructuring' or 'job design'.

Barnes (1987) contended that typical QWL philosophy revolves around creating trust, growth equity and excellence in the organisational setting. Improving the quality of working life is now recognized as a learning process. It is one which engages our full potential for extracting information from the environment and putting it to work for common-sense purposes. The learning shown by participants in QWL projects is based on the assumptions of traditional education and the role of experts.

Emery (1984) examined the conflicts as may appear in a QWL project and argued for the whole-hearted management support and decentralized approach which leads to evolving democratically structured workplaces. *Terra* (1995) found that employee participation through the implementation of self-regulating teams had a positive effect on workers' health and motivation. Another empirical study by *Wall and Clegg* (1981) focused on work redesign and found that there were significant improvements in job satisfaction and emotional distress/strain when the jobs were redesigned to provide employees with greater autonomy.

Singer (1985) opined that organizational climates which serve to recognize self-esteem, relatedness to others, self-definition, self-actualization, personal power, utilization of one's own creative talents and sense of achievement are the quality of work-life expectations of today's knowledge worker. The young engineering professional entering the world of consulting engineering expects to make an innovative and rewarding contribution to the quality of his/her organizational experience. He recommended that organizations must create clear promotional paths and compensation systems that reward creative abilities and contribute to professional career development without having to follow the traditional model of becoming a partner or manager to be considered a professional success.

Drago (1993) holds that employers are the major beneficiaries of employee involvement efforts because these programs usually require voluntary contributions of employee knowledge, a more intensive style of monitoring by peers or shifting risk to employees without an accompanying return in benefits. This leads to improvement of QWL. Similarly, whenever an organisation encounters crises such as possible plant closures or increased competition, it forces a significant change in workplace practices which help to prevent, destabilize or eliminate competing coalitions such as unions, thereby generating improved working environment (*Katz and McKersie,* 1989).

Requena (2003) undertook empirical analysis of the relationship between social capital and satisfaction and quality of life in the workplace in Spain. Social capital was considered as the set of cooperative relationships between social actors that facilitate collective action. This concept was measured based on five dimensions: trust, social relations, commitment, communication and influence. An analysis has been carried out applying regression and causal models to determine the influence on satisfaction and quality of life at work of social capital dimensions and of characteristics of the worker, work environment and company or organization. The results of the analysis indicate that the models applied are significant, which confirms the examined propositions. She argued that higher levels of social capital imply greater levels of satisfaction and quality of life at work. Social capital is a better predictor of quality of life at work and job satisfaction than the characteristics of the worker, the company or organization and the work environment.

6.1.3 Research Studies on Quality of Work Life

Most of the existing research studies on QWL are based on the assumption that an individual's satisfaction or dissatisfaction experiences define the quality of his/her work life. It is believed that objective job characteristics induce satisfaction or dissatisfaction attitudes and the association between working conditions is moderated by an individual's abilities, values and expectations (*Seashore,* 1975). However, satisfaction is only one of the many aspects of QWL (*White,* 1981; *Davis and Cherns,* 1975). The assumption in using job satisfaction has been that it can serve as a motivator through which employees change and accommodate to their jobs and environment.

Wyatt (1988) highlighted the usage of concept of QWL in various countries. He said that QWL as a way of democratizing and humanizing the work place has been investigated and applied mainly in different parts of the Western industrialized world including Europe, Canada, USA, Japan and Australia. QWL is a sense of overall well-being with the work process from the perspective of both employee and employer. QWL means a working experience that is physically and spiritually life enhancing. Thus, life-enhancing characteristics are from both the perspective of the employee and organisation. MNC's should concern them with how the local people conceive the QWL given their total life work situation.

Grothe (1991) conducted a nationwide Quality of Work Life survey of approximately 4,000 employees in a large American-based computer-manufacturing corporation. The focal age group described as the work force "vanguard" to the 21st Century (those workers who will be in their late 30s to late 50s in the year 2000) reported significantly lower quality of work life factor scores than three older comparison age groups. This result was found for 73% of the possible paired comparisons on 31 quality of work life factors. This pattern of results remained after the effects of employee tenure, hierarchical level and salary range were partialled out. Findings of the study suggest that organizations need to continue to try new work-system approaches to meet the needs of this key century-spanning group. These efforts need to move beyond the experimental stage and must become an integral part of the total organization strategy. He proposed that new educational training opportunities could be provided, especially for: (1) the focal vanguard group in cognitive self-management skills, and (2) the key human resource strategic decision-makers regarding (a) the characteristics of this century-bridging generation, and (b) new work designs that are responsive to their values and expectations.

Haines Jr. (1991) used a well-researched deterministic model from the attitude literature to empirically examine how attitudes that decision-makers hold towards various work arrangements relate to behaviours (use of the work arrangements), intended behaviours (proposed adoption of the work arrangements) and personal preference. Attitude formation and decision-making with respect to both organizational and employee quality of work life issues were considered. The results indicate that decision-makers in the public sector consider organizational issues to be more important than employee issues with respect to the selection of alternative work arrangements. Manager's intentions to implement work arrangements in the future can be predicted by their current attitudes towards these work arrangements.

Sinha and Sayeed (1980) reported that in the Indian setting work has already been initiated on QWL by many but a major headway is yet to be made. Initially, the orientation to the QWL remains sociological, but lately there has been a gradual switch over to psychological aspect of QWL.

Teo and Waters (2002) examined the occupational stress-strain relationship among a sample of 109 white-collar employees in Singapore. Participants completed a survey that assessed the presence of 8 human resource practices (job training, communication, job redesign, promotional opportunities, employee involvement, family-friendly policies, pay systems and individual-focused stress interventions (SMIs), two major stressors (role overload and responsibility), two types of strain (vocational and interpersonal) and organizational commitment. Results indicated that human resource (HR) practices did not reduce the sources of stress (role overload and responsibility) within the workplace. However, there was a direct negative relationship between HR practices and interpersonal strain. In particular, family-friendly practices, job training, and SMIs reduce interpersonal strain. An examination of vocational strain showed that it was negatively associated with SMIs and job training. In addition, organizational commitment mediated the relationship between HR practices and vocational strain. They concluded that HR practices may be effective as part of a symptom-directed approach to stress intervention.

Mohan and Mohan (1999) measured the relationship of need fulfillment with leadership styles in public and private enterprises. A study based on the Hersey and Blanchard model was conducted to identify the difference between the respondents in respect of need fulfilment (lower order needs and higher order needs), leadership styles (high task-low relationship, high task-high relationship, high relationship-low task and low relationship-low task) and leadership effectiveness.

Several empirical studies have dealt with the impact of cellular manufacturing (CM) on employees' attitudes, job satisfaction, morale and quality of work life. However, research is lacking on which desirable socio-technical job characteristics have significant impact on the success of CM implementation. *Olorunniwo and Udo* (2002) studied the socio-technical system (STS) principles to identify three major categories of variables that are likely to impact CM implementation namely top management role, job design for operators and cross-training. Three different exploratory regression models were used to identify subsets of the variables that have the most impact on CM success. The results indicate that CM implementation seems to be more successful if top management initiates the CM project and if employees are cross-trained to run various machines and read blue prints.

Greenhaus et. al. (2003) examined the relation between work-family balance and quality of life among professionals employed in public accounting. Three components of work-family balance were assessed: time balance (equal time devoted to work and family), involvement balance (equal involvement in work and family) and satisfaction balance (equal satisfaction with work and family). For individuals who invested substantial time in their combined work and family roles, those who spent more time on family than work experienced a higher quality of life than balanced individuals who, in turn, experienced a higher quality of life than those who spent more time on work than family. They observed similar findings for involvement and satisfaction.

Sashkin and Williams (1990) conducted a study that supports the idea that climates can indirectly impact organizational performance. They measured aspects of the climate such as trust, truthfulness, integrity and justice and found that these aspects are related to organizational functioning. Examining different organizations, they found that companies with a lack of trust and justice factors incurred costs in terms of employee sickness and accident compensation. The authors concluded that organizational fairness is clearly related to financial performance. They contended that by addressing issues of fairness, some companies could save millions of dollars annually through decreased costs related to employee illnesses and accidents.

Johnson (1999) suggested that companies with high quality of work life can also enjoy exceptional growth (measured by five-year asset growth and sales growth trend data) and profitability (measured by five-year return on assets and return on equity data).

Badawy (1994) investigated the job involvement of several information systems professionals to determine its impact on the quality of work life. It was shown that the level of job involvement serves as a complex moderator in the pattern of relationships of work experiences. High levels of job involvement can sometimes enhance the quality of work life but it can also have the opposite effect in other individuals.

Bradburn (1969) opined that people evaluate their level of happiness by weighing up the good and bad experiences to form an overall impression. This notion of balance between positive and negative emotional responses is also reflected in occupational research where measures of anxiety or job satisfaction are often used to assess occupational stress (*Newton*, 1989). The use of these measures implies that stress, being an unpleasant emotional state, is associated with the absence of more pleasurable emotional experiences. A person's emotional experience can be explained by the two independent dimensions of positive and negative affect (*Diener and Emmons,* 1985). Positive affect is a pleasurable emotional state characterized by terms such as enthusiasm, energy, mental alertness and determination whereas negative affect refers to the subjective experience of distress and includes emotional states such as anger, anxiety, fear, guilt and nervousness (*Watson,* 1988). Emotional responses are only one component of a person's overall quality of life. It is also necessary to consider cognitive and somatic health dimensions. Taking this broader perspective, *Headey et. al.* (1984) have made a distinction between ill-being (later termed psychological distress) and well-being.

Research into the determinants of perceived quality of life has led to the development of empirical models which relate social background factors, personality, major life-events, coping responses and domain satisfactions to one another and to both well-being and ill-being indices (*Diener,* 1984). These models suggest that positive (beneficial) and negative (adverse) life events operate differently in determining a person's level of psychological well-being. Different patterns of association often emerge, with negative events correlating more strongly with the ill-being dimension, whilst positive events tend to relate more strongly with the well-being dimension. *Headey and Wearing* (1992) have also shown that when considered simultaneously, there is no relationship between positive events and ill-being or between negative events and well-being. These findings are of particular importance because they resulted from an eight-year longitudinal study that examined both static and dynamic relationships between these variables.

Other studies also found positive associations between progressive human resource management practices, such as training and staffing selectivity and perceptual firm performance measures. Employee satisfaction is essential to implementing high-performance or high-commitment work systems, which often lead to a firm's financial performance. Financial performance cannot be sustained unless the non-financial underpinnings of employee satisfaction, innovation, productivity, product quality, customer service and customer satisfaction are measured and improved.

Guzzo and Noonan (1994) assumed that an organization's HR practices influenced employee commitment since they were communications from the employer to the employee. How employees interpreted and made sense of their employer's HR practices affected their psychological contract with their employer and ultimately their commitment to that employer.

Tuuli and Karisalmi (1999) measured Six dimensions of the quality of working life to find out the relationship of burnout and the quality of working life. Burnout was measured by emotional exhaustion from the Maslach Burnout Inventory (MBI). Some demographic variables were included in the analyses. The result shows the impact of psychological job demands on burnout in both business lines. The impact of the other five indexes (conflicts, job control, work of superior, organization of work and monotonous job) on burnout were different in these two business lines. Still variables had some impact on burnout in both the retail trade and in the metal industry. Age turned out to be a complicated factor in relation to burnout. The findings confirmed the prediction concerning burnout. Burnout was positively related to the amount of different conflicts in the work place, job demands and monotony on the job. The good features of the working community, i.e., organizational functioning, open communication, work of superior and job control were negatively correlated to the burnout. All correlations between burnout and dimensions of working life were significant.

Although a concern for improving quality of work life is one of the reasons cited for the growing body of international research into teacher stress (*Kyriacou,* 1987) there has been little theoretical attention given to the relationship between occupational stress and a teacher's quality of work life (*Worrall and May,* 1989). It seems that researchers believe improved quality of work life is brought about by reducing teachers' level of psychological distress. This would explain why teacher's stress researchers continue to focus almost exclusively on the negative aspects of teaching (*O'Connor and Clarke,* 1990; *Pierce and Molloy,* 1990). Evidence however, suggests that adverse and beneficial experiences operate independently to determine the positive and negative aspects of a person's overall quality of life (*Headey and Wearing,* 1992).

In a very innovative study, *Crouter and Garbarino* (1982) explored the role of "corporate self-reliance" in producing and maintaining a sustainable society and the QWL as an ingredient of developing such an organisation. They examined the meaning of *corporate* self-reliance: business enterprises assuming responsibility for the consequences of their operation in the social as well as the physical environment by forming partnerships with local communities and families. They presented four strategies for the development of corporate self-reliance. The first is the role of *labour-management committees* as change agents for improving the quality of community and work life. The second strategy is *worker-ownership* as a constructive community response to plant shut-downs. The third strategy involves *employer-based family support systems.* The fourth is *participative work* as a means of enhancing personal and corporate competence resulting in enhanced morale and productivity, essential components of corporate self-reliance. In all four examples, the underlying theme is the importance of investing in human resources and improving the QWL so as to gain and retain strategic advantage through human capital.

Shortridge (2003) investigated the relation between the value of a firm and employee attitudes on the firm's workplace quality—workplace attitudes. Workplace attitude refers to recognition of those organizational characteristics that enhance employee work experiences and assist employees in balancing their jobs and personal lives. *Igbaria et. al.* (1991) found that employees whose work setting was compatible with their career orientation reported higher levels of job and career satisfaction than employees whose career orientation did not match attributes of their work setting

Benkhoff (1997) conducted a study to explore the proposed link between HRM characteristics and their relationships to employee satisfaction, intention to stay and organizational performance. Commitment emerged as the central variable that was closely related to work satisfaction and intention to stay and most important, made a significant contribution to branch performance of the bank.

To be successful, employers must assure their employees a good quality of work life. Quality of work life means "having good supervision, good working conditions, good pay and benefits and an interesting, challenging and rewarding job." High quality is sought through an employee relations philosophy that encourages the use of QWL efforts, which are systematic attempts by an organization to give workers greater opportunities to affect their jobs and their contribution to the organization's overall effectiveness. Proactive managers and HR departments find ways to empower employees so that they draw on their "brains and wits," usually by getting the employees more involved in the decision-making process. (*Werther,* 1996). Employee satisfaction and involvement can be accomplished in a variety of ways. Research has shown that, if employees are happy and satisfied in the workplace, they will usually be more motivated, more productive and have positive self-esteem and improved morale.

Fritz (1993) suggested that the organization should also continue to maintain and promote a strong employee focus and high levels of job satisfaction. Barriers to employee and customer satisfaction must be identified and removed. He found that the greatest opportunity for improvement in the quality climate was in the utilization of human resources. Improving the quality of work life for employees (e.g., focus on employee health and well-being, design of effective work policies, performance appraisal, reward and recognition systems, providing opportunities for interesting and challenging work, etc.) is necessary to achieve the organization's objectives of consistently providing conducive environment for growth of employees.

The U.S. Merit Systems Protection Board (1994) found that for a sample of government employees, non-supervisors were less satisfied with their jobs than were supervisors. Within the non-supervisory group, employees in lower grade levels were less satisfied with their jobs, their pay, meaningfulness of their work and the use of their skills than employees in higher grade levels. Similarly, *Burke* (1996) carried out research in both the private and public sectors and showed that employees at higher levels are more satisfied with their jobs than those at lower levels in the organizational hierarchy. The differences in job satisfaction were particularly strong for broad assignments, challenge, interacting with senior people and opportunities for advancement. In a related study, *Jurkiewicz and Massey* (1997) found high levels of similarity between groups of supervisory and non-supervisory municipal personnel on what they want from their jobs (e.g., chance to use special abilities and learn new things, opportunities for advancement, chance to make a contribution to important decisions, challenge and variety in work assignments, etc.). However, non-supervisory employees were significantly more dissatisfied than supervisory personnel with what they were actually getting from their jobs.

In a study that employed a sample of 330 police officers, *Hart et. al.* (1993) used an occupational hassle and uplifts scale to demonstrate that positive and negative work experiences are independent and that both must be assessed in order to describe a police officer's quality of life. It was found that a police officer's negative work experiences tended to correlate more strongly with ill-being indices, whereas positive work experiences tended to correlate more strongly with well-being indices.

6.1.4 Quality of Work Life Practices in Organisations: A Review

Many organizations have designed unique, socially relevant QWL programmes to motivate and encourage their employees. Over the past several years, employers have increased their focus on organizational characteristics that enhance employee work experiences and assist employees in balancing their jobs and personal lives (*Shellenbarger,* 1998). Companies offer employees amenities such as on-site daycare, consultancy services and flexible work schedules (*Levering and Moskowitz,* 1998).

US Federal government has suggested following programs: (a) reduced cost for child care, (b) care for mildly ill children, (c) parenting support groups, and (d) a "beeper-alert" program (in which employees are loaned beepers when they have an imminent family emergency) (*Solomon,* 1992).

Many organisations have a time-off program in which parents can take time off to accompany their children on the first day of school or to attend parent-teacher conferences (*Santora*, 1992). Some instituted an interesting concept referred to as an Inter-generational Center (that is a day care for children and elder dependents of employees) (*Laabs*, 1993).

In addition to the programs listed, many organizations now offer non-traditional work arrangements such as telecommuting, flextime and job sharing to help workers cope with their personal and family-related responsibilities (*Kleinman*, 2000). Most successful organizations realize that employee satisfaction equals success. This focus on workplace quality has become significant enough for business press publications such as Fortune and Working Mother to publish annual lists of companies that excel in creating a high quality of work life for their employees.

By helping employees balance work and family responsibilities, companies can increase their overall productivity, reduce absenteeism and better retain valued employees. For instance, as the Los Angeles Department of Water and Power found that its work and family program reduced turnover and improved recruitment, it estimates that the program yields a return of $10 for each dollar invested.

Workplace support refers to policies and actions such as flexible schedules and providing child care that make employees feel supported by the organization. The most important factor mentioned by employees enhancing job quality was autonomy, meaningfulness opportunities for learning, advancement and job security.

Hughes (2001) highlighted that one of the most prevalent concepts used to create a good quality of work life is employee involvement. Employee involvement is a variety of techniques that are used to enable employees to participate in the decision-making processes that affect their working environment. Integrity and trust are important aspects of successful participative initiatives. The purpose of involving employees in the public sector in the decision-making processes relates primarily to morale, productivity and employee satisfaction. A good quality of work life allows employees the opportunity to make certain decisions about the design of their workplace, the processes to be used and the resources they need to do their jobs most effectively. In fact, an employee who has performed a particular job over several years may be in a better position to make this determination. To be effective, good quality of work life cannot be used as a device by management to disengage unions or to keep unions out of the workplace. Many successful organizations have established a policy to encourage and enable all employees to become involved in and contribute to the organization.

Different companies know gain sharing by different names, such as performance sharing, productivity incentive or as profit-sharing in the private sector. These programs generally refer to incentive plans that involve employees in a common effort to improve organizational performance and are based on the concept that the resulting incremental economic gains are shared among employees and the company. While many variants of gain sharing exist, they are all based on the same principles. First, the company must be able to measure its output and second, when employees reduce labour costs by increasing productivity, they share in the savings (*Kevin,* 1991).

When using flextime, employers must ensure that the office is covered. A sufficient number of people must be available at the worksite when needed (*Buckley et. ul.,* 1988). Flextime allows employees the option of choosing their own work hours, with certain exceptions. A basic flextime system allows employees to work the same number of hours each day, although their hours may vary. Perhaps the most important feature of flextime is that employees are permitted to strike a balance between their personal or family lives and their careers. Such work and family programs often make good business sense. By helping employees balance work and family responsibilities, companies can increase their overall productivity, reduce absenteeism and better retain valued employees.

Employee assistance programs (EAP's) are designed to help employees with a wide variety of problems that ultimately interfere with job performance. Generally speaking, these problems are related to stress, personal, emotional or financial concerns or family difficulties. The main focus of EAP programs is to help employees resolve their problems, at least to the extent that the problems are affecting the employees in the workplace environment. Treatment may come in the form of in-house assistance, counseling or referrals outside the company. Most employers provide such programs do so primarily because they value their employees.

Some employers provide on-site day care at no cost to the employee or for a moderate fee. This benefit has proven to be an effective recruitment aid, since, by providing such a service employers can reduce absenteeism. A national survey conducted by Hewitt Associates, a consulting firm, found that "85 percent of the employers surveyed extended some form of child care benefits to their employees, 13 percent offered sick/ emergency child care programs and 10 percent provided child care centers" (*Sherman*, 1998).

In addition to caring for their own children, many employees are finding themselves within the "sandwich" generation. In essence, these employees have to take on the responsibilities of caring for their elderly parents and raising small children. It is quite apparent how such responsibilities can become overwhelming, particularly when an employee is caring for an ill, elderly parent; his or her own children; and trying to pursue a career. Realizing this concern, some employers have gone one step further by extending these services not only to the employees' children, but to their disabled and elderly dependents as well.

Researches have shown that job autonomy is another tool used in organisations for improving QWL. It is considered to provide responsibility for the resulting effects of one's own work and/or accomplishments. One method in which job autonomy is normally created in organisations is through autonomous work teams. The philosophy behind this is that teams can contribute to improved performance by identifying and solving work-related problems, so as to motivate employees by having them participate in decisions that affect them and their work.

6.2 SUMMARY

The concept of the "quality of work life" encompasses a wide range of organizational phenomena. In an extensive review of the QWL literature, several correlates with job satisfaction were extracted including the intrinsic nature of the work, autonomy, democratic supervisory style, supportive supervisory style and an organizational climate which reflect support, open communication and autonomy. A totally integrated system permits the employee to strike a proper balance between work and family life. Needless to say, having a "totally integrated benefit system" is definitely becoming the wave of the future in both the private and public sector. In addition, some employers are finding that being a "family friendly" organization is not only the right thing to do but it also may be critical to the organizational culture and its viability. While job satisfaction is generally considered to be the primary indicator of the quality of work life, job involvement and organizational commitment have also been identified as important attitudinal outcomes reflective of the internal career and of the "goodness" of the quality of work life (*Loscocco and Roschelle,* 1991). Other job-related components of satisfaction which have been reported are: participative supervision, interaction with peers, high wages, opportunity for promotion, level of interest in the job, having enough authority and information to do the job, use/development of personal skills and seeing concrete evidence of an individual's efforts. One view of employee involvement claims that employee involvement is part of a transformation of the workplace from traditional hierarchical roles to an idealized "industrial democracy" in which employees, management and owners benefit from the new work structure. This "win-win" situation is seen as ethically superior because it results in stable, more satisfying jobs for employees and higher productivity for the firm (*David and Tyson,* 1991). Communication, participation in strategic planning and decision-making throughout the organization would also likely to improve; and supervisor and non-supervisor perceptions of the quality culture and organizational climate may become less disparate.

References

Agarwala, T. (2003): "Innovative Human Resource Practices and Organizational Commitment: An Empirical Investigation." *International Journal of Human Resource Management,* Vol. 14(2), pp. 175-97.

Badawy, M.K. (1994): "Work Experiences, Job Involvement and Quality of Work Life Among Information Systems Personnel." *Mis Quarterly,* 1 June.

Barnes, J. (1987): *Teaching Experience: the International Encyclopedia of Teaching and Teacher Education*, Edited by Michael, University of Sydney, Australia.

Barney, J.B. (1991): "Firm Resources and Sustained Competitive Advantage." *Journal of Management*, Vol. 17, pp. 99-120.

Benkhoff, B. (1997): "A Test of the HRM Model: Good for Employers and Employees". *Human Resource Management Journal*, Vol. 7(4), pp. 44-60.

Bradburn, N.M. (1969): *The Structure of Psychological Well-being*, Chicago: Aldine.

Buckley, F., Monks, K. and Sinnott, A. (1998): "Communications Enhancement: A Process Dividend for the Organization and the Hrm Department?" *Human Resource Management*, Vol. 37 (3/4), pp. 221-34.

Buckley, M.R., Fedor, D.B. and Kicza, D.C. (1988): "Work Patterns Altered by New Lifestyles." *Personnel Administrator*, December, pp. 40-43.

Burke, R.J. (1995): "Management Practices, Employees' Satisfaction and Perceptions of Quality of Service." *Psychological Reports*, Vol. 77, pp. 748-50.

Carless, S.A. (1981): "Improving Quality of Work Life." *Management Handbook Operating Guidelines, Techniques and Practices*, New York: Ronald Press.

Cherns, A. (1978): "The Quality of Work Life and the Productivity Menace." *Manpower Journal*, Vol. 14(2), pp. 19-30.

Cherns, A.B. (1978): "Perspective on the QWL." *International Studies of Management and Organizations*, Vol. 8, pp. 35-38.

Crouter, A.C. and Garbarino, J. (1982): "Corporate Self-reliance and the Sustainable Society." *Technological Forecasting and Social Change*, Vol. 22(2), pp. 139-151.

Cullen, J., Parboteeah, B.K.P. and Victor, B. (2003): "The Effects of Ethical Climates on Organisational Commitment: A Two-study Analysis." *Journal of Business Ethics*, Vol. 46, pp. 127-41.

David, J (1981): *QWL: Current Trends and Directions*, Toronto: Ontario Quality of Working Life Centre.

David, L. and Tyson, L.D. (1991): "Participation, Productivity and the Firm's Environment," *Paying for Productivity*, Blinder, A. Ed. Washington, The Brookings Institution, pp. 183-224.

Davis, L. and Cherns, A. (Eds) (1975): "The Quality of Working Life." Vol. 1, Free Press, New York.

Diener, E. and Emmons, R.A. (1985): "The Independence of Positive and Negative Affect." *Journal of Personality and Social Psychology*, Vol. 47, pp. 1105-17.

Diener, E. (1984): "Subjective Well-being." *Psychological Bulletin*, Vol. 95, pp. 542-75.

Drago, R. (1993): "Involving Employees: An Australian Evaluation." *Unpublished Paper, Department of Economics, University of Wisconsin, Milwaukee.*

Emery, M. (1984): "Learning and the Quality of Working Life," *Computers in Industry*, Vol. 5(4), pp. 381-87.

Fritz, S.M. (1993): "A Quality Assessment Using the Baldrige Criteria: Nonacademic Service Units in A Large University." *Unpublished Doctoral Dissertation, the University of Nebraska-lincoln.*

Fulmer, I., Gerhart, B. and Scott, K. (2005): "Are the 100 Best Better? An Empirical Investigation of the Relationship Between Being A 'Great Place To Work' and Firm Performance." *Personnel Psychology* (Forthcoming).

Graser, M.E. (1976): "Productivity Gains Through Work-life Improvements." *The Psychological Corporations*, pp. 3-4.

Greenhaus, J.H., Collins, K.M. and Shaw, J.D. (2003): "The Relation Between Work-family Balance and Quality of Life." *Journal of Vocational Behaviour*, Vol. 63(3), pp. 510-31.

Grothe, C.M. (1991): "Is the Work Force Vanguard To the 21st Century: A Quality of Work Life Deficient-prone Generation?" *Journal of Business Research*, Vol. 23(1), pp. 67-82.

Guzzo, R.A. and Noonan, K.A. (1994): "Human Resource Practices As Communications and the Psychological Contract." *Human Resource Management*, Vol. 33(3), pp. 447-62.

Haines, L.D.G. Jr. (1991): "Predicting Alternative Work Arrangements From Salient Attitudes: A Study of Decision Makers in the Public Sector." *Journal of Business Research*, Vol. 23(1), pp. 83-97.

Hart, P.M., Wearing, A.J. and Heady, B. (1993a): "Determinants of Police Well-being and Ill-being: A Dynamic Model of Personality, Coping and Work Experiences." Paper Presented At 1993 National Conference of the Australasian Society on Traumatic Stress Studies, Adelaide, South Australia, 23-25 April.

Headey, B. and Wearing, A.J. (1992): *Understanding Happiness: A Theory of Subjective Well-being*, Melbourne: Longman Cheshire.

Headey, B., Holmstrom, E. and Wearing, A.J. (1984): "Well-being and Ill-being: Different Dimensions?" *Social Indicators Research*, Vol. 14, pp. 115-39.

Hian, C.C. and Einstein, W.O. (1990): "Quality of Work Life (QWL): What Can Unions Do?" *S.A.M. Advanced Management Journal*, Vol. 55 (2), pp. 17-22.

Hughes, C. (2001): "Totally Integrated Employee Benefits." *Public Personnel Management*, 22 Sept.

Igbaria, M. and Greenhaus, J.H. (1992): "Determinants of Mis Employees' Turnover Intentions: A Structural Equation Model." *Communication of the Acm*, Vol. 35(2), pp. 35-49.

Igbaria, M. and Guimaraes, T. (1999): "Exploring Differences in Employee Turnover Intentions and its Determinants Among Telecommuters and Non-telecommuters." *Journal of Mis*, Vol. 16 (1), pp. 147-64.

Igbaria, M., Greenhaus, J.H. and Parasuraman, S. (1991): "Career Orientations of Mis Employees: An Empirical Analysis." *Mis Quarterly*, Vol. 15(2), pp. 151-69.

Jackson, S.E. (1983): "Participation in Decision-making As A Strategy for Reducing Job-related Strain." *Journal of Applied Psychology*, Vol. 68, pp. 3-19.

Jamison, C.S. Wallace, M. and Jamison, P.L. (2004): "Contemporary Work Characteristics, Tress and Ill Health." *American Journal of Human Biology*, Vol. 16(1), pp. 43-56.

Johnson, S.K. (1999): "A Longitudinal Study of Quality of Work Life and Business Performance." *South Dakota Business Review*, Vol. 29(1), p. 119.

Johnston, G.P. and Snizek, W.E. (1991): "Combining Head and Heart in Complex Organizations: A Test of Etzioni's Dual Compliance Structure Hypothesis." *Human Relations*, Vol. 44, pp. 1255-72.

Jurkiewicz, C.L. and Masey, T.K. (1997): "What Motivates Municipal Employees: A Comparison of Supervisory *v.* Non-supervisory Personnel." *Public Personnel Management*, Vol. 26 (3), pp. 367-77.

Katz, D. and Mckersie, P. (1989): "The Transformation; Clair Brown and Michael Reich, "When Does Cooperation Work? A Look At Nummi and Van Nuys," *California Management Review*, Summer, p. 2644.

Katz, D. and Kahn, R.L. (1978): *Social Psychology of Organization*, (2nd Edition). New York: John Wiley and Sons.

Kevin, M.P. (1991): "Lessons Learned From Gain-sharing." *Hr Magazine*, April, pp. 70.

Kleinman, L.S. (2000): *Human Resource Management*, South-western College Publishing New York, p. 39.

Kyriacou, C. (1987): "Teacher Stress and Burnout: An International Review." *Educational Research*, Vol. 29, pp. 146-52.

Laabs, J.J. (1993): "Family Support Makes Business Sense." *Hr Magazine*, January, pp. 38-43.

Lawler, E.E. (1986): *High-involvement Management*, San Francisco, Ca: Jossey-bass Publishers.

Levering, R. and Moskowitz, M. (1998): "The 100 Best Companies To Work for in America," *Fortune*, Vol. 138 (1), pp. 84-95.

Lines, R. (2004): "Influence of Participation in Strategic Change: Resistance, Organisational Commitment and Change Goal Achievement." *Journal of Change Management*, Vol. 4, pp. 193-215.

Loscocco, K.A. and Roschelle, A.R. (1991): "Influences on the Quality of Work and Non-work Life: Two Decades in Review," *Journal of Vocational Behaviour*, Vol. 39(2), pp. 182-225.

Mali, P. (1981): *Management Handbook Operating Guidelines, Techniques and Practices*, New York: Renold Press Publications and Sons, John Willey.

Mohan, R. and Mohan, R. (1999): "Need Fulfilment, Leadership Styles and Effectiveness: A Study of Two Indian Organisations." *Management Review*, Vol. 11(3), pp. 47-54.

Morrison, P.A. (1990): "HRM: Its Growing Scope and Future Direction." *The Futurist*, March/April, pp. 9-15.

Nadler, D.A. and Lawler, E.D. (1982): "Quality of Work Life Programs, Coordination and Productivity." *Journal of Contemporary Business*, Vol. 11, pp. 93-106.

Newton, T.J. (1989): "Occupational Stress and Coping With Stress: A Critique." *Human Relations*, Vol. 42, pp. 441-61.

O'connor, P.R. and Clarke, V.A. (1990): "Determinants of Teacher Stress." *Australian Journal of Education*, Vol. 34, pp. 41-51.

Olorunniwo, F. and Udo, G. (2002): "The Impact of Management and Employees on Cellular Manufacturing Implementation." *International Journal of Production Economics*, Vol. 76(1), pp. 27-38.

Osterman, P. (1994): "How Common is Workplace Transformation and How Can We Explain Who Adopts It?" *Industrial and Labour Relations Review*, January, pp. 173-88.

Pierce, C.M.B. and Molloy, G.N. (1990): "Relations Between School Type, Occupational Stress, Role Perceptions and Social Support." *Australian Journal of Education*, Vol. 34, pp. 330-38.

Requena, F. (2003): "Social Capital, Satisfaction and Quality of Life in the Workplace." *Social Indicators Research*, Vol. 61, pp. 331-60.

Robbins, S.P. (1989): *Organizational Behaviour: Concepts, Controversies and Applications*, New Jersey: Prentice Hall.

Santora, J.E. (1992): "Nabisco Tackles Tomorrow's Skills Gap." *Personnel Journal*, September, pp. 47-50.

Sashkin, M. (1988): "The Visionary Leader." in Conger, J.A. and Kanungo, R.N. (Eds.). *Charismatic Leadership: The Elusive Factor in Organizational Effectiveness*, pp. 122-60, San Francisco: Jossey-bass.

Seashore, S.E.(1975): "Defining and Measuring the Quality of Working Life" in the *Quality of Working Life, Vol. 1: Problems, Prospects and State of the Art*, Louis E. Davis, Albert B. Chems and Associates, New York: the Free Press.

Shellenbarger, S. (1998): "Companies Are Finding It Really Pays To Be Nice To Employees." *Wall Street Journal*, Vol. July 22, B1.

Sherman, B.S. (1998): *Managing Human Resources*, Southwestern College Publishing.

Shortridge, R.T. (2003): "Firm Value and Employee Attitudes on Workplace Quality." *Accounting Horizons*, 1 December.

Singer, J.F. (1985): "Compensation System Management Planning Considerations in Consulting Engineering." *Engineering Management International*, Vol. 39(3), pp. 183-89.

Sinha, P. and Sayeed, O.B. (1980): "Measuring Quality of Work Life: Development of An Inventory." *Indian Journal of Social Work*, Vol. 41(3), pp. 221-26.

Solomon, C.M. (1992): "Work/Family Ideas That Break Boundaries." *Personnel Journal*, Vol. Oct, pp. 112-17.

Suttle, J.L. (1977): "Improving Life At Work—Problems and Prospects," in *Behavioural Science Approaches To Organizational Change*, Hackman, J.X. and Suttle, J.L. (Eds.), Goodyear, Santa Barbara, Ca, pp. 1-29.

Teo, C. and Waters, L. (2002): "The Role of Human Resource Practices in Reducing Occupational Stress and Strain." *International Journal of Stress Management*, Vol. 9(3), pp. 207-26.

Terra, N. (1995): "The Prevention of Job Stress by Redesigning Jobs and Implementing Self-regulating Teams." in Murphy, L.R., Hurrell, J.J. Jr., Sauter, S.C. and Keita, G.P.'s *Job Stress Interventions*, pp. 265-82, Washington: Amer. Psychol. Association.

Tuuli, P. and Karisalmi, S. (1999): "Impact of Working Life Quality on Burnout." *Experimental Aging Research*, Vol. 25, pp. 441-49.

U.S. Merit Systems Protection Board (1994): *Working for America: An Update*, Washington, DC: U.S. Government Printing Office-377-070.

U.S. Merit Systems Protection Board (1998): *Federal Supervisors and Strategic Human Resources Management*, Washington, DC.

Wall, T.D. and Clegg, C.W. (1981): "A Longitudinal Study of Group Work Redesign." *Journal of Occupational Behaviour*, Vol. 2, pp. 31-49.

Walton, R.E. (1985): "From Control to Commitment in the Workplace." *Harvard Business Review*, Vol. 63 (2), pp. 77-84.

Watson, D. (1988): "Intra-individual and Inter-individual Analyses of Positive and Negative Affect: Their Relation to Health Complaints, Perceived Stress and Daily Activities." *Journal of Personality and Social Psychology*, Vol. 54, pp. 1020-30.

Werther, D. (1996): *Human Resources and Personnel Management*, McGraw-Hill Inc., New York, p. 499.

White, T.A. (1981): "The Relative Importance of Work as a Factor in Life Satisfaction." *Relations Industrielles,* Vol. 36(l), pp. 179-91.

Worrall, N. and May, D. (1989): "Towards A Person-in-situation Model of Teacher Stress." *British Journal of Educational Psychology,* Vol. 59, pp. 174-86.

Wright, P., Dunford, B. and Snell, S.A. (2001): "Human Resources and the Resource-based View of the Firm." *Journal of Management,* Vol. 27, pp. 701-21.

Wyatt, T.A. (1988): "Quality of Work Life: Cross-cultural Considerations." *Asia Pacific Journal of Management,* Vol. 6(1), pp. 129-40.

Zornitsky, J.J. (995): "Making Effective HRM a Hard Business Issue." *Compensation and Benefits Management,* Vol. 2(1), pp. 16-24.

CHAPTER

Dimensions and Objectives of the Research

7.1 GAPS IN EXISTING STUDIES

Perusal of the existing literature reveals that the studies involving leadership behaviour patterns and its influences on the subordinates have mostly been done in the developed countries. As it has been conclusively proved that leadership is situational, it becomes important that the studies are conducted in India so as to have direct impact on the management practices. Moreover, the studies have been done on quality of work life as well as organisational commitment *per se*. However, there is scarce literature available highlighting the influence of leadership behaviour on the quality of work life as well as organisational commitment. Hence, the rationale for the present study. The leadership has also been studied in its various facets like the leadership styles, factors affecting leadership effectiveness, challenges facing leadership, etc. There is thus a need to study the extent to which leader's Behaviour influences organisational commitment among subordinates as well as its impact on quality of work life. It may also be worthwhile to study whether any significant difference exists between organisational commitment exhibited by the subordinates and the leader.

7.2 NEED FOR THE STUDY

Although the concept of job involvement, its antecedents and outcomes have been researched extensively by organizational researchers, little attention has been devoted to exploring job involvement and its relationship to the work experiences and job attitudes of white goods industry personnel. The dearth of research in this area is surprising in light of prior findings that these professionals have high need for achievement and growth and place a high value on interesting work, job challenges and growth opportunities. The job design literature provides extensive evidence that job involvement is associated positively with the five "core" elements: job characteristics or job scope; need for achievement; growth as well as job satisfaction; performance and organizational commitment. These factors underscore the importance of examining the work experiences and other factors related to the job involvement of employees and the relationship of involvement with favourable job and organizational outcomes, reflecting their quality of work life. Studies on the antecedents of commitment (*Cohen*, 1992) showed that job involvement and its relationship to organizational commitment differ significantly across occupational groups. Viewed in conjunction with previous findings (*Igbaria and Greenhaus*, 1992) organizational commitment is the most proximal determinant of turnover intentions of employees. These studies reinforce the importance of investigating the job involvement of employees and the role of involvement in influencing the quality of work life.

Systematic evaluation of QWL in the consumer industry has not occurred. The existence of rapid environmental changes and competitive pressures in the industry suggested the importance of determining the extent to which QWL activity, if any, existed in the industry. Furthermore, it was deemed desirable to understand which components of working life were perceived as important within different employee groups and with which aspects satisfaction existed.

7.3 DEFINITION OF THE RESEARCH PROBLEM

Quality of Work Life and Organisational Commitment Among Employees in Relation to Leadership Behaviour

7.4 RESEARCH OBJECTIVES OF THE STUDY

(1) To study the leadership Behaviour pattern as exhibited by the managers in terms of Initiative and Consideration parameters.
(2) To study the difference in the leadership behaviour pattern as perceived by managers and their subordinates' perception about them.
(3) To study the impact of Leadership Behaviour on perceived quality of work life among the subordinates.
(4) To examine the impact of Leadership Behaviour on organisational commitment among the subordinates.
(5) To find out whether any significant difference exists between the quality of work life as perceived by the manager and the subordinates.
(6) To examine whether any significant difference exists between the manager and the subordinates in terms of organisational commitment.
(7) To examine the influence of individual-centered variables, viz., age, educational qualification of the managers and the subordinates on the leadership behaviour pattern, organisational commitment and QWL as perceived by self and the subordinates.

7.5 RESEARCH HYPOTHESES

Following hypotheses were formulated and tested to achieve the desired research objectives:

(1) There is significant difference in the Leadership Behaviour pattern of managers as perceived by self and the subordinates on the total Leadership Behaviour Description Index.

(2) There is significant difference in the Leadership Behaviour of managers in terms of initiative and consideration dimensions as perceived by self and the subordinates.

(3) There is significant difference in the perceived Leadership Behaviour pattern of managers above 35 years of age and the managers below 35 years of age.

(4) There is significant difference in the perceived Leadership Behaviour pattern of managers with post-graduate qualifications from the managers with graduate qualifications.

(5) There is significant difference in the perceived Leadership Behaviour pattern of managers as perceived by subordinates above 35 years of age and the subordinates below 35 years of age.

(6) There is significant difference in the perceived Leadership Behaviour pattern of managers as perceived by subordinates with post-graduate qualifications from the subordinates with graduate qualifications.

(7) There is a significant difference in terms of organisational commitment among the managers and the subordinates working in the same organisation.

(8) There is a significant difference in terms of organisational commitment among the managers above 35 years of age from the managers below 35 years of age.

(9) There is a significant difference in terms of organisational commitment among the managers with post-graduate qualifications from the managers with graduate qualifications.

(10) There is a significant difference in terms of organisational commitment among the subordinates above 35 years of age from the subordinates below 35 years of age.

(11) There is a significant difference in terms of organisational commitment among the subordinates with post-graduate qualifications from the subordinates with graduate qualifications.

(12) There is a significant difference in terms of perceived quality of work life among the managers and the subordinates working in the same organisation.

(13) There is a significant difference in terms of perceived quality of work life among the managers above 35 years of age from the managers below 35 years of age.

(14) There is a significant difference in terms of perceived quality of work life among the managers with post-graduate qualifications from the managers with graduate qualifications.

(15) There is a significant difference in terms of perceived quality of work life among the subordinates above 35 years of age from the subordinates below 35 years of age.

(16) There is a significant difference in terms of perceived quality of work life among the subordinates with post-graduate qualifications from the subordinates with graduate qualifications.

7.6 RESEARCH DESIGN

For the present study, the descriptive research method was considered appropriate as the focus was on studying human behaviour which can be better studied through descriptive rather than experimental research. Moreover, the parameters to be studied, viz, leadership behaviour, quality of work life and the organisational commitment develop over a period of time and may not be appropriately studied under experimental conditions.

The data was collected on the basis of convenience-cum-quota sampling wherein 425 employees working in consumer durable industry were contacted. The quota was drawn in terms of age, educational qualifications, marital status of the respondent, the length of service rendered in the organisation, job profile and ownership pattern and size of the organisation. The method of contact was personal visits/mailing. The managers supervising these employees in each organisation were also contacted to elicit their views. 398 response sheets were found complete in all respects and were finally analysed.

The domain of the study was restricted to employees serving in the geographical area of North India including the states of New Delhi, Punjab, Haryana, Himachal Pradesh, Jammu and Kashmir, Rajasthan, Western U.P. and Union Territory of Chandigarh. Incidentally, this provided opportunity to personally contact majority of the field staff.

The break-up of the responses finally analysed is as under:

Managerial Cadre comprising of Branch Managers, Regional Managers, Territory Managers, Zonal Managers, Assistant General Managers and above.

Subordinates comprising of Salesman, Sales officers, Regional Sales officers, Sales Executives, Regional Sales Executives, etc.

Total Managerial cadre who responded to the survey and whose responses were finally included in the analysis was 151.

The break up of these *151 managerial cadre* personnel is as under:

Managerial cadre below the age of 35 years as on September 30, 2005	86
Managerial cadre above the age of 35 years as on September 30, 2005	65
Managerial cadre with Graduate Qualifications	77
Managerial cadre with Post Graduate Qualifications	74
Total Subordinates who responded to the survey and whose responses were finally included in the analysis	247

The break up of *247 subordinates* is as under :

Subordinates below the age of 35 years as on September 30, 2005	98

Subordinates above the age of 35 years as on September 30, 2005	149
Subordinates with Graduate Qualifications	192
Subordinates with Post-Graduate Qualifications	55

The information was obtained through three research instruments:

1. *Leadership Behaviour Description Questionnaire (LBDQ) of Halpin and Winer* (1957).
2. *Organizational Commitment Questionnaire (OCQ) developed by Meyer, Allen and Smith* (1993).
3. *Quality of Work Life Inventory developed by Sinha and Sayeed* (1980).

The various items in these scales were tested for, among other things, issues of accuracy, relevance, readability, grammar, potential for offensiveness and appearance of social, cultural or gender bias. After development these instruments were pre-tested on a small group of staff at four of the participating organizations. This pre-testing was done to ensure that individuals could follow the instructions associated with the format, to obtain estimates of the time required to complete the survey instrument, to identify items that were poorly written or ambiguous, and devise appropriate implementation strategy for data collection. The questionnaires and implementation strategies were revised accordingly. All closed-ended (or quantitative) responses were entered directly from the questionnaires into SPSS (version 10.0.5 for windows, SPSS, Inc., Chicago, 1999). Prior to data analysis, all the survey questions were re-coded.

The collected data was statistically analysed using SPSS/ Minitab packages which have been considered as very flexible and popular due to the ease in their usage (*Punch,* 1998).

(a) The Descriptive statistics like percentages, mean, median, Kurtosis, standard deviations were employed.
(b) Correlation coefficient and t-test were employed to determine the relationship between leadership

behaviour and quality of work life as well as organisational commitment.

(c) Test of significance was employed to determine whether any significant difference exists between the managers and the subordinates in terms of quality of work life as well as organisational commitment indices.

7.6.1 Leadership Behaviour Description Questionnaire (LBDQ)

Leadership Behaviour Description Questionnaire (LBDQ) was originally developed by Personnel Research Board at the Ohio State University and has since been modified many times. *Halpin and Winer* (1952) identified the basic dimensions of leadership as *Initiating Structure and Consideration.*

In their description, *Consideration* refers to the "behaviour indicative of friendship, mutual trust, respect and warmth in relationship between the leader and the members of his staff."

Initiating structure refers to the "leader's behaviour in delineating the relationship between him and the members of his work group and in endeavouring to establish well-defined patterns of organization, channels of communication and methods and procedures."

For the present study, same description of these two dimensions was used. Review of literature has reported high validity of LBDQ as a method whereby group members describe the leadership behaviour of designated leaders in formal organizations. This questionnaire contains 30 short statements that describe specific ways in which leaders behave. Each of the two dimensions contains fifteen likert-type scale items ranging from Always Behave to Never Behave descriptions.

The scale was pretested in Indian scenario in order to validate the sequence and the wording of the statements. Scores were computed for total LBDQ index as well as its constituent elements, viz., consideration as well as the initiative indices.

The Reliability: *Reliability for LBDQ was determined by the split-half method. The estimated reliability co-efficient using this method was found to be 0.83 for initiating structure scores and 0.92 for consideration scores* (Halpin, *1966).*

The Validity: *The validity of the leadership behaviour questionnaire has been tested through extensive use in leadership research in management.* Halpin *(1966) has provided evidence of concurrent criterion validity of the LBDQ and invalidity study conducted under well-controlled laboratory conditions.* Stogdill *(1970) has also supported the validity of the LDBQ subtests of initiating structure and consideration.*

This instrument has been administered in wide variety of situations. This is considered to be one of the most popular and widely used instruments for describing leadership behaviour. *Greenberg* (1996), *Halpin* (1956, 1957), *Hemphill* (1955), *Hemphill and Coons* (1957), *Shartle* (1966), *Stogdill* (1963, 1970), *Nolan* (1969), *Kunz and Hoy* (1976) have used the scale in their research.

7.6.2 Organisational Commitment Scale Developed by Meyer, Allen and Smith (1993)

Organisational Commitment Scale developed by Meyer, Allen and Smith (1993) was used. This seven point scale measures three themes through 18 items classified under three heads:

Affective commitment, i.e. extent to which employees remains with the organization because they want to.

Continuance commitment, i.e. extent to which employees remains with the organization because they need to.

Normative commitment, i.e. extent to which employees remains with the organization because they feel they ought to do so.

7.6.3 The Quality of Work Life Inventory by Sinha and Sayeed (1980)

The Quality of Work Life Inventory by Sinha and Sayeed (1980) is a scale having 17 dimensions to measure various aspects of work life. In all there are 85 items in the inventory measuring 17 dimensions of Quality of Work Life.

Operational definition of Dimensions of QWL

1. *Economic Benefits (EB)*: Receiving adequate monetary income and financial rewards.
2. *Physical Working Condition (PWC)*: conditions affecting physical comfort and convenience on and at the job.
3. *Mental State (MS)*: feeling good *v*. feeling of depression or being upset at work.
4. *Career Orientation (CO)*: progressing for career objectives and having opportunity for progress.
5. *Advancement on Merit (AM)*: the extent to which rewards and punishments are based on merit.
6. *Effect on Personal Life (EPL)*: effect of job on personal life. The hangover effect on the individual which may be positive or negative.
7. *Union-Management Relation (UMR)*: the relationship between union and management and consideration of each other's point of view.
8. *Self Respect (SR)*: the feeling of being treated as an adult with respect and due dignity.
9. *Supervisory Relationship (RS)*: the relationship with the supervisor and mutual understanding.
10. *Intra-group Relations (IGR)*: the way workers in a group interact.
11. *Sense of Achievement* v. *Apathy (A)*: the workers concern and ambition for work.
12. *Confidence in Management (CM)*: beliefs that the management is aware of and concerned about workers problems and interests.
13. *Meaningful Development (MD)*: opportunity to learn more and apply skills and abilities meaningfully and in a challenging way.
14. *Control, Influence and Participation (CIP)*: the extent to which workers are involved in decision-making, their influence and control.
15. *Employee Commitment (EC)*: loyalty to company and concern for its future.
16. *General Life Satisfaction (GLS)*: fulfilment of 'life' needs apart from the work situation, i.e. in family, in society and so on.

17. *Organisational Climate (OC)*: the Organisational outlook and approach in the interest of the workers for the betterment of the industry.

These statements pertained to certain characteristics related to work and working conditions. Respondents were requested to assign weightages to these in terms of how much of these are present in their job. *The alpha reliability of the inventory was found to be 0.97. The inventory has been successfully used in India by Sayeed and Sinha* (1981), *Anantharaman and Ravindranath* (1982) *and Rana* (1989).

7.6.4 Classification of Data

Classification of Data was undertaken on the following criteria:

(a) Designation of the respondent.
(b) Age of the respondent.
(c) Educational Qualifications of the respondent.
(d) Average Monthly Income.
(e) Marital Status.
(f) Length of Service in Present Organisation.
(g) Length of Service in Consumer Durable Industry.
(h) Number of persons directly reporting to the respondent.

7.7 LIMITATIONS OF THE STUDY

The present research study has been conducted to understand perceptual differences towards the leadership behaviour of the managers and their subordinates. Thus, it requires willingness as well as the ability of the respondents to reply honestly to the administered questionnaire.

The study has been conducted in the Northern India. Thus, the findings my not be exactly replicable in other parts of the country.

The opinions and the perceptions of the managers and the subordinates working in the consumer durable industry have been elicited. These may not be replicable in other industries. Thus, the findings are specific to only consumer durable industry. However, many of the findings and recommendations may have general applicability.

Although every effort has been made to contact entire population consisting of workforce employed in the Consumer Durable industry in North India, yet there may be differences in the opinions and perceptions of those who responded to the questionnaire and those whose responses could not be ascertained.

Due to time and money constraints, study has been conducted by contacting employees working only in North India. Incidentally, this provided control over the data collection and validation of the data, thereby enhancing reliability of the study.

References

Anantharaman, R.N. and Ravindranath, K.V. (1982): Need Satisfaction and its Importance Among Bank Employees. *Managerial Psychology*, Vol. 3(1), 49-55.

Becker, B. and Huselid, M. (1998): "High Performance Work Systems and Firm Performance: A Synthesis of Research and Managerial Implications." *Research in Personnel and Human Resources*, Edited By Ferris, G.F., Vol. 16, pp. 53-101: Jai Press Inc., Greenwich, CT.

Blau, G.J. (1985a): "The Measurement and Prediction of Career Commitment." *Journal of Occupational Psychology*, Vol. 58(4), pp. 277-88.

Blau, G.J. (1985b): "A Multiple Study Investigation of the Dimensionality of Job Involvement." *Journal of Vocational Behaviour*, Vol. 27(1), pp. 19-36.

Blau, P. (1964): *Exchange and Power in Social Life*. Wiley Publications, New York.

Cohen, A. (1992): "Antecedents of Organizational Commitment Across Occupational Groups: A Meta Analysis." *Journal of Organizational Behaviour*, Vol. 13(6), pp. 539-58.

Greenberg, J. (1996): *Managing Behaviour in Organizations*. Upper Saddle River, New Jersey: Prentice-hall.

Halpin, A.W. and Winer, B.J. (1952): "The Leader Behaviour of the Airplane Commander." *Technical Report III* Prepared for Human Resources Laboratory Department of the Air Force Under Contracts Af33.

Halpin, A.W. and Winer, B.J. (1957): "A Factorial Analysis of the Leader Behaviour Descriptions." In: Stogdill, R.M. and Coons, A.E. (Eds.). *Leader Behaviour: Its Description and Measurement: Res. Monographs*. Bureau of Business Research, Ohio State University, Columbus, Ohio (U.S.).

Halpin, A.W. (1956): "The Leadership Behaviour of School Superintendents." *College of Education,* Ohio State University, Columbus, Ohio (U.S.).

Halpin, A.W. (1957): *Manual for the Leader Behaviour Description Questionnaire,* Ohio State University, Columbus, Ohio (U.S.).

Halpin, A.W. (1966): *Theory and Research in Administration.* Mcmillan Co. Ltd., New York.

Hemphill, J.K. and Coons, A.E. (1950): *Leader Behaviour Description Questionnair,.* Personnel Research Board, Ohio State University, Ohio, Columbus (U.S.).

Hemphill, J.K. and Coons, A.E. (1957): "Development of the Leader Behaviour Description Questionnaire." *Journal of Social Issues,* Vol. 12, pp. 41-49.

Hemphill, J.K. (1955): "Leadership Behaviour Associated With the Administrative Reputation of College Department." *Journal of Educational Psychology,* Vol. 46(7), pp. 38-51.

Igbaria, M. and Greenhaus, J.H. (1992): "Determinants of Mis Employees' Turnover Intentions: A Structural Equation Model." *Communication of the Acm,* Vol. 35(2), pp. 35-49.

Kanungo, R. (1979): "The Concept of Alienation and Involvement Revisited." *Psychological Bulletin,* Vol. 86(1), pp. 119-38.

Kanungo, R. (1982): "Measurement of Job and Work Involvement." *Journal of Applied Psychology,* Vol. 67(3), pp. 341-49.

Kunz, D.W. and Hoy, W.K. (1976): "Leadership Styles of the Principal and the Professional Zone of Acceptance of the Teachers." *Journal of Educational Administration Quarterly,* Vol. 1(3), pp. 49-64.

Lev, B. (2002): *Intangibles: Management, Measurement, and Reporting,* Brookings Institution Press, Washington, D.C.

Meyer J.P., Allen, N.J. and Smith, C.A. (1993): "Commitment To Organizations and Occupations: Extension and Test of a Three-component Conceptualization." *Journal of Applied Psychology,* Vol. 78(4), pp. 538-51.

Morrow, P.C. (1983): "Concept Redundancy in Organizational Research: The Case of Work Commitment," *Academy of Management Review,* Vol. 8(3), pp. 486-500.

Nolan, J.S. (1969): *"The Leadership Behaviour and the Administrative Action, Patterns of Principals of Public Elementary Schools of State of New Jersey."* Unpublished Ph.D. Thesis Submitted to Fordman University, New York.

Punch, K.F. (1998): *Introduction to Social Research: Quantitative and Qualitative Approaches,* Sage Publications, London.

Rabinowitz, S. and Hall, D.T. (1977): "Organizational Research on Job Involvement." *Psychological Bulletin,* Vol. 84(2), pp. 265-88.

Rana, A. (1989): *A Cross-cultural Study of Indian and Nepalese Managers. Job Satisfaction in Relation to Managerial Style, Quality of Working Life, Personality, Locus of Control and Need Satisfaction.* Unpublished Ph.D. Thesis, Panjab University, Chandigarh.

Sayeed, O.B. and Sinha, P. (1981): "Quality of Working Life in Relation to Job Satisfaction and Performance in two Organizations". *Managerial Psychology,* Vol. 2(1), pp. 15-30.

Shartle, C.L. (1966): *Executive Performance and Leadership*. McGraw-Hill Publications, New York.

Sinha, P. and Sayeed, O.B. (1980): "Measuring QWL: Development of An Inventory." *Indian Journal of Social Work*, Vol. 41(3), pp. 219-26.

Stogdill, R.M. (1963): *Manual for Leadership Behaviour Description Questionnaire. Form XII: An Experimental Approach*. Ohio State University, College of Commerce and Administration, Columbus.

Stogdill, R.M. (1970): *A Review of the Research on Leadership Behaviour Description Questionnaire*, Ohio State University, College of Commerce and Administration, Columbus.

Stogdill, R.M. (1974): *Handbook of Leadership: A Survey of Theory and Research*, The Free Press, New York.

CHAPTER

Leadership Behaviour—Analysis and Interpretation

8.1 INTRODUCTION

The main issue addressed in this chapter and subsequent two chapters concerns the relationship between managerial practices on the one hand and employees' commitment and quality of work life on the other. Assessment of managerial practices and their implications in terms of commitment and job satisfaction appear to be of theoretical and empirical relevance with regard to the performance of employees in the consumer durable sector. Leadership, job satisfaction and commitment are closely interrelated. Job satisfaction and commitment are immediate antecedents of intention to leave the workplace and turnover: the higher an employees' commitment, the lower their intention to leave. Among antecedents of job satisfaction and commitment, leadership plays a central role along with other human resource management practices. Leadership is positively correlated with employees' job satisfaction and with commitment towards the institution and its missions.

Parry (1998) has defined leadership as "*the presentation by a leader of some identifiable goal or vision or future state that people can desire; and the generation of a willingness within those people to follow the leader along a socially responsible and mutually beneficial course of action toward that goal.*" Included in this definition are a number of components:

- The idea that leadership includes the presentation of a *future*—a leader must be going 'somewhere'.
- The idea of others *following* the leader.
- The idea of *willing following*—people being willing to follow rather than being coerced.
- A *desirable future state*—a goal that motivates the followers.
- An *attainable future state*—goals that are not too difficult (or too easy) to discourage followers.
- A *mutually beneficial* course of action—the intended outcome of the leadership journey is beneficial to both leader and followers.
- The idea that the leadership journey involves a *socially responsible and ethical* course of action—this is said to differentiate real leadership from influence.
- Leadership is translated into both *actions and words*.

Three propositions were the basis of undertaking this study so as to make humble efforts to add to the existing body of knowledge in this area:

1. Any lack of alignment or disconnect between the formal goals and strategy and implementation decision-making by the managers of an organisation is likely to have the most significant impact on strategic leadership efforts and the organisation's strategic performance.
2. Managing the context for leadership in business organisations is a vital component of strategic leadership efforts of the managers.
3. Both transformational and transactional leadership approaches are required in effective strategic leadership in business organisations with an emphasis

on transformational approaches. However, specific interventions need to be tailored for the particular context of the organisation.

How the work is delivered relies to varying extents on the decisions, skills, attitudes and behaviours of the supporting staff. Therefore, influencing the staff carrying out the work so that they understand how their roles and work relates to the outcomes and strategy set by the managers becomes vital. This can involve overcoming professional biases, traditional methods of delivery or particular established interests among other barriers. This is where leadership and in particular strategic leadership can play an important role in influencing staff to perform in a manner best suited to achieving the organisation's desired outcomes.

Key behavioural components of emerging leadership which have been analysed in the present study include:

- *Envisioning*—creation of an attractive vision of the future that is challenging, meaningful, credible and worthy of pursuit.
- *Energizing*—generation of motivation to act among organisation members through personal enthusiasm, leveraging the enthusiasm of others and celebrating successes.
- *Enabling*—helping people to perform in the face of challenging goals by providing support and expressing confidence.

Besides the perception of the subordinates regarding 'instrumental leadership'; qualities as measured by the following components were also analysed:

- *Structuring*—creating structures (e.g. setting goals, standards and roles) that make clear required behaviours.
- *Controlling*—creation of systems and processes to monitor, measure and assess behaviour and results, and to administer corrective action.

- *Rewarding*—administering contingent rewards and punishments.

Yukl (2002) provided a working definition of leadership: "*Leadership is the process of influencing others to understand and agree about what needs to be done and how it can be done effectively and the process of facilitating individual and collective efforts to accomplish the shared objectives.*" This definition is process rather than outcome focused and does not incorporate *willing following* and *social responsibility* as necessary components.

Internalisation means that the leader's proposal or request becomes integrated with the follower's own values and beliefs, leading to commitment to the ideas regardless of reward or punishment. Personal identification involves identification with and commitment to the leader rather than the idea and is probably driven by the follower's needs for acceptance and self-esteem (*Yukl,* 2002).

Organisations are facing a turbulent environment, increasing demands and pressure from stakeholders. In order to succeed in this environment, leaders must "*build a culture with a core competency which values and excels at adaptation.*" Leadership is integral to organisations adapting and surviving in their environment. Tasks of today's leaders include preparing "*the members of their organisations to cope with and adapt to changes of mission environment and/or direction.*" Thus, the challenge of leadership is the development of an adaptive organisational culture as the organisation's primary core competence.

8.2 PRESENTATION, ANALYSIS AND INTERPRETATION OF FINDINGS REGARDING LEADERSHIP BEHAVIOUR

For the present study, *Leadership Behaviour Description Questionnaire (LBDQ)* as validated by *Halpin* (1957) has been used which identified the basic dimensions of leadership as *Initiating Structure and Consideration. Consideration* refers to the "behaviour indicative of friendship, mutual trust, respect and warmth in relationship between the leader and the members of his staff." *Initiating Structure* refers to the "leader's behaviour in delineating the relationship between him and the members of his work group and in endeavouring to establish well-defined patterns of organization, channels of communication and methods and procedures."

Table 8.1 presents the statistical analysis of the Leadership Behaviour Description Index (LBD) and its constituent Components (Initiation and Consideration Indices) as perceived by Self (Managers) and by their Subordinates (Non-managers). The purpose was to compare the score on the total LBD index as well as its individual components. The table indicates that the mean scores of managers on the total LBD index are almost similar to the perception of the subordinates about their manager. However, there is a difference on the individual components. Managers perceive themselves to be high on consideration index whereas the subordinates feel that the managers are high on initiative index and low on consideration.

The mean scores of Leadership Behaviour Description Index have been graphically represented in Figure 8.1.

Leaders must concentrate less on "concrete task and performance direction", and more on "framing and guiding the work tasks so that they align with the organisation's mission and focus." Vision and goals, rather than rules and procedures, are seen as key tools for co-ordination and control. Clear vision helps people understand the purpose, objectives and priorities of an organisation, gives work meaning and fosters a sense of common purpose. Our respondents have shown that successful change leaders, among other things, communicate a clear vision and enlist others to help achieve it. Thus managers have an impact in organisations through promulgating vision which attracts commitment and energises people, creates meaning, establishes a standard of excellence and bridges the present with the future.

Managerial cadre need to be initiative oriented so as to lead from the front. This has to be matched with consideration so as to generate empathy towards the subordinate. This humane attitude can instill confidence in the subordinates to undertake calculated risks. Managers need to conceptualise major work characteristics (i.e. staffing, training, assigning work, appraising performance, allocating rewards, etc.) within a human resource framework, so as to make subordinates aware about their responsibilities regarding work groups. This could

TABLE 8.1

Statistical Parameters of Leadership Behaviour Description Index (LBD) and its Constituent Components (Initiation and Consideration Indices) as perceived by Self (Managers) and by their Subordinates (Non-managers)

Sample			*Consideration Index*	*Initiation Index*	*Total Leadership Behaviour Description score*
(1)	*(2)*	*(3)*	*(4)*	*(5)*	*(6)*
Managerial Cadre	151	average	58.159	51.304	109.464
		stdev	6.166	7.478	12.101
		median	60.000	52.000	110.000
		max	68.000	67.000	132.000
		min	43.000	29.000	75.000
		skewness	-0.525	-0.710	-0.593
		kurtosis	-0.550	0.630	-0.017
Non-manager's perception about their manager	247	average	56.298	53.048	109.345
		stdev	6.373	4.844	9.081
		median	57.000	53.000	109.000
		max	68.000	66.000	132.000

		min	38.000	42.000	89.000
		skewness	-0.731	0.500	0.063
		kurtosis	0.137	0.236	-0.044
Total	398	average	57.137	52.261	109.399
		stdev	6.329	6.212	10.514
		median	58.000	52.000	110.000
		max	68.000	67.000	132.000
		min	38.000	29.000	75.000
		skewness	-0.631	-0.593	-0.371
		kurtosis	-0.093	1.506	0.164

FIG. 8.1

Mean Scores of Leadership Behaviour Description Index (LBD) and its Constituent Components (Initiation and Consideration Indices) as perceived by Self (Managers) and by their Subordinates

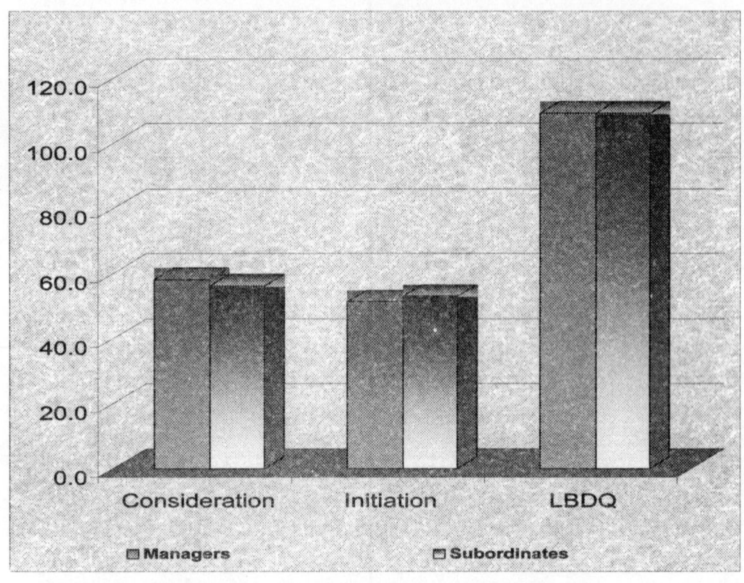

be achieved through the decentralisation of power so as to make them responsible for their team functioning in well-adapted working conditions.

The Leadership Behaviour Index was also analysed on the basis of age of the respondents (Table 8.2). Comparison of the managerial cadre on the basis of age of the respondents reveals that the managerial cadre below the age of 35 consider themselves to be low on consideration index as compared to managerial cadre respondents above the age of 35, whereas the initiativeness is also perceived to be high in managerial cadre above the age of 35 as compared to the mangers of lower age bracket.

Opinion of the subordinates about their managers was also collected. Subordinates below the age of 35 have almost the same perception as that of the subordinates above the age of 35 on both consideration as well as initiative indices.

The means scores of Leadership Behaviour Description Index and its Constituent Components, i.e. Initiation and Consideration as perceived by Manager and their subordinates classified on the basis of age has been graphically represented in Figure 8.2.

FIG. 8.2

Mean Scores of Leadership Behaviour Description Index (LBD) and its Constituent Components (Initiation and Consideration Indices) as perceived by Self (Managers) and by their Subordinates classified on the basis of the Age-group (Below 35 years and Above 35 years respectively)

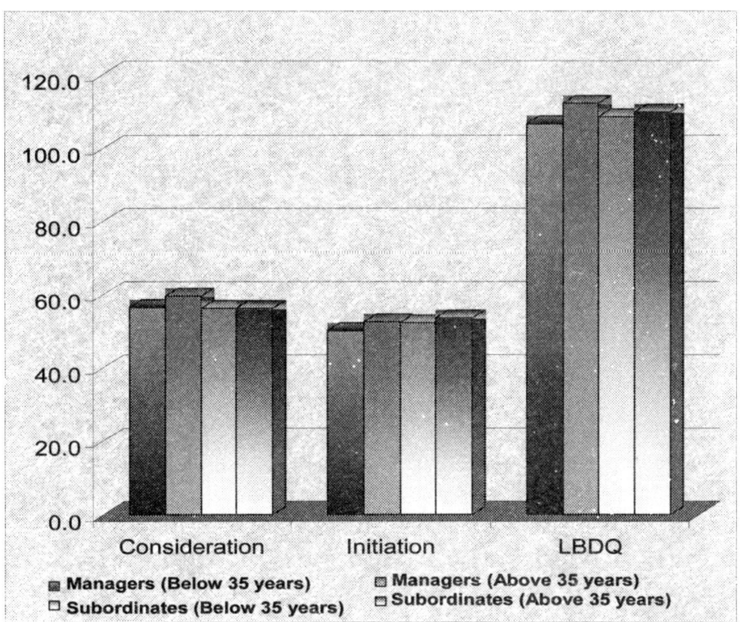

Similarly, segmented analysis of the Leadership Behaviour Index on the basis of educational qualifications was undertaken. Findings reveal that the managerial cadre with Post-graduate qualifications consider themselves to be high on total Leadership Behaviour Index as well as on both consideration as well as initiative indices compared to managers with only graduate qualifications.

Subordinates with Post-graduate qualifications have no difference in opinion than the subordinates with the Post-Graduate qualifications in terms of their perception on the Leadership Behaviour Index as well as its constituent elements, viz, consideration and initiative indices.

The means scores of Leadership Behaviour Description Index and its Constituent components, i.e. Initiation and Consideration as perceived by Manager and their subordinates classified on the basis of Educational Qualifications have been graphically represented in Figure 8.3.

FIG. 8.3

Mean Scores of Leadership Behaviour Description Index (LBD) and its Constituent Components (Initiation and Consideration Indices) as perceived by Self (Managers) and by their Subordinates classified on the basis of Educational Qualifications (Graduate and Post-Graduate)

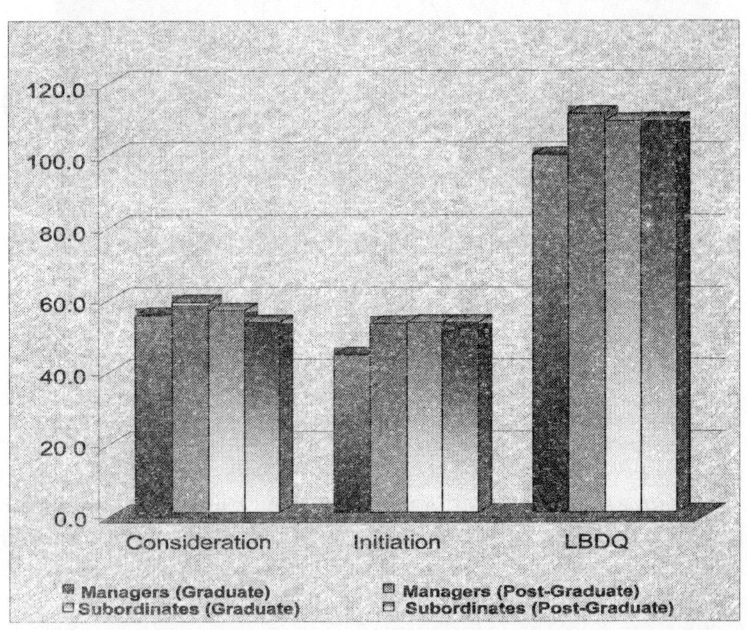

These findings reveal that the main challenges for today's managers are to build a long-term vision, to increase

TABLE 8.2

Statistical Parameters of Leadership Behaviour Description Index (LBD) and its Constituent Components (Initiation and Consideration Indices) as perceived by Self (Managers) and by their Subordinates (Non-managers) classified on the basis of the age of the respondents

Sample			*Consideration*		*Initiation*		*Total Leadership Behaviour Description score*	
			Age		*Age*		*Age*	
			Below 35 (86)	*Above 35 (65)*	*Below 35 (86)*	*Above 35 (65)*	*Below 35 (86)*	*Above 35 (65) (66)*
(1)	*(2)*	*(3)*	*(4)*	*(5)*	*(6)*	*(7)*	*(8)*	*(9)*
Managerial cadre	151	average	56.607	59.676	50.250	52.622	106.857	112.297
		stdev	6.746	5.159	7.662	7.041	12.880	10.767
		median	56.000	60.000	51.000	54.000	109.500	114.000
		max	67.000	68.000	67.000	64.000	130.000	132.000
		min	43.000	48.000	29.000	35.000	75.000	83.000
		skewness	-0.356	-0.448	-0.657	-0.897	-0.586	-0.727
		kurtosis	-0.944	-0.250	1.518	0.825	-0.024	0.740

(Contd.)

TABLE 8.2 (Contd.)

			Below 35 (98)	*Above 35 (149)*	*Below 35 (98)*	*Above 35 (149)*	*Below 35 (98)*	*Above 35 (149)*
(1)	*(2)*	*(3)*	*(4)*	*(5)*	*(6)*	*(7)*	*(8)*	*(9)*
Subordinates perception about their manager	247	average	56.406	56.275	52.281	53.647	108.688	109.922
		stdev	6.628	6.331	4.848	4.787	9.107	9.136
		median	59.000	57.000	51.000	54.000	109.000	110.000
		max	66.000	68.000	66.000	65.000	132.000	129.000
		min	38.000	40.000	45.000	42.000	92.000	89.000
		skewness	-1.100	-0.519	0.772	0.358	0.081	0.013
		kurtosis	0.682	-0.095	0.355	0.571	0.104	0.029

TABLE 8.2a

Summary of Statistical Parameters of Leadership Behaviour Description Index (LBD) and its Constituent Components (Initiation and Consideration Indices) as perceived by Self (Managers) and by their Subordinates classified on the basis of the age of the respondents

Sample			*Consideration*		*Initiation*		*Total Leadership Behaviour Description score*	
			Age		*Age*		*Age*	
			Below 35 (184)	*Above 35 (214)*	*Below 35 (184)*	*Above 35 (214)*	*Below 35 (184)*	*Above 35 (214)*
(1)	(2)	(3)	(4)	(5)	(6)	(7)	(8)	(9)
Total	398	average	56.500	57.705	51.333	53.216	107.833	110.920
		stdev	6.627	6.075	6.345	5.826	10.970	9.866
		median	58.000	58.000	51.000	54.000	109.000	112.000
		max	67.000	68.000	67.000	65.000	132.000	132.000
		min	38.000	40.000	29.000	35.000	75.000	83.000
		skewness	-0.725	-0.589	-0.545	-0.623	-0.480	-0.314
		kurtosis	-0.165	0.085	2.311	1.465	0.409	0.189

TABLE 8.3

Statistical Parameters of Leadership Behaviour Description Index (LBD) and its Constituent Components (Initiation and Consideration Indices) as perceived by Managers and by their Subordinates classified on the basis of the educational qualifications of the respondents

Sample			*Consideration*		*Initiation*		*Total Leadership Behaviour Description score*	
			Qualification		*Qualification*		*Qualification*	
			Graduate	*Post-graduate*	*Graduate*	*Post-graduate*	*Graduate*	*Post-graduate*
(1)	*(2)*	*(3)*	*(4)*	*(5)*	*(6)*	*(7)*	*(8)*	*(9)*
Managerial Cadre	151	average	55.889	58.750	44.000	52.821	99.889	111.571
		stdev	4.167	6.230	7.550	6.606	10.398	11.443
		median	56.000	60.000	41.000	52.500	101.000	113.000
		max	60.000	68.000	54.000	67.000	114.000	132.000
		min	49.000	43.000	36.000	29.000	86.000	75.000
		skewness	-0.699	-0.671	0.235	-0.931	-0.039	-0.938
		kurtosis	-0.721	-0.300	-2.257	2.646	-1.531	1.246

Subordinates perception about their manager	247	average	56.286	56.382	53.102	53.147	109.388	109.529
		stdev	6.484	6.391	4.806	4.931	8.942	9.433
		median	57.000	57.000	53.000	53.000	110.000	108.500
		max	67.000	68.000	66.000	65.000	132.000	129.000
		min	38.000	40.000	45.000	42.000	92.000	89.000
		skewness	-0.809	-0.672	0.472	0.535	-0.036	0.134
		Kurtosis	0.113	0.354	0.080	0.741	0.036	0.047

(Contd.)

TABLE 8.3 (*Contd.*)

Summary of Statistical Parameters of Leadership Behaviour Description Index (LBD) and its Constituent Components (Initiation and Consideration Indices) as perceived by Managers and by their Subordinates classified on the basis of the educational qualifications of the respondents

Sample			*Consideration*		*Initiation*		*Total Leadership Behaviour Description score*	
			Qualification		*Qualification*		*Qualification*	
			Graduate	*Post-graduate*	*Graduate*	*Post-graduate*	*Graduate*	*Post-graduate*
(1)	*(2)*	*(3)*	*(4)*	*(5)*	*(6)*	*(7)*	*(8)*	*(9)*
Total	398	average	56.224	57.856	51.690	52.944	107.914	110.800
		stdev	6.153	6.361	6.205	6.001	9.723	10.719
		median	57.000	59.000	52.000	53.000	109.000	110.500
		max	67.000	68.000	66.000	67.000	132.000	132.000
		min	38.000	40.000	36.000	29.000	86.000	75.000
		skewness	-0.798	-0.641	-0.512	-0.672	-0.194	-0.613
		kurtosis	0.238	-0.094	0.821	2.652	-0.042	0.782

commitment, to build teams and coalitions in order to fully realize the skills of the team. To reach goals of the organization, they should focus on motivating, inspiring and empowering their employees. In work settings, the supervisor is often the most salient person and is therefore likely to both represent the organisation's culture and to exert a direct influence upon subordinates' behaviours. Superiors assigning tasks, specifying procedures, and clarifying expectations have been shown to result in reduced role ambiguity and increased job satisfaction among employees. Leaders who are perceived to closely monitor their subordinates in order to prevent mistakes tend to evoke higher levels of emotional exhaustion among their staff. Close monitoring may be perceived as a lack of trust in the staff.

Emotional support and adequate feedback provision about subordinates' performance would be a better strategy and may lead to an increase in employees' self-esteem. Thus, not only they need to have high initiative and consideration, they should also be perceived to be so by their subordinates.

The Leadership Behaviour Index and its constituent elements (viz., consideration and initiative) were also analysed by applying t-test of significance

$$t = \frac{\overline{X}_1 - \overline{X}_2}{S}\sqrt{\frac{n_1 n_2}{n_1 + n_2}}$$

where,

$\overline{X}_1$ = mean of the first sample (managers)

$\overline{X}_2$ = mean of the second sample (non-managers)

n_1 = number of observations in the first sample (managers)

n_2 = number of observations in the second sample (subordinates)

S = combined standard deviation

The t-test on the difference in the perception of the managerial cadre and the subordinate's perception about their supervisor on the consideration index (Table 8.4) reveals that the perceptual difference is significant. Managers consider

TABLE 8.4

Test of Significance (t-test) on the Difference of Managers' perception about self and Subordinates' perceptions about their Manager on the Consideration Index

	Sample Size	*Mean*	*Std. Deviation*	*t-value*	*Tabulated Value*	*Significance*
Managers	151	58.159	6.166			
Subordinates' Perception	247	56.298	6.373	2.848	2.576	Significant
Total	398	57.137	6.329			

themselves to be significantly more considerate than the subordinate's perceptions about them. Thus, managers not only should be considerate towards their team but must also command respect for such a behaviour. Managerial cadre need be more sensitive to the needs and wants of the subordinates so as to build a team of dedicated and loyal subordinates who value the command of their executive. Such a behavioural intervention will go a long way in instilling bon homie in the team so as to have cohesiveness.

Table 8.5 reveals that the subordinates consider their managers to be having more initiative than the perception of the managers about themselves. One possible explanation could be the lower involvement of the subordinates in goal setting and decision-making, thereby making employees feel that the

TABLE 8.5

Test of Significance (t-test) on the Difference of Managers' perception about self and Subordinates' perceptions about the Manager on the Initiation Index

	Sample Size	*Mean*	*Std. Deviation*	*t-value*	*Tabulated Value*	*Significance*
Managers	151	51.304	7.478			
Subordinates' Perception	247	53.048	4.844	2.7166	2.576	Significant
Total	398	52.261	6.212			

manager has more initiative as he takes most of the decisions. Such a perception may lead to poor development of the subordinate as he may not take initiative himself and may look towards the manager for problem-solving.

Comparative analysis of the managerial cadre's perception about the total leadership behaviour score as well as the subordinates perception about them (Table 8.6) reveals that the difference is not significant. Thus, the subordinates have similar perception about their executive as that of the executives themselves. Leadership is a process of social interaction that is ultimately founded in cognitive processes. Consideration is a people-related dimension defined as "the degree to which a leader acts in a friendly and supportive manner, shows concern for subordinates and looks out for their welfare" (*Yukl,* 1994). Leaders high on consideration tend to focus on the needs of the stakeholder, both physical and psychological. Conversely, initiating structure behaviours are more task focused and are defined as "the degree to which a leader defines and structures his or her own role and the roles of subordinates toward attainment of the group's formal goals" (*Yukl,* 1994). Leaders high on initiating structure exhibit behaviours, which provide direction and clarify goals. The initiating structure style focuses less on how stakeholders feel, and more on creating systems for efficiently performing job tasks. Based on the process of automatic categorization and the general preference for homogeneity, it is conceivable that subordinates in certain industries which have shorter chains of command may evaluate

TABLE 8.6

Test of Significance (t-test) on the Difference of Managers' perception about self and Subordinates' perceptions about the Manager on the Leadership Behaviour Index

	Sample Size	*Mean*	*Std. Deviation*	*t-value*	*Tabulated Value*	*Significance*
Managers	151	109.464	12.101			
Subordinates' Perception	247	109.345	9.081	0.1091	2.576	Insignificant
Total	398	109.399	10.514			

their leaders more readily and optimistically than in other industries which have longer chains of command. This is evidenced by the fact that past research has consistently shown that a consideration behaviour either alone or in conjunction with structuring behaviour is related to job satisfaction. Consequently, a positive employee appraisal lends itself to the consideration style.

Comparative analysis was also undertaken to analyse whether there is any significant difference in the perception of the managers in different age groups on the consideration index. Managerial cadre in the age group above 35 years has statistically significant scores on the consideration index than the managers in the age group below 35 years. As the managers reach higher age groups, consideration towards the well-being of the subordinates take precedence (Table 8.7).

TABLE 8.7

Test of Significance (t-test) on the Difference of Managers' perception about self on the Consideration Index (comparison between Managers below 35 years and Managers above 35 years)

	Sample Size	*Mean*	*Std. Deviation*	*t-value*	*Tabulated Value*	*Significance*
Managers Below 35 years	86	56.607	6.746	3.0411	2.576	Significant
Managers Above 35 years	65	59.676	5.159			

Similarly, perception of the subordinates about their manager was also compared across different age groups. However, no significant difference was noticed. Thus, subordinates across different age groups have no difference in their perception about their manager on the consideration index (Table 8.8).

It may be explained that the subordinates tend to focus on the readily visible and identifiable task related behaviour of the leader, in turn yielding a greater perception of structuring behaviour. Decision-making may have been perceived to be

TABLE 8.8

Test of Significance (t-test) on the Difference of Subordinates' perception about their Manager on the Consideration Index (comparison between Subordinates below 35 years and Subordinates above 35 years)

	Sample Size	*Mean*	*Std. Deviation*	*t-value*	*Tabulated Value*	*Significance*
Subordinates Below 35 years	98	56.406	6.628	-0.1584	2.576	Insignificant
Subordinates Above 35 years	149	56.275	6.331			

largely centralized and procedures may have been highly structured.

Similarly, difference of managers perception across different age groups on the initiative index (Table 8.9) was statistically insignificant. Subordinates across different age groups also had similar opinion about their managers (Table 8.10). Thus, managers as well as their subordinates perceive them to have similar level of initiativeness.

TABLE 8.9

Test of Significance (t-test) on the Difference of Managers' perception about self on the Initiation Index (comparison between Managers below 35 years and Managers above 35 years)

	Sample Size	*Mean*	*Std. Deviation*	*t-value*	*Tabulated Value*	*Significance*
Managers Below 35 years	86	50.250	7.662	1 9380	2.576	Insignificant
Managers Above 35 years	65	52.622	7.041			

This notion is supported by the work of *Rogers* (1995) who proposed that higher levels of trust are associated with people-oriented leader behaviours including listening, seeking employee involvement and encouraging mutual team support

TABLE 8.10

Test of Significance (t-test) on the Difference of Subordinates' perception about their Manager on the Initiation Index (comparison between Subordinates below 35 years and Subordinates above 35 years)

	Sample Size	*Mean*	*Std. Deviation*	*t-value*	*Tabulated Value*	*Significance*
Subordinates Below 35 years	98	52.281	4.848	2.1678	2.576	Insignificant
Subordinates Above 35 years	149	53.647	4.787			

and praise. These are consistent with consideration style behaviours and recommendations for supportive behaviours.

Another hypothesis which was tested was whether there is any significant difference on the total Leadership Behaviour Description Index between manager below the age of 35 and those managers above the age of 35. It was found that managers above the age of 35 consider themselves to have higher Leadership Behaviour score as compared to the managers below 35 years (Table 8.11)

TABLE 8.11

Test of Significance (t-test) on the Difference of Managers' perception about self on the Leadership Behaviour Description Index (comparison between Managers below 35 years and Managers above 35 years)

	Sample Size	*Mean*	*Std. Deviation*	*t-value*	*Tabulated Value*	*Significance*
Managers Below 35 years	86	106.857	12.880	2.747	2.576	Significant
Managers Above 35 years	65	112.297	10.767			

In order to test whether their subordinates also have similar perception about their superiors, difference on Leadership Behaviour Description Index of the subordinates of different age groups was computed. Subordinates across different age groups have similar opinion about their manager on the total Leadership Behaviour Description Index as no significant difference exists across age groups (Table 8.12).

TABLE 8.12

Test of Significance (t-test) on the Difference of Subordinates' perception about their Manager on the Leadership Behaviour Description Index (comparison between Subordinates below 35 years and Subordinates above 35 years)

	Sample Size	*Mean*	*Std. Deviation*	*t-value*	*Tabulated Value*	*Significance*
Subordinates Below 35 years	98	108.688	9.107	1.0448	2.576	Insignificant
Subordinates Above 35 years	149	109.222	9.136			

Another hypothesis tested was whether managers of different qualifications vary on the total Leadership Behaviour Description Index. It was found that the managers with Post-graduate qualifications were higher on the total Leadership Behaviour Description Index as compared to the managers with

TABLE 8.13

Test of Significance (t-test) on the Difference of Managers' perception about self on the Leadership Behaviour Description Index (comparison between Managers with Graduate Qualifications and Managers with Post-graduate Qualifications)

	Sample Size	*Mean*	*Std. Deviation*	*t-value*	*Tabulated Value*	*Significance*
Managers (Graduate Qualifications)	77	99.889	10.398	5.8996	2.576	Significant
Managers (Post-graduate Qualifications	74	111.571	11.443			

graduate qualifications and this difference was statistically significant.

Another hypothesis tested was whether the subordinates with different levels of qualifications also have perceptual difference about the Leadership Behaviour Description Index of their supervisor. However, this difference was not statistically significant. Thus, subordinates have similar opinion about their manager irrespective of their level of qualifications. (Table 8.14).

TABLE 8.14

Test of Significance (t-test) on the Difference of Subordinates' perception about their Manager on the Leadership Behaviour Description Index (comparison between Subordinates with Graduate Qualifications and Subordinates with Post-graduate Qualifications)

	Sample Size	*Mean*	*Std. Deviation*	*t-value*	*Tabulated Value*	*Significance*
Subordinates (Graduate Qualifications)	192	109.3888	8.942	0.1199	2.576	Insignificant
Subordinates (Post-graduate Qualifications	55	109.529	9.433			

Another comparative analysis was undertaken on the consideration index between managers of graduate qualifications and the managers with post-graduate qualifications. Managers with higher qualifications had statistically significantly higher consideration index than managers with graduate qualifications (Table 8.15). However, subordinates with post-graduate qualifications had no significant difference in their opinion about their manager's on consideration index than subordinates with only graduate qualifications (Table 8.16). Thus, subordinates have similar opinion about their managers on consideration index irrespective of their level of educational qualifications.

Comparative analysis of the managers across educational qualifications was also undertaken on the initiation index. It was found out that the managers with post-graduate

TABLE 8.15
Test of Significance (t-test) on the Difference of Managers' perception about self on the Consideration Index (comparison between Managers with Graduate Qualifications and Managers with Post-graduate Qualifications)

	Sample Size	*Mean*	*Std. Deviation*	*t-value*	*Tabulated Value*	*Significance*
Managers (Graduate Qualifications)	77	55.889	4.167	2.8356	2.576	Significant
Managers (Post-graduate Qualifications	74	58.750	6.230			

TABLE 8.16
Test of Significance (t-test) on the Difference of Subordinates' perception about their Manager on the Consideration Index (comparison between Subordinates with Graduate Qualifications and Subordinates with Post-graduate Qualifications)

	Sample Size	*Mean*	*Std. Deviation*	*t-value*	*Tabulated Value*	*Significance*
Subordinates (Graduate Qualifications)	192	56.286	6.484	0.1166	2.576	Insignificant
Subordinates (Post-graduate Qualifications	55	56.382	6.391			

qualifications had significantly higher score on the initiation index than the managers with graduate qualifications (Table 8.17).

Analysis of the perception of the subordinates about their manager's initiation index revealed that there is no statistical difference between subordinate across different educational qualifications, i.e. subordinate with graduate qualifications had similar opinion about their manager's initiativeness as that of the subordinates with post-graduate qualifications. (Table 8.18)

TABLE 8.17

Test of Significance (t-test) on the Difference of Managers' perception about self on the Initiation Index (comparison between Managers with Graduate Qualifications and Managers with Post-graduate Qualifications)

	Sample Size	*Mean*	*Std. Deviation*	*t-value*	*Tabulated Value*	*Significance*
Managers (Graduate Qualifications)	77	44.000	7.550	7.2086	2.576	Significant
Managers (Post-graduate Qualifications	74	52.821	6.606			

TABLE 8.18

Test of Significance (t-test) on the Difference of Subordinates' perception about their Manager on the Initiation Index (comparison between Subordinates with Graduate Qualifications and Subordinates with Post-graduate Qualifications)

	Sample Size	*Mean*	*Std. Deviation*	*t-value*	*Tabulated Value*	*Significance*
Subordinates (Graduate Qualifications)	192	53.102	4.806	0.0715	2.576	Insignificant
Subordinates (Post-graduate Qualifications	55	53.147	4.931			

Leaders are now perceived to have ability to transform the thought processes of their subordinates. Managers have to lead from the front by being high on both consideration as well as initiativeness. Not only they should be high on both these parameters but must also be perceived to be so by their subordinates. Transformational features are seen as adding to leadership's effectiveness. It attempts to "*engage the follower in true commitment and involvement in the effort at hand*" (Bass, 1998).

He has identified four components of transformational leadership:

- *Charismatic leadership*—involves leaders being role models for followers. Leaders are seen as having extraordinary capabilities, persistence and determination; they display ethical and moral courage and do the "right thing".
- *Inspirational motivation*—leaders behave in ways that people want to emulate; they inspire by providing meaning in work; they develop clear visions for the future and get followers envisioning the future; leaders communicate expectations clearly; they develop commitment of followers.
- *Intellectual stimulation*—leaders stimulate followers to be innovative and creative; followers are included in the process of addressing problems and finding solutions; followers' ideas are not criticised but rather new approaches are encouraged.
- *Individualised consideration*—special attention is paid to individual followers' needs for growth and achievement; differences in followers are recognised; interactions between leaders and followers are personalised.

Based on the findings of this study, following strategies could be used for enhancing follower adaptability:

- Uncertainty resolution through training and development and slow implementation of change.
- Resource provision—Organisational developments aimed at increasing coping skills and changing the perceptions of followers.
- Provision of access to a wide range of experiences.
- Communication of desirable messages.

References

Bass, B.M. (1998): *Transformational Leadership: Industrial, Military and Educational Impact*, Lawrence Erlbaum, Mahwah, New Jersy.

G.A. Yukl : *Leadership in Organizations*, Englewood Cliffs, NJ: Prentice-Hall (1994).

Parry, K.W. (1998): "Leadership Challenges for the Public Sector: A Preliminary Assessment and Conclusions for Research," *Public Sector*, 21 (4), pp. 17-18).

Rogers, R.W. (1995): "The Psychological Contract of Trust: Part II". *Executive Development*, Vol. 8, pp. 7-15.

S.P. Brown and R.A. Peterson, Antecedents and Consequences of Salesperson Job Satisfaction: Meta-analysis and Assessment of Causal Effects. *Journal of Marketing Research* 30 (1993), pp. 63-77.

Yukl, G.A. (1994): *Leadership in Organizations*, (3rd ed.), Englewood Cliffs, New Jersy: Prentice-Hall.

Yukl, G. (2002): *Leadership in Organizations*, (5th ed.), Upper Saddle River, New Jersy: Prentice-Hall.

CHAPTER

Organisational Commitment— Analysis and Interpretation

9.1 PRESENTATION, ANALYSIS AND INTERPRETATION OF FINDINGS REGARDING ORGANISATIONAL COMMITMENT

This section highlights the salient findings of the survey on the Organisational Commitment among the managers and the subordinates. The scale developed by *Meyer, Allen and Smith* (1993) has been used.

It has been recognised that individual, organisational and task characteristics exist which may act as moderators on leadership effectiveness. Among these moderators, are *individual characteristics of subordinates* (ability and training; high need for independence; professional orientation; indifference toward organisational rewards), *task characteristics* (methodologically invariant tasks; task-provided feedback; intrinsically satisfying tasks) and finally, *organisational characteristics* (organisational formalisation; organizational inflexibility; highly specified and active advisory and staff functions; cohesive work groups; organisational rewards not within the leader's control; spatial distance between a superior and subordinates) (*Kerr and Jermier*, 1978).

Campion et. al. (1993) also insisted that characteristics such as job design, interdependence, team composition, environmental context and process (e.g. workload sharing, communication/cooperation within groups, potency and social support) better account for effectiveness criteria (such as productivity and satisfaction). In an international sample, the influence of cultural factors cannot be ruled out (*Hofstede*, 1980).

Although each of these components increases the likelihood that the employee will choose to remain within the organisation, the nature of these psychological ties differs from one another.

Affective commitment refers to the degree to which the employee identifies with, is involved in and is emotionally attached to the organisation. Affectively committed employees believe in the goals and values of the organisation and enjoy being a member of it. Employees with strong affective commitment remain with the organisation because they *want* to do so.

Affective commitment refers to the degree to which the employee recognizes that costs associated with leaving the organisation tie him or her to the organisation. Such employees remain within the organisation because they *have* to do so. People who think high costs are involved (finding another job, moving to another city) are less likely to leave the organisation.

Normative commitment refers to the degree to which the employee feels an obligation to the organisation; staying within the organisation is the right and moral thing to do. Employees remain within the organisation because they feel they *ought* to do so.

All components of commitment are positively related to the decision whether to stay or leave the organisation. As commitment influences levels of satisfaction, it is of significance to continuously monitor the organisational commitment level of the employees in order to prevent their premature leaving.

Table 9.1 highlights the various statistical parameters of the total Organisational Commitment index as well as its constituent components, viz., affective, continuance and

TABLE 9.1

Statistical Parameters of Organisational Commitment Index (OC) and its Constituent Components (Affective Index, Continuance Index and Normative Index) as perceived by Managers and their Subordinates

	Sample Size		*Affective Index*	*Continuance Index*	*Normative Index*	*Total Organisational Commitment score*
(1)	*(2)*	*(3)*	*(4)*	*(5)*	*(6)*	*(7)*
Managers	151	average	24.406	23.130	28.942	76.478
		stdev	3.431	5.638	4.668	9.102
		median	24.000	24.000	29.000	78.000
		max	33.000	34.000	41.000	97.000
		min	17.000	11.000	19.000	57.000
		skewness	0.172	-0.386	0.367	-0.027
		kurtosis	-0.105	-0.576	-0.159	-0.682
Subordinates	247	average	26.000	25.881	27.333	79.214
		stdev	4.889	5.617	4.848	11.146
		median	26.000	25.500	28.000	80.000

(Contd.)

TABLE 9.1 (Contd.)

(1)	(2)	(3)	(4)	(5)	(6)	(7)
		max	37.000	39.000	36.000	100.000
		min	8.000	11.000	11.000	43.000
		skewness	-0.233	-0.083	-0.588	-0.758
		kurtosis	1.053	-0.081	0.679	0.583
Total	398	average	25.281	24.641	28.059	77.980
		stdev	4.354	5.774	4.819	10.333
		median	24.000	25.000	28.000	78.000
		max	37.000	39.000	41.000	100.000
		min	8.000	11.000	11.000	43.000
		skewness	0.034	-0.204	-0.194	-0.445
		kurtosis	0.976	-0.165	0.584	0.069

normative indices. The findings have been presented in a comparative manner in the table.

Similarly, the various statistical parameters have been computed across different age groups of the respondents and presented in Table 9.2. The comparative analysis of the responses of managerial and the non-managerial cadre across different educational qualifications have been presented in Table 9.3.

Perusal of these findings reveals that the non-managerial cadre exhibited higher level of organisational commitment as compared to the managerial cadre. Non-managers scored higher on the affective and continuance dimensions of the organisational commitment whereas managers scored higher on the normative index. Thus, it could be said that the non-managers felt obliged to the organisation and/or felt that the opportunity cost of leaving the organisation may be higher. It could also be due to lack of perceived better opportunities in other organizations. Managers by exhibiting higher scores on the normative index showed their concern toward moral aspects of continuing with the organisation.

Figure 9.1 represents graphically the mean scores of organisational commitment Index and its Constituents Components, i.e. affective, continuance and normative indices as perceived by managers and their subordinates.

Analysis was also undertaken on the organisational commitment across different age groups. Managers below the age of 35 exhibited more commitment score than managers above 35 years. On the other hand, non-managers in the higher age groups were more committed. This could be explained for fewer opportunities to elderly personnel at the lower hierarchies (Table 9.2)

Figure 9.2 represents graphically the mean scores of organisational commitment Index and its Constituents Components, i.e. affective, continuance and normative indices as perceived by managers and their subordinates as classified on the basis of age.

Organisational Commitment among managers with graduate qualifications was higher than that of the managers with post-graduate qualifications. This could be explained for lack of many opportunities to non-professionals at upper

TABLE 9.2

Statistical Parameters of Organisational Commitment Index (OC) and its constituent Components (Affective Index, Continuance Index and Normative Index) as perceived by Managers and their Subordinates in different age groups

	Sample Size		*Affective Index*		*Continuance Index*		*Normative Index*		*Total Organisational Commitment score*	
			Age		*Age*		*Age*		*Age*	
			Below 35 (86)	*Above 35 (65)*	*Below 35 (86)*	*Above 35 (65)*	*Below 35 (86)*	*Above 35 (65)*	*Below 35 (86)*	*Above 35 (65)*
(1)	*(2)*	*(3)*	*(4)*	*(5)*	*(6)*	*(7)*	*(8)*	*(9)*	*(10)*	*(11)*
Managers	151	average	24.357	24.459	23.571	23.054	29.821	28.324	77.750	75.838
		stdev	3.129	3.548	5.990	5.307	4.823	4.637	9.332	8.751
		median	24.000	24.000	24.500	23.000	29.500	28.000	79.500	76.000
		max	33.000	31.000	34.000	32.000	41.000	39.000	95.000	97.000
		min	18.000	18.000	11.000	11.000	21.000	19.000	62.000	57.000
		skewness	0.556	0.190	-0.274	-0.532	0.385	0.396	-0.132	0.124
		kurtosis	1.125	-0.498	-0.723	-0.290	0.136	-0.384	-1.186	-0.168

			Below 35 (98)	*Above 35 (199)*	*Below 35 (98)*	*Above 35 (199)*	*Below 35 (98)*	*Above 35 (199)*	*Below 35 (98)*	*Above 35 (199)*
(1)	*(2)*	*(3)*	*(4)*	*(5)*	*(6)*	*(7)*	*(8)*	*(9)*	*(10)*	*(11)*
Subordinates	247	average	24.594	26.922	24.531	26.686	26.938	27.647	76.063	81.255
		stdev	5.387	4.413	5.875	5.391	5.500	4.453	12.861	9.637
		median	24.000	27.000	24.500	27.000	28.000	28.000	77.000	83.000
		max	37.000	36.000	35.000	39.000	36.000	36.000	100.000	94.000
		min	8.000	18.000	11.000	16.000	11.000	15.000	43.000	56.000
		skewness	-0.221	-0.009	-0.250	0.152	-0.723	-0.402	-0.650	-0.564
		kurtosis	2.335	-0.756	0.037	-0.468	0.855	0.205	0.356	-0.301

(*Contd.*)

TABLE 9.2 (Contd.)

Summary of Statistical Parameters of Organisational Commitment Index (OC) and its constituent Components (Affective Index, Continuance Index and Normative Index) as perceived by Managers and their Subordinates in different age groups

	Sample Size		*Affective Index*		*Continuance Index*		*Normative Index*		*Total Organisational Commitment score*	
			Age		*Age*		*Age*		*Age*	
			Below 35 (184)	*Above 35 (65)*	*Below 35 (86)*	*Above 35(65)*	*Below 35 (86)*	*Above 35 (65)*	*Below 35 (86)*	*Above 35 (65)*
(1)	*(2)*	*(3)*	*(4)*	*(5)*	*(6)*	*(7)*	*(8)*	*(9)*	*(10)*	*(11)*
Total	398	average	24.483	25.886	24.083	25.159	23.283	27.932	76.850	78.977
		stdev	4.444	4.230	5.898	5.622	5.352	4.518	11.291	9.607
		median	24.000	25.500	24.500	25.000	29.000	28.000	78.500	79.000
		max	37.000	36.000	35.000	39.000	41.000	39.000	100.000	97.000
		min	8.000	18.000	11.000	11.000	11.000	15.000	43.000	56.000
		skewness	-0.075	0.199	-0.256	-0.097	-0.375	-0.038	-0.593	-0.215
		kurtosis	3.111	-0.627	-0.389	-0.001	1.031	0.000	0.385	-0.628

TABLE 9.3

Statistical Parameters of Organisational Commitment Index (OC) and its constituent Components (Affective Index, Continuance Index and Normative Index) as perceived by Managers and their Subordinates across different educational qualifications

	Sample Size		Affective Index		Continuance Index		Normative Index		Total Organisational Commitment score	
			Qualification		Qualification		Qualification		Qualification	
			Graduate	Post-graduate	Graduate	Post-graduate	Graduate	Post-graduate	Graduate	Post-graduate
(1)	(2)	(3)	(4)	(5)	(6)	(7)	(8)	(9)	(10)	(11)
Managers	151	average	23.667	24.536	25.000	23.000	29.778	28.839	78.444	76.375
		stdev	2.121	3.506	2.345	5.896	7.014	4.343	7.213	9.261
		median	24.000	24.000	24.000	23.000	29.000	29.000	80.000	77.000
		max	26.000	33.000	30.000	34.000	39.000	41.000	88.000	97.000
		min	20.000	18.000	23.000	11.000	19.000	21.000	68.000	57.000
		skewness	-0.348	0.259	1.346	-0.257	0.024	0.446	-0.103	0.072
		kurtosis	-0.797	-0.241	1.556	-0.811	-1.113	-0.071	-1.065	-0.752

(*Contd.*)

TABLE 9.3 (Contd.)

			Graduate	*Post-graduate*	*Graduate*	*Post-graduate*	*Graduate*	*Post-graduate*	*Graduate*	*Post-graduate*
(1)	*(2)*	*(3)*	*(4)*	*(5)*	*(6)*	*(7)*	*(8)*	*(9)*	*(10)*	*(11)*
Subordinates	247	average	25.551	26.706	25.510	26.353	27.653	26.971	78.714	80.029
		stdev	5.168	4.509	5.831	5.415	4.893	4.865	12.184	9.756
		median	24.000	28.000	25.000	25.500	28.000	27.500	81.000	80.000
		max	37.000	35.000	36.000	39.000	36.000	36.000	100.000	94.000
		min	8.000	18.000	11.000	16.000	11.000	15.000	43.000	56.000
		skewness	-0.186	-0.250	-0.242	0.294	-0.888	-0.238	-0.788	-0.571
		kurtosis	1.866	-0.916	-0.078	-0.270	1.564	-0.080	0.539	-0.020

TABLE 9.3 (Contd.)

Summary of Statistical Parameters of Organisational Commitment Index (OC) and its Constituent Components (Affective Index, Continuance Index and Normative Index) as perceived by Managers and their Subordinates across different educational qualifications

	Sample Size		Affective Index		Continuance Index		Normative Index		Total Organisational Commitment score	
			Qualification		Qualification		Qualification		Qualification	
			Graduate	Post-graduate	Graduate	Post-graduate	Graduate	Post-graduate	Graduate	Post-graduate
(1)	(2)	(3)	(4)	(5)	(6)	(7)	(8)	(9)	(10)	(11)
Total	398	**average**	25.259	25.356	25.431	24.267	27.983	28.133	78.672	77.756
		stdev	4.858	4.032	5.426	5.919	5.260	4.611	11.503	9.564
		median	24.000	24.500	25.000	24.000	28.000	28.000	80.000	78.000
		max	37.000	35.000	36.000	39.000	39.000	41.000	100.000	97.000
		min	8.000	18.000	11.000	11.000	11.000	15.000	43.000	56.000
		skewness	-0.045	0.173	-0.202	-0.131	-0.463	0.062	-0.778	-0.148
		kurtosis	2.201	-0.680	0.268	-0.332	0.960	0.162	0.745	-0.692

FIG. 9.1

Mean Scores of Organisational Commitment Index (LBD) and its constituent Components (Affective; Continuum and Normative Indices) as perceived by Managers and by their Subordinates

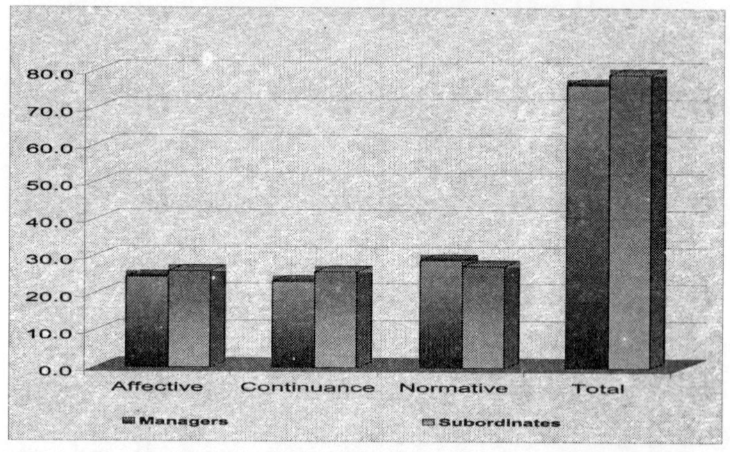

FIG. 9.2

Mean Scores of Organisational Commitment Index (LBD) and its constituent Components (Affective; Continuum and Normative Indices) as perceived by Managers and by their Subordinates classified on the basis of Age (Below 35 years and Above 35 years respectively)

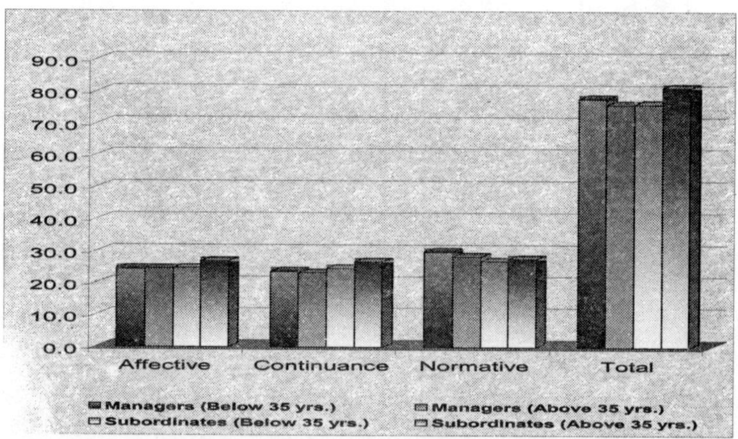

ladders of the hierarchy. Post-graduate Qualifications may open new vistas for growth. Hence, managers with Post-graduate Qualifications tend to move from the organizations faster, thereby exhibiting lower Organisational Commitment. Non-managers with Post-graduate Qualifications scored higher on the Organisational Commitment index than the non-managers with simple graduate qualifications (Figure 9.3).

Figure 9.3 represents graphically the mean scores of organisational commitment Index and its Constituents Components, i.e. affective, continuance and normative indices as perceived by managers and their subordinates and as classified on the basis of educational qualification.

FIG. 9.3

Mean Scores of Organisational Commitment Index (LBD) and its constituent Components (Affective; Continuance and Normative Indices) as perceived by Managers and by their Subordinates classified on the basis of Educational Qualifications (Graduate and Post-graduate)

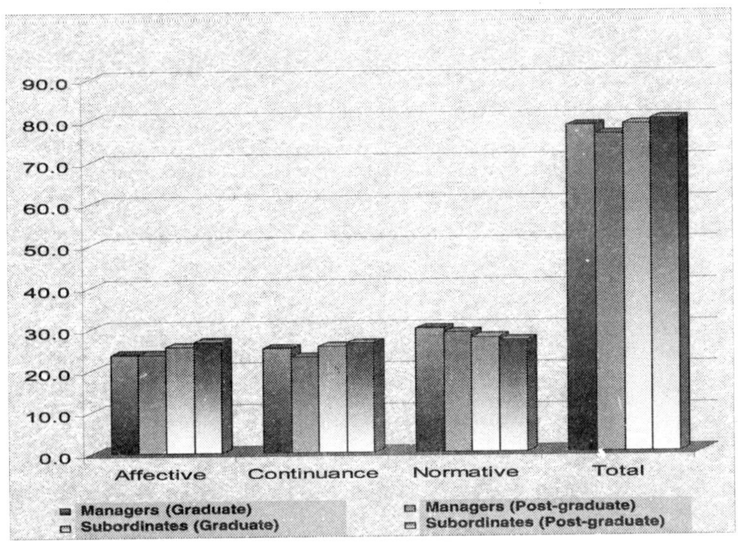

It can be argued that developmental prospects are more strongly related to commitment among managers whereas advancement prospects have a positive effect on organizational commitment among the non-managers. Job involvement among the non-manager groups also enhances organisational commitment. It could also be hypothesized that role stressors as well as role conflicts have negative effects on organizational commitment. Organisations need to clearly define areas of operations and reduce role ambiguity so as to ensure higher organisational commitment among the subordinates.

Effort was also made to statistically analyse whether there is any significant difference in the organisational commitment levels of the managers and the subordinates. The findings reveal that the difference in the total organisational commitment scores is not statistically significant. (Table 9.4) The organisational commitment level among the consumer durable industry jobs could be attributed to the higher levels of intrinsic and extrinsic rewards including salary and entail more extensive boundary-spanning activities and greater role stress than the jobs held by employees of other durable industries with low and/or moderate involvement. These experiences are also differentially related to career expectations and indicators of the quality of work life among individuals in this high involvement industry. Moreover, these high-involvement employees display greater commitment to their employing organizations than other industries as reported in the other studies using the same scale. Furthermore, jobs high in both intrinsic (e.g., autonomy, challenge) and extrinsic (e.g., opportunities for recognition) rewards have progressively stronger positive effects on the job satisfaction and career satisfaction of individuals with high job involvement. The results of previous studies (quoted in the review of literature section) also show differential effects of

TABLE 9.4

Test of Significance (t-test) on the Difference between Managers and their Subordinates' perceptions on the Total Organisational Commitment (OC) Index

	Sample Size	*Mean*	*Std. Deviation*	*t-value*	*Tabulated Value*	*Significance*
Managers	151	76.4783	9.102	-2.5633	2.576	Insignificant
Subordinates	247	79.2143	11.146			
Total	398	77.9804	10.333			

salary on job and career satisfaction and commitment to the organization.

It appears that high levels of job involvement can exacerbate the negative effects of role conflict on quality of work life. These findings are analogous to those documented in the literature (*Greenhaus and Beutell,* 1985) that high levels of job involvement and family involvement heighten the level of work-family conflict experienced by individuals and its aversive effects on individuals' well-being.

Analysis on each of three constituent elements of the commitment index was also undertaken. It revealed that the non-managers have significantly higher levels of affective commitment as well as continuance commitment as compared to the managers (Tables 9.5 and 9.6).

TABLE 9.5

Test of Significance (t-test) on the Difference between Managers and their Subordinates' perceptions on the Affective Commitment Index

	Sample Size	*Mean*	*Std. Deviation*	*t-value*	*Tabulated Value*	*Significance*
Managers	151	24.4058	3.4313	-3.545	2.576	Significant
Subordinates Perception	247	26.00	4.8891			
Total	398	25.2810	4.3535			

TABLE 9.6

Test of Significance (t-test) on the Difference between Managers and their Subordinates' perceptions on the Continuance Commitment Index

	Sample Size	*Mean*	*Std. Deviation*	*t-value*	*Tabulated Value*	*Significance*
Managers	151	23.1304	5.6384	-4.6115	2.576	Significant
Subordinates Perception	247	25.8809	5.6171			
Total	398	24.6405	5.7738			

On the other hand, managers have significantly higher scores on the normative commitment index than the non-managers. It could be explained that the subordinates feel more loyal to the organisation and also have a perception that it may be difficult to get another job having similar level of status and monetary gains as the present one. Managers on the other hand by exhibiting higher normative commitment scores feel they are morally obliged to continue as the organisation may have offered them so much in terms of self-esteem, positions in the hierarchy and involvement in the decision-making. (Table 9.7)

TABLE 9.7

Test of Significance (t-test) on the Difference between Managers and their Subordinates' perceptions on the Normative Commitment Index

	Sample Size	*Mean*	*Std. Deviation*	*t-value*	*Tabulated Value*	*Significance*
Managers	151	28.942	4.6680	3.2313	2.576	Significant
Subordinates Perception	247	27.333	4.8479			
Total	398	28.058	4.8194			

There should be more focus on empowered work groups and a movement away from the traditional rigid, hierarchical system of management in organizations. The researcher is of the opinion that as supervisors assumes the role of "coach," employee involvement and performance will improve. Managerial cadre need to communicate clear performance objectives, provide immediate feedback, assist in developing self-improvement plans, recognize and reward high performance and build warm positive relationships with subordinates. It has been found out that most managers do a good job of performing the technical work of their units but experience much more difficulty with the human resource management tasks that are necessary to achieve organizational effectiveness (e.g., rewarding and encouraging good performance, handling conduct problems, empowering their staff and involving them in goal-setting and decision-making etc.). Managers need to develop teams, achieving positive business results (i.e., improved organizational efficiency and effectiveness) through increased organisational commitment.

Comparison on each of the individual constituents of organizational commitment was carried out between employees below and above the age of 35 years. There was no significant difference between managers of different age groups on affective index (Table 9.8), whereas subordinates above the age of 35 years had significantly higher scores on the affective index as compared to the subordinates below the age of 35 years. Thus, employees in the higher age groups tend to associate more closely with the organization, its objectives and goals as compared to the non-managerial cadre of lower age groups.

TABLE 9.8

Test of Significance (t-test) on the Difference of Managers' perception about self on the Affective Index (comparison between Managers below 35 years and Managers above 35 years)

	Sample Size	*Mean*	*Std. Deviation*	*t-value*	*Tabulated Value*	*Significance*
Managers Below 35 years	86	24.3571	3.1290	0.1822	2.576	Insignificant
Managers Above 35 years	65	24.4594	3.5480			

TABLE 9.9

Test of Significance (t-test) on the Difference of Subordinates' perception on the Affective Index (comparison between Subordinates below 35 years and Subordinates above 35 years)

	Sample Size	*Mean*	*Std. Deviation*	*t-value*	*Tabulated Value*	*Significance*
Subordinates Below 35 years	98	24.594	5.387	3.6608	2.576	Significant
Subordinates Above 35 years	149	26.921	4.413			

The organization should also continue to maintain and promote a strong organizational culture and high levels of job satisfaction; barriers to employee satisfaction must be identified and removed. Improving the quality of work life for employees (e.g., focus on employee health and well-being, design of effective work policies, performance appraisal, reward and recognition systems, providing opportunities for interesting and challenging work, etc.) may be considered necessary to achieve the organization's objectives of consistently providing exceptional organizational environment for mutual growth and thereby achieving positive financial results.

Comparative analysis of the managers of different age groups on the continuance index revealed that there is no significant impact of the age on the continuance index. Managers of different age groups have similar scores on the continuance index (Table 9.10). On the other hand, elderly subordinates had significantly higher scores on the continuance index as compared to the subordinates of younger age groups (Table 9.11). It implies that the subordinates of higher age groups feel it necessitated to continue with the organisation as there may be fewer opportunities of switching the jobs. Thus, compulsion to continue with the present organisation was higher among the subordinates in senior age group.

TABLE 9.10

Test of Significance (t-test) on the Difference of Managers' perception about self on the Continuance Index (comparison between managers below 35 years and Managers above 35 years)

	Sample Size	*Mean*	*Std. Deviation*	*t-value*	*Tabulated Value*	*Significance*
Managers Below 35 years	86	23.571	5.990	0.5607	2.576	Insignificant
Managers Above 35 years	65	23.054	5.307			

Third dimension of organisational commitment, i.e. normative index was also compared across different age groups.

TABLE 9.11

Test of Significance (t-test) on the Difference of Subordinates' perception on the Continuance Index (comparison between Subordinates below 35 years and Subordinates above 35 years)

	Sample Size	*Mean*	*Std. Deviation*	*t-value*	*Tabulated Value*	*Significance*
Subordinates Below 35 years	98	24.5312	5.8749	2.949	2.576	Significant
Subordinates Above 35 years	149	26.6863	5.3907			

There was no significant difference on the normative index for both managers as well as the subordinates of different age groups. Managers as well as subordinates of different age groups have similar perceived moral need to continue with their present organisation. This may emerge from the industry or organizational features, its mission and goals and their alignment with the employee's own aspirations. (Tables 9.12 and 9.13)

TABLE 9.12

Test of Significance (t-test) on the Difference of Managers' perception about self on the Normative Index (comparison between Managers below 35 years and Managers above 35 years)

	Sample Size	*Mean*	*Std. Deviation*	*t-value*	*Tabulated Value*	*Significance*
Managers Below 35 years	86	29.821	4.823	-1.9598	2.576	Insignificant
Managers Above 35 years	65	28.3243	4.637			

In a study of salesperson-sales manager relationships, *Flaherty and Pappas* (2000) found that greater trust lead to increased job satisfaction and organizational commitment. This is consistent with past research which suggests that job

TABLE 9.13

Test of Significance (t-test) on the Difference of Subordinates' perception about self on the Normative Index (comparison between Subordinates below 35 years and Subordinates above 35 years)

	Sample Size	*Mean*	*Std. Deviation*	*t-value*	*Tabulated Value*	*Significance*
Subordinates Below 35 years	98	26.9375	5.5004	1.1254	2.576	Insignificant
Subordinates Above 35 years	149	27.6471	4.4534			

satisfaction is highly associated with organizational commitment *(Brown and Peterson,* 1993). It is conceivable that as a leader fulfils the needs of his followers, greater commitment will take place as well *(Brown and Peterson, 1993).*

Effort was also made to compare the organisational commitment levels across different age groups. It was found that there is no significant difference on the organisational commitment index between managers of different age groups (Table 9.14). On the other hand, subordinates of higher age group exhibited significantly higher organisational commitment scores, meaning thereby that elder subordinates are more committed towards the organisation as compared to subordinates of younger age group (Table 9.15)

TABLE 9.14

Test of Significance (t-test) on the Difference of Managers' perception about self on the Organisational Commitment Index (comparison between Managers below 35 years and Managers above 35 years)

	Sample Size	*Mean*	*Std. Deviation*	*t-value*	*Tabulated Value*	*Significance*
Managers Below 35 years	86	77.75	9.3318	1.2838	2.576	Insignificant
Managers Above 35 years	65	75.83	8.7512			

TABLE 9.15

Test of Significance (t-test) on the Difference of Subordinates' perception about self on the Organisational Commitment Index (comparison between Subordinates below 35 years and Subordinates above 35 years)

	Sample Size	*Mean*	*Std. Deviation*	*t value*	*Tabulated Value*	*Significance*
Subordinates Below 35 years	98	76.0625	12.8614	3.5817	2.576	Significant
Subordinates Above 35 years	149	81.2549	9.6371			

Among antecedents of job satisfaction and commitment, leadership plays a central role, along with other human resource management practices. Leadership was found to be positively correlated with employees' job satisfaction and with commitment towards the institution and its missions (*Dunham,* 2000; *Stordeur et. al.* 2000; *Morrison et al.,* 1997).

In a study conducted on nurses, it was found that nurses rated superior's abilities to plan teamwork, to solve conflicts, to give priority to nurses' development as important antecedents to job satisfaction. The researcher explained it to a constellation of historical and structural factors and corporate culture. He opined that in the health care system the evolution of values, structures and professions is very slow and may vary among countries (*Genevieve,* 2003).

Another basis of comparison in the present study was the impact of educational qualifications on the constituents of organisational commitment. Table 9.16 reveals that there is no significant difference among managers with Graduate Qualifications from those managers having Post-graduate qualifications on the affective components of organisational commitment. Subordinates also exhibited similar responses. There was no significant difference on the affective index among subordinates having different levels of educational qualifications. (Table 9.17)

Lower affective commitment scores have been shown to be related to higher absenteeism and intention to leave and actual

TABLE 9.16

Test of Significance (t-test) on the Difference of Managers' perception about self on the Affective Index (comparison between Managers with Graduate Qualifications and Managers with Post-graduate Qualifications)

	Sample Size	*Mean*	*Std. Deviation*	*t-value*	*Tabulated Value*	*Significance*
Managers (Graduate Qualifications)	77	23.6667	2.1213	1.5477	2.576	Insignificant
Managers (Post-graduate Qualifications	74	24.5357	3.5056			

TABLE 9.17

Test of Significance (t-test) on the Difference of Subordinates' perception about self on the Affective Index (comparison between Subordinates with Graduate Qualifications and Subordinates with Post-graduate Qualifications)

	Sample Size	*Mean*	*Std. Deviation*	*t-value*	*Tabulated Value*	*Significance*
Subordinates (Graduate Qualifications)	192	25.5510	5.1683	1.8162	2.576	Insignificant
Subordinates (Post-graduate Qualifications	55	26.7059	4.5094			

turnover and fewer organisational citizenship behaviours (*Farrell and Stamm*, 1988; *Mathieu and Zajac*, 1990; *Meyer and Allen*, 1991; *Tett and Meyer*, 1993).

Finegan (2000) found that affective commitment is highest when there is a congruence between an individual's personal values and those of the organisation in which they worked. This was not the case for normative commitment, where there was a closer relationship between an individual's personal value system and normative commitment, with the organisational culture playing little or no part in the relationship. Commitment scores in her study were not predicted by person-organisation value fit. Thus, it may be reasonable to assume that an employee's affective commitment is influenced by the fit between an organisation's value system and that of the employee (*Edwards and Rothbard,* 1999).

Similar impact of educational qualifications on the continuance index of organisational commitment was studied. Here also no significant difference was observed between managers with Post-graduate qualifications and the managers with Graduate qualifications (Table 9.18). Subordinates also exhibited similar trend as subordinates with Post-graduate qualifications did not significantly differ from the subordinates with Graduate qualifications (Table 9.19).

TABLE 9.18

Test of Significance (t-test) on the Difference of Managers' perception about self on the Continuance Index (comparison between Managers with Graduate Qualifications and Managers with Post-graduate Qualifications)

	Sample Size	*Mean*	*Std. Deviation*	*t value*	*Tabulated Value*	*Significance*
Managers (Graduate Qualifications)	77	25	2.3452	2.167	2.576	Insignificant
Managers (Post-graduate Qualifications	74	23	5.8961			

The impact of educational qualifications on the normative component of organisational commitment was also studied. Here also no significant difference was observed between managers with Post-graduate or Graduate qualifications (Table 9.20) as well as non-managers (Table 9.21). Thus, educational qualifications had no significant impact on the normative index. The urge to remain in the organisation due to moral obligations is similar whether managers have Post-graduate or Graduate qualifications. Similar is the response exhibited by subordinates. There is similar feeling of moral

TABLE 9.19

Test of Significance (t-test) on the Difference of Subordinates' perception on the Continuance Index (comparison between Subordinates with Graduate Qualifications and Subordinates with Post-graduate Qualifications)

	Sample Size	*Mean*	*Std. Deviation*	*t-value*	*Tabulated Value*	*Significance*
Subordinates (Graduate Qualifications)	192	25.5102	5.8314	1.1536	2.576	Insignificant
Subordinates (Post-graduate Qualifications	55	26.3529	5.4154			

TABLE 9.20

Test of Significance (t-test) on the Difference of Managers' perception about self on the Normative Index (comparison between managers with Graduate Qualifications and Managers with Post-graduate Qualifications)

	Sample Size	*Mean*	*Std. Deviation*	*t-value*	*Tabulated Value*	*Significance*
Managers (Graduate Qualifications)	77	29.7778	7.0139	1.2286	2.576	Insignificant
Managers (Post-graduate Qualifications	74	28.8323	4.3433			

responsibility towards organisation in subordinates whether they have Post-graduate or Graduate qualifications. (Table 9.21)

Leatt and Schneke (1982) found that structure, size, technology, internal and external environments can influence employees' attitudes and behaviour. When providing home/residential care, for example, employees work more independently without the permanent control of superiors who naturally have to delegate a part of the organisation and coordination of functions. Consequently, employees can feel empowered, having better control over their activity. Their

TABLE 9.21

Test of Significance (t-test) on the Difference of Subordinates' perception about self on the Normative Index (comparison between Subordinates with Graduate Qualifications and Subordinates with Post-graduate Qualifications)

	Sample Size	*Mean*	*Std. Deviation*	*t value*	*Tabulated Value*	*Significance*
Subordinates (Graduate Qualifications)	192	27.6531	4.8928	1.0824	2.576	Insignificant
Subordinates (Post-graduate Qualifications	55	26.9706	4.8647			

perception of leadership quality will be higher under these circumstances.

The impact of educational qualifications on the total organisational commitment scores was tested. It was found out that educational qualifications have no significant impact on the organisational commitment level among both managers as well as non-managers. They exhibited similar organisational commitment scores. (Tables 9.22 and 9.23)

TABLE 9.22

Test of Significance (t-test) on the Difference of Managers' perception about self on the Organisational Commitment Index (comparison between Managers with Graduate Qualifications and Managers with Post-graduate Qualifications)

	Sample Size	*Mean*	*Std. Deviation*	*t-value*	*Tabulated Value*	*Significance*
Managers (Graduate Qualifications)	77	78.444	7.2130	1.3894	2.576	Insignificant
Managers (Post-graduate Qualifications	74	76.375	9.2609			

TABLE 9.23
Test of Significance (t-test) on the Difference of Subordinates' perception on Organisational Commitment Index (comparison between Subordinates with Graduate Qualifications and Subordinates with Post-graduate Qualifications)

	Sample Size	*Mean*	*Std. Deviation*	*t-value*	*Tabulated Value*	*Significance*
Subordinates (Graduate Qualifications)	192	78.7142	12.1843	0.9072	2.576	Insignificant
Subordinates (Post-graduate Qualifications	55	80.0294	9.7560			

It has been noticed that if the organisation is facing rapid change with a requirement for reactivity which alters job characteristic and work-unit values, the "fit" may become a mismatch which might predict a fall in AC scores. As organisational values appear not to influence NC or AC directly one might suggest that internal organisational functioning changes may not impact on these facets of commitment (*Finegan*, 2000).

Literature review has suggested that commitment to an organisation results when individuals publicly commit themselves to a specific course of action, namely to being an employee of a particular organisation, and to supporting the goals of that organisation. Some employees may become committed to using specific procedures in the pursuit of these organisational goals and are likely to resist actively any changes proposed by management to either the goals or procedures.

Commitment among subordinates working in the branch level was observed to be higher than that of the subordinates working at the divisional or head offices as decisiveness is more dominant and the organisation is more bureaucratic and hierarchical at the corporate level. The highest scores for organisational commitment were found at the branch levels as at this work setting, the amount of opportunities to interact with the markets are higher and more freedom available to plan one's strategies. Leadership is viewed as an important predictor of job satisfaction and commitment, beside the other work setting characteristics. Leadership quality is a core element of management. It is not only strongly related to the amount of employee commitment but it is also logically linked to organisational performance (*Rogg et al,* 2001).

Considine and Callus (2009) found low levels of organisational commitment with a sample of police officers from South Australia. She suggested that this was consistent with their dissatisfaction with organisational factors (pay, promotional opportunities and the organisation itself) and that it may have reflected a lack of understanding of organisational goals, or of the external factors which influenced management. She hypothesised that improvement of the organisational commitment of these officers would impact upon organisational effectiveness and the ability to face the challenges inherent in future changes.

When the employees perceive the organisation and even the profession as a place where they can fulfil work-related desires, the *intent to stay* will increase. Quality of leadership is also positively related to the amount of job satisfaction and productivity. It is recommendable that supervising staff in the consumer durable sector pays more attention to individual differences in order to increase the person-job match. As the amount of affective commitment develops mainly in one's earlier career stages, it is extremely important to start paying attention to the work-related abilities, needs and desires of subordinates, in order to adjust leadership style, work-related demands and developmental plans. During one's entire career, the future employability should be considered in order to prevent premature loss of capabilities, knowledge and commitment.

According to *Gaertner* (1999), supervisory support and promotional chances could be directly related to organisational commitment over and above job satisfaction. It is also important to point out that, compared to organisational commitment, job satisfaction varies more directly and instantaneously with changing working conditions (*Mowday et al,* 1982).

Moreover, if managers would conceptualize major work characteristics (i.e. staffing, training, assigning work, appraising performance, allocating rewards, etc.) within a human resource framework, it might enhance employees awareness in human resource departments of their responsibilities regarding work groups (*Campion et. al.,* 1993); this could favour the decentralisation of power in baseline managers hands, who would be more suitable to work as leaders, responsible for their team functioning in well-adapted working conditions.

Employees who are committed demonstrate a strong acceptance of the organisation's values, tasks and working manner. Subordinates who firmly believe in these values are likely to manifest them in the performance. They keep these values in mind when preparing their plans and implementing them. These employees are also more conscious of their conduct and work attitudes, as they want to set good examples for their peers.

References

Campion, M.A., Medsker, G.J. and Higgs, A.C. (1993) Relations between Work Group Characteristics and Effectiveness: Implications for Designing Effective Work Groups. *Personnel Psychology,* Vol. 46, pp. 823-50.

Dunham, T.J. (2000): "Nurse Executive Transformational Leadership Found in Participative Organizations." *Journal of Nursing Administration,* Vol. 30(5), pp. 241-50.

Edwards, J.R. and Rothbard, N.F. (1999): "Work and Family Stress and Well-being: An Examination of Person-environment Fit in the Work and Family Domains." *Organizational Behaviour and Human Decision Processes,* Vol. 77(2), pp. 85-29.

Farrell, D., and Stamm, C.L. (1988): "Meta-analysis of The Correlates of Employee Absence." *Human Relations,* Vol. 41, pp. 211-27.

Finegan, J.E. (2000): "The Impact of Person and Organizational Values on Organizational Commitment." *Journal of Occupational and Organizational Psychology,* Vol. 73, pp. 149-69.

Flaherty, K.E. and Pappas, J.M. (2000): "The Role of Trust in Salesperson-sales Manager Relationships". *Journal of Personal Selling and Sales Management* Vol. 20, pp. 271-78.

Gaertner, S. (1999): "Structural Determinants of Job Satisfaction and Organizational Commitment in Turnover Models." *Human Resource Management Review,* Vol. 9(4), pp. 479-93.

Genevieve, L. (2003): "Dare to be Different: Transformational Leadership May Hold the Key to Reducing the Nursing Shortage." *Journal of Nursing Management,* Vol. 11, pp. 73-79.

Greenhaus, J.H. and Beutell, N.J. (1985): "Sources of Conflict Between Work and Family Roles." *Academy of Management Review,* Vol. 10(1), pp. 76-88.

Hofstede, G. (1980): *Culture's Consequences.* Beverly Hills, Ca: Sage Publications.

Kerr, S. and Jermier, J.M. (1978), Substitutes for Leadership: Their Meaning and Measurement. *Organizational Behaviour and Human Performance,* Vol. 22, pp. 375-403.

Leatt, P. and Schneck, R. (1982): "Technology, Size, Environment and Structure in Nursing Sub-Units." *Organization Studies,* Vol. 3(3), pp. 221-42.

Mathieu, J. and Zajac, D.M. (1990): "A Review and Meta-analysis of the Antecedent, Correlates and Consequences of Organizational Commitment Among Professionals and Non-professionals." *Journal of Vocational Behaviour,* Vol. 34, pp. 299-317.

Stordeur, S., Vandenberghe, C. and D'hoore, W. (2000): "Leadership Styles Across Hierarchical Levels in Nursing Departments." *Nursing Research,* Vol. 49(1), pp. 37-43.

Tett, R.P. and Meyer, J.P. (1993): "Job Satisfaction, Organizational Commitment, Turnover Intention and Turnover: A Path Analysis Based on Meta-analytic Findings." *Personnel Psychology,* Vol. 46, pp. 259-93.

CHAPTER 10

Quality of Work Life—Analysis and Interpretation

10.1 PRESENTATION, ANALYSIS AND INTERPRETATION OF FINDINGS REGARDING QUALITY OF WORK LIFE

The results of this survey were intended to assist decision-makers in identifying key workplace issues, as perceived by employees, in order to develop strategies to address and improve the quality of working conditions for staff within consumer durable industry in particular and business enterprises as a whole. The Quality of Work Life inventory developed by *Sinha and Sayeed* (1980) was considered appropriate as it has been extensively used in Indian conditions (as evidenced in Chapters 3 and 4). The findings have been analysed on total quality of work life scores as well as individual dimensions of the quality of work life. The results and discussion have been supplemented with the implications for the management as well as the employees. Effort has also been made to suggest suitable strategies for enhancing perceived quality of work life for both managers and subordinate.

Quality of work life is a dynamic multi-dimensional construct that currently includes such concepts as job security, reward systems, training and career advancement opportunities, and participation in decision-making. As such quality of work life has been defined as the workplace strategies, operations and environment that promote and maintain employee satisfaction with an aim to improve working conditions for employees and organizational effectiveness for employers (*Lau and Bruce,* 1998).

Walton (1975) has proposed eight conceptual categories relating to the quality of working life. These being:

1. Adequate and fair compensation
2. Safe and healthy working conditions
3. Immediate opportunity to use and develop human capabilities
4. Opportunity for continued growth and security
5. Social integration in the work organisation
6. Constitutionalism in thc work organisation (rights to privacy, free speech and equitable treatment and due process)
7. Work and total life space
8. Social relevance of work life

Table 10.1 summarises various statistical parameters on the quality of work life index as computed for the managers and their subordinates. The findings reveal that the subordinates perceive their quality of work life to be much better than the perception of the managers. Thus, subordinates rate organizational culture and work environment to be much more conducive than the managers who do not express higher scores on the quality of work life index.

The quality of work life index was computed for both managers and non-managers for different age groups as well as educational qualifications. The higher average scores expressed by Non-managerial cadre is indicative of higher levels of quality of work life perceived by the subordinates compared to the managerial cadre (Table 10.2).

TABLE 10.1

Statistical Parameters of Quality of Work Life (QWL) Index as perceived by Managers and their Subordinates

	Cadre	
	Managers	*Subordinates*
average	378.623	402.569
stdev.	72.612	79.883
median	408.000	417.000
max	532.000	541.000
min	140.000	153.000
skewness	-1.829	-1.526
kurtosis	3.659	2.839

One of the most significant findings was the difference in employee opinion based on the age of respondents. The experiences and expectations of younger workers (those under 35 years) were compared to those of prime age (35 to 45) and to mature age workers (45 and above). To control for the impact of different working time arrangements, only full-time workers were selected for the purpose of age comparisons. Amongst full-time workers, there were significant differences on a number of key factors. The most telling finding concerned the levels of *dissatisfaction* amongst older full-time managers. Within the managerial cadre, younger age group expressed higher QWL scores as compared to the higher age group managers. One possible explanation could be the exposure to many different organizations which the elderly aged managers have served spanning across their careers thereby having a good idea of working conditions of many organisations, whereas the experiences of the younger managers may have been limited to few organizations. Another explanation could be higher expectations of the senior aged managers arising out of family compulsions, stress levels due to comparative inability to move to different organizations and locational constraints, etc. (Table 10.2)

On the other hand, senior aged non-managers were more satisfied with the Quality of work life in their present

TABLE 10.2

Statistical Parameters of Quality of Work Life (QWL) Index as perceived by Managers and their Subordinates (classified on the Basis of Age Below 35 years and Above 35 years)

	Managers		*Subordinates*	
	Below 35 yrs.	*Above 35 yrs.*	*Below 35 yrs.*	*Above 35 yrs.*
average	166.362	150.833	195.986	247.238
stdev	9.898	8.8106	6.789	9.967
median	171.000	154.000	232.000	275.500
max	530.000	510.000	532.000	541.000
min	109.000	102.000	126.000	149.000
skewness	0.547	0.657	0.177	-0.241
kurtosis	-1.583	-1.472	-1.859	-1.816

organisation than the younger aged subordinates. This could arise with the satisfaction, reconciliation with their present status, understanding of the job market imperfections, family liabilities making them more realistic, etc.

The quality of work life index was also compared across different levels of educational qualifications (Table 10.3). Managers with Graduate qualifications had a higher perceived quality of work life scores compared to the managers with post-graduate qualifications. Similar pattern was observed for the non-managers. One possible explanation could be the enhanced expectancy levels due to higher qualification, leading to increased dissatisfaction with present state of affairs. Another reason could be the difficulties in switching jobs which are in consonance with one's academic excellence. While job insecurity and declining working conditions are of paramount importance to employee groups, perceived employee dissatisfaction and the concomitant effects on productivity and on-costs are of concern to employers.

Each of the seventeen constituent elements of the quality of work life index was statistically analysed. The comparisons on the basis of age as well as academic qualifications were also undertaken.

TABLE 10.3

Statistical Parameters of Quality of Work Life (QWL) Index as perceived by Managers and their Subordinates (classified on the Basis of Graduate and Post-graduate Qualifications)

	Managers		*Subordinates*	
	Graduate	*Post-graduate*	*Graduate*	*Post-graduate*
average	291.130	249.217	237.083	160.988
stdev	13.561	18.379	21.033	20.294
median	257.000	298.000	271.000	189.000
max	500.000	532.000	513.000	541.000
min	132.000	147.000	138.000	172.000
skewness	2.407	-0.920	-0.150	0.556
kurtosis	4.200	-0.744	-1.879	-1.578

Table 10.4 highlights the perception on the Economic Benefits component of the quality of work life index. Managerial cadre with Post-graduate qualifications and age above 35 years exhibited highest scores on the economic benefit component. Invariably such managers occupied the positions of divisional heads or equivalent. For the non-managerial cadre, graduates in the age group of 35 years and above had the highest scores. One explanation could be realism that salaries and perks as in consonance with one's caliber and expertise.

Table 10.5 summarizes the Physical Working Conditions (PWC) component of the quality of work life index as perceived by managers and their subordinates. These two categories have been classified on the basis of age below 35 years and above 35 years as well as Graduate and Post-graduate Qualifications. Managers expressed higher scores on the Physical Working Conditions index than the non-managers. Within the managerial cadre, managers in the higher age group and with graduate qualifications expressed higher scores. Within the non-managerial cadre, subordinates with younger age group and with graduate qualifications were more satisfied with the working conditions.

Table 10.6 highlights the perception of the managers and the subordinates on the Mental State component of the quality

TABLE 10.4

Statistical Parameters of Economic Benefits Component of Quality of Work Life (QWL) as perceived by Managers and their Subordinates (classified on the Basis of Age Below 35 years and Above 35 years as well as Graduate and Post-graduate Qualifications)

	Managers					Subordinates				
	Total	Below 35	Above 35	Graduate	Post-graduate	Total	Below 35	Above 35	Graduate	Post-graduate
(1)	(2)	(3)	(4)	(5)	(6)	(7)	(8)	(9)	(10)	(11)
average	24.56522	22.14286	25.83784	22.66667	25.85714	22.72619	23	20.2549	23.87755	20.4375
stdev	6.839501	5.133148	7.135644	6.244998	6.365899	4.755089	4.990313	4.603664	4.512172	5.84718
median	23.067	21.380	23.590	23.784	23.692	24.341	23.584	25.592	23.439	24.481
max	27	27	26	27	24	27	27	23	27	23
min	7	8	7	8	7	8	8	9	8	9
skewness	-1.97662	-1.0106	-2.39187	-1.63691	-2.25104	-0.98672	-1.15955	-0.92811	-1.28119	-0.51425
kurtosis	3.956332	1.704069	5.513594	4.49474	5.76575	1.50492	1.439785	1.809143	2.480389	-0.3566

TABLE 10.5

Statistical Parameters of Physical Working Conditions (PWC) Component of Quality of Work Life (QWL) as perceived by Managers and their Subordinates (classified on the Basis of Age Below 35 years and Above 35 years as well as Graduate and Post-graduate Qualifications)

	Managers					*Subordinates*				
	Total	*Below 35*	*Above 35*	*Graduate*	*Post-graduate*	*Total*	*Below 35*	*Above 35*	*Graduate*	*Post-graduate*
(1)	*(2)*	*(3)*	*(4)*	*(5)*	*(6)*	*(7)*	*(8)*	*(9)*	*(10)*	*(11)*
average	15.043	13.678	16.189	17.111	12.286	13.964	14.274	12.125	14.041	13.824
stdev	7.912	6.526	7.823	6.642	7.507	5.378	5.1562	5.3201	5.240	5.723
median	15.583	13.720	16.481	71.672	12.472	14.472	15.639	13.483	15.769	14.648
max	17	15	17	17	15	15	15	14	15	14
min	5	8	5	8	5	6	6	8	6	8
skewness	-1.29174	-0.64691	-1.70381	-0.410	-1.506	-0.50485	-0.447	-0.9201	-0.624	-0.357
kurtosis	1.676965	0.447605	2.481505	-0.062	2.568	0.155995	0.581933	1.389778	0.146	0.239

TABLE 10.6

Statistical Parameters of Mental State Component of Quality of Work Life (QWL) as perceived by Managers and their Subordinates (classified on the Basis of Age Below 35 years and Above 35 years as well as Graduate and Post-graduate Qualifications)

	Managers					Subordinates				
	Total	*Below 35*	*Above 35*	*Graduate*	*Post-graduate*	*Total*	*Below 35*	*Above 35*	*Graduate*	*Post-graduate*
(1)	*(2)*	*(3)*	*(4)*	*(5)*	*(6)*	*(7)*	*(8)*	*(9)*	*(10)*	*(11)*
average	33.522	33.679	31.189	35.222	31.750	31.762	33.438	31.275	33.204	30.147
stdev	7.563	6.527	7.824	6.476	6.850	4.998	5.847	5.150	4.920	5.188
median	35.730	35.03	34.06	37.02	32.17	31.97	34.07	32.36	34.03	31.05
max	35.000	35.000	34.000	34.000	35.000	35.000	32.000	35.000	32.000	35.000
min	12.000	8.000	12.000	11.000	12.000	9.000	10.000	9.000	9.000	10.000
skewness	-1.915	-0.647	-1.704	-1.406	-2.229	-1.047	-0.514	-0.447	-1.058	-1.081
kurtosis	3.776	0.448	2.482	2.442	6.059	1.975	-0.357	0.582	1.946	2.362

of work life index. It can be noticed that the managers perceive themselves to be in a better mental state than the subordinates. Within managers, the managers who are below the age of 35 years have better scores on the Mental state component. Similarly, managers with Graduate qualifications have better scores than the managers with Post-graduate qualifications. One possible cause could be the higher; levels of the job responsibilities associated with the senior positions. Also, the family life positions and responsibilities of senior aged managers could be the contributing factors towards lowering the scores on the mental state component. Within the subordinates category, those subordinates who were below the age of 35 had better perception about their mental state than the older age group subordinates. Subordinates with Graduate qualifications had better scores on the mental state component.

These increasing levels of dissatisfaction reflected in lower scores on the mental state in part, reflect the changing nature of work and the manner in which these issues are linked. Dissatisfaction with career prospects amongst prime age and mature age workers was perhaps not surprising given the extent of downsizing in organisations in the late 1990s. By the late 1990s, almost half of consumer durable organisations had downsized. A consequence of this dramatic downsizing has been the demise of traditional career paths that employees could once have expected.

Table 10.7 summarises perceptions of the employees on the Career Orientation (CO) component of Quality of Work Life (QWL). The data has been classified and computed on the basis of age below 35 years and above 35 years as well as Graduate and Post-graduate qualifications. The findings reveal that managers perceive that their organization is more conscious towards their need for careers than the perception of the subordinates. This feeling is even more pronounced in the subordinates in older age groups, especially with Post-graduate qualifications. This disillusionment requires urgent attention of the human resource managers as career planning must incorporate justifiable aspirations of the employees.

Older workers were also more likely to have higher levels of dissatisfaction with the amount of work they had to do, their

Table 10.7

Statistical Parameters of Career Orientation (CO) Component of Quality of Work Life (QWL) as perceived by Managers and their Subordinates (classified on the Basis of Age Below 35 years and Above 35 years as well as Graduate and Post-graduate Qualifications)

	Managers					Subordinates				
	Total	*Below 35*	*Above 35*	*Graduate*	*Post-graduate*	*Total*	*Below 35*	*Above 35*	*Graduate*	*Post-graduate*
(1)	*(2)*	*(3)*	*(4)*	*(5)*	*(6)*	*(7)*	*(8)*	*(9)*	*(10)*	*(11)*
average	14.652	14.964	13.189	14.000	14.071	12.452	13.125	11.176	13.204	11.235
stdev	8.201	4.435	8.082	7.000	7.750	6.272	5.320	4.844	5.427	7.329
median	15.273	15.231	14.537	14.371	14.386	13.362	14.342	13.210	14.958	12.427
max	17	14	17	16	17	17	16	17	16	17
min	5	5	6	6	7	7	9	9	7	9
skewness	-1.401	-1.039	-1.925	-0.633	-1.567	-0.678	-0.920	-1.161	0.012	-0.955
kurtosis	2.192	2.509	3.759	-0.971	3.376	1.585	1.390	2.776	-0.215	1.644

career prospects and their level of pay relative to other employees doing similar work in other industries.

Table 10.8 reveals surprising findings on the Advancement on Merit (AM) component of Quality of Work Life (QWL) as perceived by managers and their subordinates. Here also classification was done on the basis of age as well as educational qualifications. Findings reveal that almost 33% of the employees, whether managerial or non-managerial feel that merit is not the only consideration for promotions. Extraneous factors play a predominant role in deciding the promotions. Managers in senior age groups, especially with Post-graduate qualifications are even more pronounced in their feelings. Subordinates in the senior age group and with Post-graduate qualifications are still more pessimistic in their expressions. This is contrary to the general perception that merit is the predominant factor in the private sector, especially in the multinational organizations.

Figure 10.1 summarises the Mean Scores of QWL Index as perceived by Managers and their subordinates.

FIG.. 10.1

Mean Scores of Quality of Work Life (QWL) Index as Perceived by Managers and their Subordinates

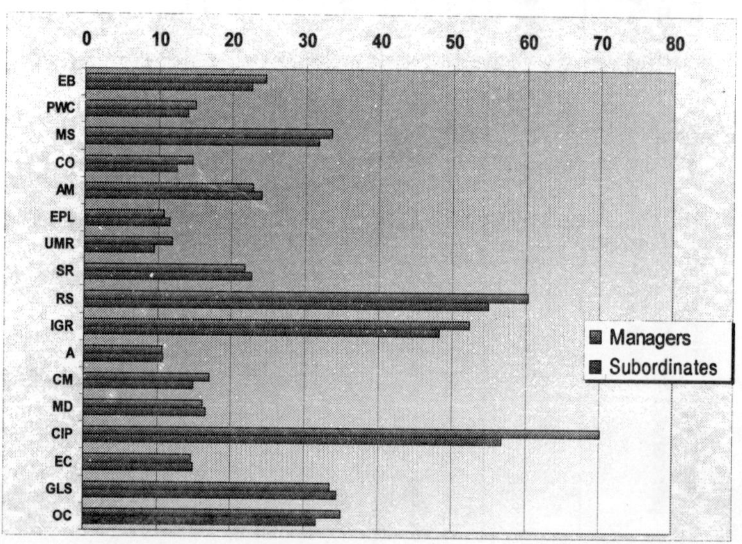

TABLE 10.8

Statistical Parameters of Advancement on Merit (AM) Component of Quality of Work Life (QWL) as perceived by Managers and their Subordinates (classified on the Basis of Age Below 35 years and Above 35 years as well as Graduate and Post-graduate Qualifications)

	Managers					Subordinates				
	Total	Below 35	Above 35	Graduate	Post-graduate	Total	Below 35	Above 35	Graduate	Post-graduate
(1)	(2)	(3)	(4)	(5)	(6)	(7)	(8)	(9)	(10)	(11)
average	22.899	25.429	21.784	24.444	20.179	24.107	23.906	20.235	24.898	20.971
stdev	7.871	5.217	8.213	6.483	7.418	6.157	6.337	6.163	5.569	6.926
median	23.058	26.073	24.078	26.529	25.589	24.437	24.449	25.731	25.674	23.549
max	31	31	28	31	28	29	29	28	29	28
min	10	13	10	13	11	10	5	9	15	10
Skewness	-1.455	-0.665	-1.407	-0.723	-1.569	-1.445	-1.013	-1.762	-1.319	-1.448
kurtosis	2.277	-0.066	2.204	-0.196	3.284	3.493	2.280	4.720	3.491	3.145

Table 10.9 highlights the Effect on Personal Life (EPL) component of Quality of Work Life (QWL) as perceived by managers and their subordinates. The classification has been undertaken on the basis of age as well as educational qualifications. Non-managers had higher average score than the managers. Within the non-managerial cadre, respondents in the age group upto 35 years and with Graduate qualifications had the highest scores.

Table 10.10 summarises perceived union-management relations. The managers perceived that the relations are cordial to a greater degree than the perception of the subordinates. Within the managerial cadre, younger age group managers were even more strong in their conviction that the union-management relations are cordial than the managers in senior age groups. Similarly, managers with graduate qualifications gave higher scores on the relations within the organisation than the manners with Post-graduate qualifications. In the non-managerial category also, similar pattern was observed.

Self-respect component of the quality of work life index was also computed for both managers as well as non managers. The findings reveal that non-managers felt that self-respect was enhanced by association with the organisation to a greater extent than the feelings of the managerial cadre. The subordinates with graduate qualifications gave higher scores on self-respect component than the non-managers with Post-graduate qualifications. Such self-esteem augurs well with the consumer durable industry as it reflects pride felt by the subordinates for being associated with the organization (Table 10.11).

The results for younger and mature age workers also provided some insight into the more positive attitude of the younger workers. Younger workers were extremely unlikely to work more than 45 hours a week and therefore unlikely to feel the same work pressures with regard to the amount of work to be done and the unfairness of remuneration as older workers. Further, it is possible that younger workers may either have lower expectations of career advancement at this stage of their working life or may feel more positive about their career prospects over the long-term. The positive attitude of younger workers was also reflected in their opinions on the self-respect

Table 10.9

Statistical Parameters of Effect on Personal Life (EPL) Component of Quality of Work Life (QWL) as perceived by Managers and their Subordinates (classified on the Basis of Age Below 35 years and Above 35 years as well as Graduate and Post-graduate Qualifications)

	Managers					*Subordinates*				
	Total	*Below 35*	*Above 35*	*Graduate*	*Post-graduate*	*Total*	*Below 35*	*Above 35*	*Graduate*	*Post-graduate*
(1)	*(2)*	*(3)*	*(4)*	*(5)*	*(6)*	*(7)*	*(8)*	*(9)*	*(10)*	*(11)*
average	10.681	10.143	10.351	10.24	10.231	11.488	11.969	11.020	12.796	10.853
stdev	0.247	0.508	0.371	0.225	0.870	0.403	0.255	0.617	0.930	0.046
median	10.378	10.239	10.935	10.986	10.536	12.023	12.352	12.382	13.031	10.237
max	11	12	11	12	11	13	11	13	13	11
min	7	9	7	7	9	7	8	7	8	7
skewness	-1.388	-0.822	-1.602	0.152	-1.559	-1.279	-0.843	-1.534	-0.963	-1.514
kurtosis	2.081	0.035	3.171	-0.389	2.994	2.716	0.820	3.834	0.962	3.70

TABLE 10.10

Statistical Parameters of Union-Management Relations (UMR) Component of Quality of Work Life (QWL) as perceived by Managers and their Subordinates (classified on the Basis of Age Below 35 years and Above 35 years as well as Graduate and Post-graduate Qualifications)

	Managers					Subordinates				
	Total	*Below 35*	*Above 35*	*Graduate*	*Post-graduate*	*Total*	*Below 35*	*Above 35*	*Graduate*	*Post-graduate*
(1)	*(2)*	*(3)*	*(4)*	*(5)*	*(6)*	*(7)*	*(8)*	*(9)*	*(10)*	*(11)*
average	11.884	13.393	11.351	12.333	12.214	09.464	10.688	09.961	10.939	09.794
stdev	1.835	1.374	1.480	1.387	1.665	1.184	1.881	1.885	1.308	1.309
median	11.876	14.327	11.453	13.234	13.037	10.231	10.724	10.237	11.934	10.832
max	14	14	13	14	13	12	12	11	12	11
min	7	7	8	8	7	7	9	7	8	7
skewness	-1.869	-0.563	-1.867	-1.316	-1.944	-1.162	-0.489	-1.406	0.021	-1.515
kurtosis	4.008	0.325	3.522	1.458	4.726	4.633	3.211	4.606	1.686	4.144

TABLE 10.11

Statistical Parameters of Self-Respect (SR) Component of Quality of Work Life (QWL) as perceived by Managers and their Subordinates (classified on the Basis of Age Below 35 years and Above 35 years as well as Graduate and Post-graduate Qualifications)

	Managers					Subordinates				
	Total	*Below 35*	*Above 35*	*Graduate*	*Post-graduate*	*Total*	*Below 35*	*Above 35*	*Graduate*	*Post-graduate*
(1)	*(2)*	*(3)*	*(4)*	*(5)*	*(6)*	*(7)*	*(8)*	*(9)*	*(10)*	*(11)*
average	21.855	23.964	20.757	24.778	21.714	22.798	23.375	20.059	24.265	20.118
stdev	3.548	3.660	3.711	3.167	3.241	3.581	3.470	3.743	5.074	2.333
median	23.949	25.793	22.942	25.946	22.453	25.472	23.589	25.045	25.032	25.082
max	23	23	22	23	22	24	22	24	22	24
min	9	11	9	11	9	12	9	12	9	12
skewness	-1.324	-0.681	-1.422	-0.473	-1.348	-1.513	-1.274	-1.689	-1.285	1.599
kurtosis	2.036	-0.361	2.490	0.911	2.440	3.993	2.392	5.231	2.737	4.404

constituent of quality of work life index. Almost two-thirds of workers under the age of 35 believed that their quality of work life would improve compared to just under half of all non-managers above the age of 35 years.

A high level of satisfaction with employees' treatment by immediate managers was explained by having workers' efforts recognized by immediate managers. However, other contributing factors included having high levels of trust in senior management, control over the way in which work is done, a suitable amount of work to be done, not having problems with discrimination or harassment in the workplace and the perception that remuneration is fair and reasonable. All these factors may have enhanced the self-respect component of quality of work life.

Figure 10.2 graphically represents the mean scores of QWL index as perceived by managers above 35 years and the managers below 35 years.

FIG. 10.2

Mean Scores of Quality of Work Life (QWL) Index as Perceived by Managers below 35 Years and Managers Above 35 years

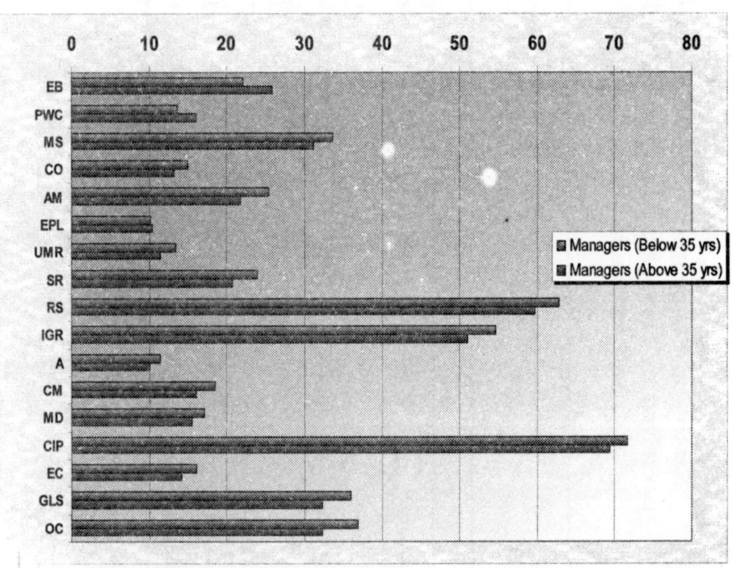

The perceived relations with their supervisors was analysed for both the managerial as well as non-managerial cadre (Table 10.12). On a positive note, the survey found that the majority of workers believed that relationships amongst co-workers *were* positive. In total 70 per cent of employees indicated that they either agreed or strongly agreed that people at their workplace got on well together. Managers perceived that their relations are cordial with their subordinates whereas the perception of the subordinates is not to the same intensity. Average scores of the managerial cadre was around 77% whereas subordinates gave much lower averages. These findings are in conformity with the findings on the consideration component of the LBDQ index. The managers need to be more benevolent and develop interpersonal relations with their subordinates. Distrust of senior management increased significantly with age, while only 21 per cent of younger workers (below 35 years) did not trust senior management, 30 per cent of workers in the age of 35 to 44 year old and mature aged workers (45 and older) expressed lower scores on supervisory relationship.

Table 10.13 highlights another related factor on inter-group relations in organizations. Here again, managers perceptions about cordial nature of relations in the organizations is much higher than the perceptions of the subordinates. The feeling of bon home in the organizations is more in the younger age group and with Graduate qualification, whether they are managers or subordinates.

Researchers have highlighted important factors that make work a positive experience are *'co-workers getting along together'* and *'interesting and satisfying work'*. Most of the workers believed that having interesting and satisfying work was as important a factor as getting on well together at the workplace in contributing to a positive work experience These two indicators complement the factors typically attributed to employee satisfaction such as having your efforts recognised, having control over the way you do work, being treated well by your immediate supervisors or even having fair and reasonable pay.

Figure 10.3 graphically represents the mean scores of quality of work life as perceived by subordinates below 35 years and subordinates above 35 years.

TABLE 10.12

Statistical Parameters of Supervisory Relationship (RS) Component of Quality of Work Life (QWL) as perceived by Managers and their Subordinates (classified on the Basis of Age Below 35 years and Above 35 years as well as Graduate and Post-graduate Qualifications)

	Managers					Subordinates				
	Total	Below 35	Above 35	Graduate	Post-graduate	Total	Below 35	Above 35	Graduate	Post-graduate
(1)	(2)	(3)	(4)	(5)	(6)	(7)	(8)	(9)	(10)	(11)
average	60.217	62.893	59.703	61.444	59.518	54.857	58.563	52.078	56.143	51.508
stdev	3.711	3.065	3.353	4.157	3.800	3.666	3.701	3.764	2.934	3.440
median	23.546	23.893	22.493	22.562	23.382	23.385	23.562	23.806	23.072	22.557
max	65	65	64	65	64	65	65	67	67	65
min	45	47	45	45	47	42	45	42	45	42
skewness	-1.489	-0.678	-1.476	-0.244	-1.587	-1.370	-1.411	-1.401	-1.490	-1.268
kurtosis	1.876	1.079	1.068	-1.254	2.136	2.964	3.261	3.170	3.328	2.968

TABLE 10.13

Statistical Parameters of Intragroup Relations (IGR) Component of Quality of Work Life (QWL) as perceived by Managers and their Subordinates (classified on the Basis of Age Below 35 years and Above 35 years as well as Graduate and Post-graduate Qualifications)

	Managers					*Subordinates*				
	Total	*Below 35*	*Above 35*	*Graduate*	*Post-graduate*	*Total*	*Below 35*	*Above 35*	*Graduate*	*Post-graduate*
(1)	*(2)*	*(3)*	*(4)*	*(5)*	*(6)*	*(7)*	*(8)*	*(9)*	*(10)*	*(11)*
average	52.290	54.607	50.973	53.444	51.393	48.298	52.156	43.490	53.510	43.147
stdev	4.169	4.779	4.269	3.747	3.143	3.971	3.604	3.649	3.442	3.382
median	53.538	55.856	52.453	54.439	52.558	49.082	51.035	44.782	55.091	44.078
max	59	59	56	59	56	54	54	49	54	49
min	29	29	27	29	27	26	26	27	26	27
skewness	-1.712	-1.102	-1.479	-1.520	-1.782	-1.495	-1.049	-1.983	-1.418	-1.868
kurtosis	2.550	2.312	1.291	4.772	2.890	3.028	1.715	4.917	2.695	4.727

FIG. 10.3
Mean Scores of Quality of Work Life (QWL) Index as Perceived by Subordinates below 35 Years and Subordinates above 35 Years

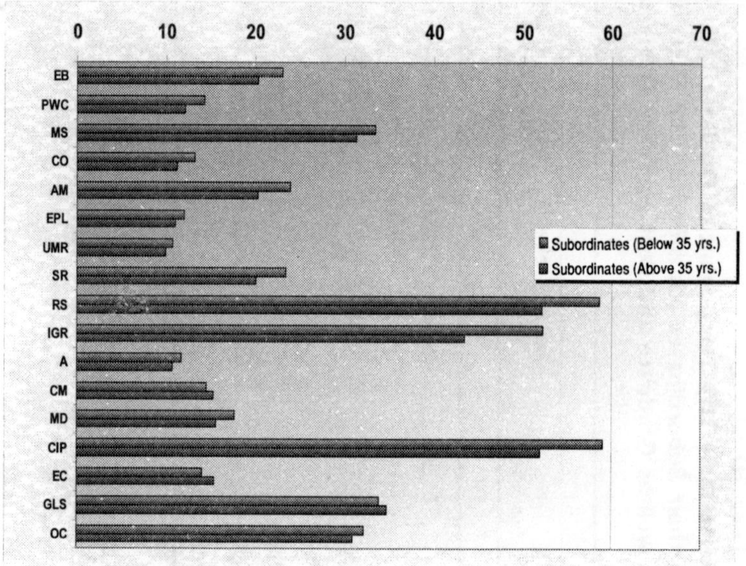

More importantly, these results were consistent across different employee groups showing that regardless of employee characteristics, employee satisfaction could be most effectively managed by addressing relationships in the workplace and by providing suitably interesting and challenging work tasks.

The implication of these results is that Human Resource managers can with a high degree of confidence, direct attention towards these two aspects of working life that can make a substantially greater difference to employee satisfaction than other general issues

Managers and the subordinates expressed similar sentiments regarding feeling of achievement by being associated with their present organizations (Table 10.14). Here again, higher sense of elation was noticed in the younger age group on the Graduate qualifications, irrespective of whether it was managerial or non-managerial cadre.

TABLE 10.14

Statistical Parameters of Sense of Achievement v. Apathy (A) Component of Quality of Work Life (QWL) as perceived by Managers and their Subordinates (classified on the Basis of Age Below 35 years and Above 35 years as well as Graduate and Post-graduate Qualifications)

	Managers					Subordinates				
	Total	Below 35	Above 35	Graduate	Post-graduate	Total	Below 35	Above 35	Graduate	Post-graduate
(1)	(2)	(3)	(4)	(5)	(6)	(7)	(8)	(9)	(10)	(11)
average	10.565	11.393	10.054	11.889	10.250	10.750	11.656	10.765	11.735	10.706
stdev	3.889	2.934	3.592	2.339	3.426	2.338	3.723	3.827	3.807	3.248
median	11.035	11.024	10.962	12.036	10.672	11.472	12.063	11.167	12.035	11.534
max	13	12	13	13	12	13	13	13	13	13
min	8	9	8	9	8	9	9	9	9	9
skewness	-1.606	-0.784	-1.657	-0.457	-1.879	-1.638	-1.770	-1.588	-2.074	-1.264
kurtosis	2.281	0.821	2.211	0.528	3.726	3.221	4.767	2.774	5.731	1.447

Confidence in Management index was computed for both the categories of employees (Table 10.15). Managers expressed greater confidence in their superiors as compared to the non-managerial cadre. This feeling was more pronounced in the managers below 35 years and with Post-graduate qualifications. Managers need to cultivate trust of their subordinates by involving them more in the decision-making, decentralizing and developing teams, etc.

Another parameter analysed was the development of employees in the organization (Table 10.16). The feeling about meaningful developments in the organisation is almost identical in both managerial and the non-managerial cadre. Younger age workers felt that there are more avenues for learning than the older aged employees. Existence of a certain set of organizational conditions and practical such as enriched positions, participation of the employees in the processes of decision-taking, safe conditions of work all contribute to make the development of individuals more meaningful.

The task design literature points to autonomy, task significance, feedback, task identity and skill variety as attributes of the task that impact motivation. These authors claim that work redesign provides a strategy for enhancing internal work motivation (i.e., the individual does the work because it interests or challenges him/her). In terms of the self-concept, the degree of autonomy would affect an individual's opportunity to attribute outcomes to his/her traits, competencies and values. The significance of a task and one's contribution to the success of the task would determine how important the feedback (task for inner-directed and social for other-directed) is to traits, competencies and values that comprise a role-specific identity that may be crucial to an individual's self-concept. Task feedback is a necessary ingredient in reinforcement or affirmation of self-perception and one's ability to identify with a task would affect how important that feedback is to an individual's self-concept. Skill variety would provide information regarding a number of traits, competencies and values that comprise different role specific identities. Goal internalization is the motivating source when the successful completion of a task helps fulfil important organizational goals that the individual has internalized into

TABLE 10.15

Statistical Parameters of Confidence in Management (CM) Component of Quality of Work Life (QWL) as perceived by Managers and their Subordinates (classified on the Basis of Age Below 35 years and Above 35 years as well as Graduate and Post-graduate Qualifications)

	Managers					Subordinates				
	Total	*Below 35*	*Above 35*	*Graduate*	*Post-graduate*	*Total*	*Below 35*	*Above 35*	*Graduate*	*Post-graduate*
(1)	*(2)*	*(3)*	*(4)*	*(5)*	*(6)*	*(7)*	*(8)*	*(9)*	*(10)*	*(11)*
average	17.072	18.464	16.189	16.889	17.214	14.929	14.531	15.294	15.061	14.912
stdev	0.305	0.474	0.141	0.555	0.422	0.485	0.229	0.723	0.403	0.751
median	18.094	18.099	17.021	17.00	18.02	15.382	15.020	15.902	15.521	15.934
max	20	19	20	19	20	17	17	16	17	16
min	16	18	16	18	16	12	15	12	15	12
skewness	-0.776	0.298	-0.743	1.106	-0.814	-0.540	-0.330	-0.716	-0.601	-0.542
kurtosis	0.572	-0.208	-0.026	2.704	0.541	0.081	0.364	0.166	0.523	-0.230

TABLE 10.16

Statistical Parameters of Meaningful Development (MD) Component of Quality of Work Life (QWL) as perceived by Managers and their Subordinates (classified on the Basis of Age Below 35 years and Above 35 years as well as Graduate and Post-graduate Qualifications)

	Managers					*Subordinates*				
	Total	*Below 35*	*Above 35*	*Graduate*	*Post-graduate*	*Total*	*Below 35*	*Above 35*	*Graduate*	*Post-graduate*
(1)	*(2)*	*(3)*	*(4)*	*(5)*	*(6)*	*(7)*	*(8)*	*(9)*	*(10)*	*(11)*
average	16.188	17.143	15.595	17.556	15.393	16.679	17.719	15.627	17.918	15.294
stdev	0.531	0.973	0.871	0.307	0.309	0.825	0.158	0.747	0.129	0.553
median	16.782	17.895	16.093	17.992	16.732	17.723	18.302	16.631	18.003	16.704
max	18	18	18	18	18	17	19	17	19	17
min	11	12	11	12	11	12	13	12	13	12
skewness	-1.090	-0.227	-1.117	-0.572	-1.149	-1.549	-1.823	-1.377	-1.947	-0.863
kurtosis	1.325	-0.512	1.212	-0.659	1.850	2.784	3.633	2.479	4.310	0.329

his/her own value system. Therefore, the task system induces motivation from all four of these sources (i.e., intrinsic process, internal and external self-concept, and goal internalization) in significant ways. Developmental efforts of the organisation were perceived to be higher by the managers as compared to the non-managers. Hence, organisation must make efforts to convince and involve the subordinates in conduct of the developmental programmes.

Table 10.17 highlights the perception of employees in terms of control, influence and participation they undertake in their organizations. Here, the comparison is more stark. There is a marked difference in the way managers and the non-managers perceive. Managers below the age of 35 and having graduate qualifications feel more involved. On the other hand, subordinates with Post-graduate qualifications and above the age of 35 more disillusioned as compared to subordinates with lower Qualifications or younger age group.

Table 10.18 summaries the employee commitment component of quality of work life. There is not much perceived difference in the scores of managers or non-managers. Similarly, there is not a substantial difference on the basis of age or educational Qualifications.

Table 10.19 highlights findings of General Life Satisfaction (GLS) component of Quality of Work Life (QWL) as perceived by managers and their subordinates. The classification has been undertaken on the basis of age below 35 years and above 35 years as well as graduate and Post-graduate qualifications. The findings reveal there is no significant difference on the general satisfaction level among the managers or the non-managers. Similarly, there is not much influence of educational qualifications.

Figure 10.4 graphically represents the mean scores of quality of work life as perceived by managers with graduate and Post-graduate qualifications.

Table 10.20 reveals that the non-managers do not consider organizational climate to be as conducive as the strong feelings of the managers. This feeling of disillusionment is more pronounced among the senior aged subordinates. The subordinates with Post-graduate qualifications are equally pessimistic.

Table 10.17

Statistical Parameters of Control, Influence and Participation (CIP) Component of Quality of Work Life (QWL) as perceived by Managers and their Subordinates (classified on the Basis of Age Below 35 years and Above 35 years as well as Graduate and Post-graduate Qualifications)

	Managers					*Subordinates*				
	Total	*Below 35*	*Above 35*	*Graduate*	*Post-graduate*	*Total*	*Below 35*	*Above 35*	*Graduate*	*Post-graduate*
(1)	*(2)*	*(3)*	*(4)*	*(5)*	*(6)*	*(7)*	*(8)*	*(9)*	*(10)*	*(11)*
average	70.087	71.607	69.432	71.889	70.125	56.726	59.000	51.941	60.347	51.471
stdev	2.020	3.618	2.500	2.723	2.229	2.607	2.385	2.546	3.812	2.335
median	72.035	73.578	71.067	73.090	72.084	71.562	60.081	53.064	61.672	53.583
max	74	72	74	73	74	68	68	64	68	64
min	34	34	34	34	34	33	32	33	33	32
skewness	-1.053	-0.898	-1.062	-1.364	-0.981	-0.826	-0.635	-1.141	-0.983	-0.649
kurtosis	0.954	0.948	0.904	1.708	0.742	1.182	1.388	2.084	1.749	0.448

TABLE 10.18

Statistical Parameters of Employee Commitment Component of Quality of Work Life (QWL) as perceived by Managers and their Subordinates (classified on the Basis of Age Below 35 years and Above 35 years as well as Graduate and Post-graduate Qualifications)

	Managers					Subordinates				
	Total	*Below 35*	*Above 35*	*Graduate*	*Post-graduate*	*Total*	*Below 35*	*Above 35*	*Graduate*	*Post-graduate*
(1)	*(2)*	*(3)*	*(4)*	*(5)*	*(6)*	*(7)*	*(8)*	*(9)*	*(10)*	*(11)*
average	14.594	16.107	14.216	14.111	15.179	14.929	14.031	15.471	14.612	15.353
stdev	2.690	2.672	2.537	2.541	2.242	2.728	2.337	2.398	2.348	1.913
median	14.583	17.428	14.873	15.023	16.037	14.950	15.093	16.021	16.023	16.022
max	19	17	19	17	19	19	16	19	16	19
min	6	5	6	8	4	7	7	8	7	8
skewness	-1.726	-0.935	-1.783	-0.612	-2.050	-1.715	-1.562	-1.846	-1.870	-1.120
kurtosis	2.635	1.661	2.443	-0.391	4.303	3.759	2.982	4.826	4.003	1.596

TABLE 10.19

Statistical Parameters of General Life Satisfaction (GLS) Component of Quality of Work Life (QWL) as perceived by Managers and their Subordinates (classified on the Basis of Age Below 35 years and Above 35 years as well as Graduate and Post-graduate Qualifications)

	Managers					Subordinates				
	Total	*Below 35*	*Above 35*	*Graduate*	*Post-graduate*	*Total*	*Below 35*	*Above 35*	*Graduate*	*Post-graduate*
(1)	*(2)*	*(3)*	*(4)*	*(5)*	*(6)*	*(7)*	*(8)*	*(9)*	*(10)*	*(11)*
average	33.464	35.964	32.324	33.667	33.929	34.464	33.875	34.824	34.449	34.471
stdev	2.806	2.941	2.519	2.471	2.368	2.917	2.517	2.635	2.497	2.210
median	25.362	26.432	24.474	24.850	26.348	25.485	25.347	26.723	25.342	25.509
max	35	35	31	34	31	34	34	34	34	34
min	9	9	11	9	12	12	14	12	14	12
skewness	-1.375	-0.888	-1.307	-0.539	-1.620	-1.465	-1.438	-1.484	-1.727	-0.765
kurtosis	1.673	1.150	1.274	-0.248	2.847	2.855	2.596	3.272	3.511	0.490

FIG. 10.4
Mean Scores of Quality of Work Life (QWL) Index as perceived by Managers with Graduate and Post-graduate Qualifications

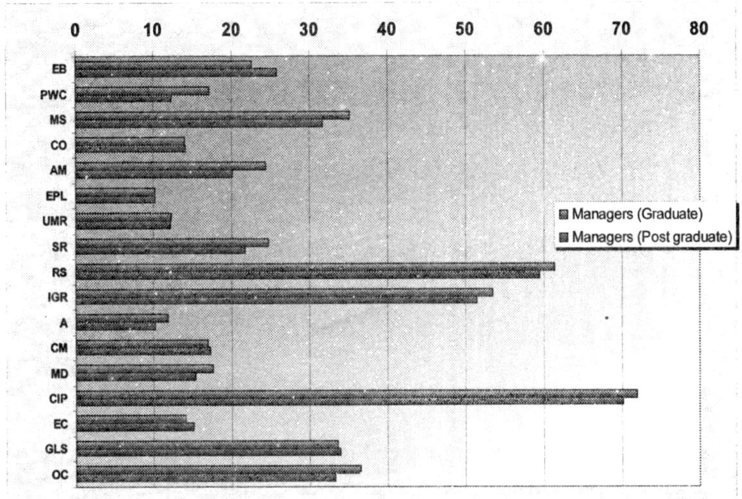

The impact of restructuring which most of the consumer durable organizations have undertaken, was also reflected in the older employee's level of dissatisfaction with the amount of work they are expected to do. Work intensification and longer hours were other legacies of corporate restructuring as survivors of downsizing efforts felt that they have to do the work of those who were retrenched. Normally full-time employed persons in consumer durable industry usually work more than 44 hours per week. Furthermore, one-third of those working more than 49 hours per week do so as they feel it is an expectation of the job and another one in five say that extra hours are necessary to get the job done. Dissatisfaction with the amount of work also goes some way to explaining dissatisfaction with the organizations policies and procedures and the compensation packages. Almost 70% workers feel that the amount of work they have to do is more and they expected that they could be more adequately remunerated for their efforts.

Table 10.20

Statistical Parameters of Organisational Climate (OC) Component of Quality of Work Life (QWL) as perceived by Managers and their Subordinates (classified on the Basis of Age Below 35 years and Above 35 years as well as Graduate and Post-graduate Qualifications)

	Managers					*Subordinates*				
	Total	*Below 35*	*Above 35*	*Graduate*	*Post-graduate*	*Total*	*Below 35*	*Above 35*	*Graduate*	*Post-graduate*
(1)	*(2)*	*(3)*	*(4)*	*(5)*	*(6)*	*(7)*	*(8)*	*(9)*	*(10)*	*(11)*
average	34.943	36.929	32.297	36.556	33.250	31.667	32.219	30.980	32.429	30.059
stdev	2.546	2.218	2.156	2.055	2.269	2.948	2.250	2.875	2.283	2.628
median	35.064	37.034	33.090	37.372	34.043	32.341	32.523	31.077	33.067	31.045
max	35	35	35	35	35	34	34	34	34	34
min	12	10	12	10	14	11	11	14	14	11
skewness	-1.353	-0.752	-1.410	0.272	-1.561	-1.429	-1.642	-1.324	-1.802	-0.737
kurtosis	1.823	1.118	1.763	-1.555	2.603	2.763	3.264	2.695	3.941	0.172

Figure 10.5 graphically represents the mean scores of quality of work life as perceived by subordinates with graduate and Post-graduate qualifications.

FIG. 10.5

Mean Scores of Quality of Work Life (QWL) Index as perceived by Subordinates with Graduate and Post-graduate Qualifications

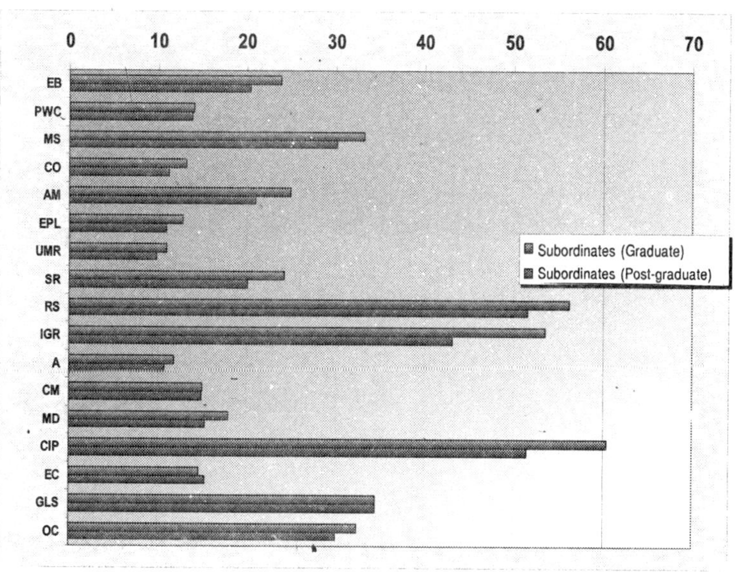

REFERENCES

Edwards, J.R. and Rothbard, N.F. (1999): "Work and Family Stress and Well-being: An Examination of Person-environment fit in the Work and Family Domains." *Organizational Behaviour and Human Decision Processes*, Vol. 77(2), pp. 85-129.

Farrell, D., and Stamm, C.L. (1988): "Meta-analysis of the Correlates of Employee Absence." *Human Relations*, Vol. 101, pp. 211-27.

Greenhaus, J.H., Collins, K.M. and Shaw, J.D. (2003): "The Relation Between Work–Family Balance and Quality of Life." *Journal of Vocational Behaviour*, Vol. 63(3), pp. 510-31.

Flaherty, K.E. and Pappas, J.M. (2000): "The Role of Trust in Salesperson-Sales Manager Relationships". *Journal of Personal Selling and Sales Management*, Vol. 20, pp. 271-78.

Lau, R.S.M., and Bruce, E.M. (1998): "A Win-Win Paradigm for Quality of Work Life and Business Performance". *Human Resource Development Quarterly*, 9(3), 211-26.

Rogers, R.W. (1995): "The Psychological Contract of Trust: Part II". *Executive Development*, Vol. 8, pp. 7-15.

S.P. Brown and R.A. Peterson, Antecedents and Consequences of Salesperson Job Satisfaction: Meta-analysis and Assessment of Causal Effects. *Journal of Marketing Research*, 30 (1993), pp. 63-77.

Walton R.E. (1975) 'Criteria for Quality of Working Life' in Davis, L. and Cherns, A. (eds.) (1975), *The Quality of Working Life*, Vol. 1, Free Press, New York, 91-1010.

Williams, R., Zyzanski, S.J. and Wright, A.L. (1992): "Life Events and Daily Hassles and Uplifts as Predictors of Hospitalization and Outpatient Visitation." *Social Science and Medicine*, Vol. 310, pp. 763-68.

CHAPTER

11

Gaining Competence through Bridging LB, QWL and OC

This section summarizes the findings of the inter-relationship between the three variables. For computing correlation coefficient, following formula of Product Moment Correlation was used:

$$r = \frac{\sum xy}{n\sigma_x \sigma_y}$$

$x = (X - \overline{X})$; $y = (Y - \overline{Y})$

σ_x = Standard deviation of series X

σ_y = Standard deviation of series Y

n = Number of pairs of observations

r = The (product moment) correlation coefficient

Table 11.1 reveals that the relationship between total leadership behaviour description index (LBDQ) and organisational commitment (OC) index as perceived by the Managers and their subordinates about their managers is positive for both managers as well as the subordinates. However, the intensity of correlation is more for the managers as compared to the subordinates. This implies that those leaders who exhibit higher leadership behavioural patterns also have higher commitment towards their organizations. Subordinates feel that those subordinates who work under leaders exhibiting higher leadership behaviour indices are more committed towards their organizations.

TABLE 11.1

Correlation Coefficients to determine Correlation between total Leadership Behaviour Description Index (LBDQ) and Organisational Commitment (OC) index as perceived by the Managers and their Subordinates

	Sample Size (n)	*Standard Deviation*		*Correlation Coefficient (r)*
		LBDQ	*OC*	
Managers	151	12.10	9.101	0.202
Subordinates	247	9.081	11.146	0.176

Table 11.2 highlights the correlation between consideration component of the leadership behaviour description index (LBDQ) and organisational commitment (OC) index as perceived by the managers and their subordinates. The relationship is also positively correlated. However, the managers feel there is a stronger correlation between these two parameters, whereas subordinate's perception is not that stronger. This means that managers feel that those managers who are more considerate also exhibit more organisational commitment. Subordinates feel that those managers who are considerate instill organisational commitment among the subordinates. Managers need to offer better career prospects, more interesting and satisfying work, greater recognition of efforts and remuneration to generate organisational commitment

Positive correlation was also noticed between initiation component of LBD index and Organisational commitment index (Table 11.3). This correlation was higher for the subordinates

TABLE 11.2

Correlation Coefficients to determine Correlation between Consideration Component of the Leadership Behaviour Description Index (LBDQ) and Organisational Comm'tment (OC) index as perceived by the Managers and their Subordinates

	Sample Size (n)	*Standard Deviation*		*Correlation Coefficient (r)*
		Consideration	*OC*	
Managers	151	6.165	9.101	0.1396
Subordinates	247	6.173	11.146	0.044

TABLE 11.3

Correlation Coefficients to determine Correlation between Initiation Component of the Leadership Behaviour Description Index (LBDQ) and Organisational Commitment (OC) index as perceived by the Managers and their Subordinates

	Sample Size (n)	*Standard Deviation*		*Correlation Coefficient (r)*
		Initiation	*OC*	
Managers	151	7.478	9.101	0.212
Subordinates	247	4.844	11.146	0.272

than the managers, implying thereby that the subordinates exhibit more commitment towards their organisation if the manager is initiative-oriented.

Self-concept motivation is internally based when the individual is primarily inner-directed. Internal self-concept motivation takes the form of the individual setting internal standards that become the basis for the ideal self. The individual tends to use fixed rather than ordinal standards of self-measurement as he/she attempts to first reinforce perceptions of competency and later achieve higher levels of competency. This need for achieving higher levels of competency is similar to what *McClelland* (1961) refers to as a high need for achievement.

The motivating force for individuals who are inner-driven and motivated by their self-concept is task feedback. It is important to these individuals that their efforts are vital in achieving outcomes and that their ideas and actions are instrumental in performing a job well. It is not important that others provide reinforcing feedback as is true for other-directed individuals. Such managers generate respect from their subordinates for their initiativeness as reflected in this survey. Another possible explanation could be the experiential learning subordinates undertake under such managers, thereby enhancing their organisational commitment levels.

Table 11.4 highlights the correlation between leadership behaviour description index (LBDQ) and affective component of the oganisational commitment (OC) index as perceived by the Managers and their Subordinates. Higher score indicates that degree, to which the employee identifies with, is involved in and emotionally attached to the organisation. Affectively committed employees believe in the goals and values of the organisation and enjoy being a member of it. Thus, subordinates exhibit higher level of affective commitment than the managers.

TABLE 11.4

Correlation Coefficients to Determine Correlation between Leadership Behaviour Description Index (LBDQ) and Affective Component of the Organisational Commitment (OC) index as perceived by the Managers and their Subordinates

	Sample Size (n)	*Standard Deviation*		*Correlation Coefficient (r)*
		LBDQ	*Affective*	
Managers	151	12.10	3.431	0.111
Subordinates	247	9.081	4.889	0.120

A positive correlation was also noticed between leadership behaviour index and continuance index (Table 11.5) Thus, the degree to which the employee recognizes that costs associated with leaving the organisation tie him or her to the organization is more for managers than the subordinates. Such managers feel

TABLE 11.5

Correlation Coefficients to determine Correlation between Leadership Behaviour Description Index (LBDQ) and Continuance Component of the Organisational Commitment (OC) index as perceived by the Managers and their Subordinates

	Sample Size (n)	*Standard Deviation*		*Correlation Coefficient (r)*
		LBDQ	*Continuance*	
Managers	151	12.10	5.638	0.183
Subordinates	247	9.081	5.617	0.0886

they have to remain within the organisation because they *have* to do so. Subordinates exhibited positive correlation between continuance index and the manager's leadership behaviour scores. However, such a correlation is not very strongly positive. Thus, subordinates need to be told that their organisation is committed to maximizing their potential and know that their contribution is making a meaningful difference to the organization.

Subordinates expressed higher normative commitment when working under leaders exhibiting higher leadership behaviour scores. Thus, those subordinates who work under leaders with higher leadership behaviour index feel morally obliged to continue in the organization. Such employees feel an obligation to the organisation; staying within the organisation is the right and moral thing to do. Employees remain within the organisation because they feel they *ought* to do so. (Table 11.6).

These findings reveal that all three components of Organisational commitment are positively correlated with leadership behaviour. Thus, those workers who are working under leaders with higher leadership behaviour index have all the three components of commitment positively correlated. Such correlations are indicative of the decision whether to stay or leave the organisation.

Table 11.7 highlights the correlation between total leadership behaviour description index (LBDQ) and quality of Work Life (QWL) index as perceived by the Managers and their

TABLE 11.6

Correlation Coefficients to determine Correlation between Leadership Behaviour Description Index (LBDQ) and Normative Component of the Organisational Commitment (OC) index as perceived by the Managers and their Subordinates

	Sample Size (n)	*Standard Deviation*		*Correlation Coefficient (r)*
		LBDQ	*Normative*	
Managers	151	12.101	4.668	0.092
Subordinates	247	9.081	4.848	0.181

TABLE 11.7

Correlation Coefficients to determine Correlation between total Leadership Behaviour Description Index (LBDQ) and Quality of Work Life (QWL) index as perceived by the Managers and their Subordinates

	Sample Size (n)	*Standard Deviation*		*Correlation Coefficient (r)*
		LBDQ	*QWL*	
Managers	151	12.101	72.617	0.4356
Subordinates	247	9.081	79.8834	0.1321

Subordinates. Findings reveal that those leaders having higher leadership behaviour index also have better quality of work life. Positive correlation also exists between these two variables for subordinates, albiet to a lesser extent. Thus, this subordinate who work under leaders exhibiting higher Leadership Behaviour perceive that they have better Quality of Work Life. Leadership style, in terms of conditional/unconditional feedback, impacts one's self-perception as well as one's self-esteem. It is affected by the employee's ability to attribute task results to him/herself, depending on whether the leader is autocratic or participative.

These results highlight the interactive nature of many of the factors that impact on working life. Although being treated well by immediate managers was obviously strongly related to having one's efforts recognised by senior management, it was also perceived to be very much dependent on a number of other organisational factors. That is, the way in which immediate managers treat employees was perceived to be reliant on a trustworthy senior management team and an organisational culture that encourages autonomy and respect.

This inducement system of any organisation also energizes, directs and sustains behaviour through a number of sources. Leadership in business organizations is primarily based on exchange relationships and is best utilized with individuals who are primarily instrumentally motivated. Such organisations provide an important source of social feedback, and is especially effective with other-directed individuals. Leadership style provides inner-directed individuals with important task feedback regarding traits, competencies and values. Such managers motivate by appealing to values and interests of the organization that have been internalized by the employees.

Table 11.8 highlights correlation between consideration component of leadership behaviour description index (LBDQ) and quality of work life (QWL) index as perceived by the Managers and their Subordinates. A very strong positive correlation has been observed for the managers. Thus, those managers having higher consideration also perceive that they have higher quality of work life. A very moderate positive correlation had been noticed between quality of work life perceived by subordinates who work under considerate

TABLE 11.8

Correlation Coefficients to determine Correlation between Consideration Component of Leadership Behaviour Description Index (LBDQ) and Quality of Work Life (QWL) index as perceived by the Managers and their Subordinates

	Sample Size (n)	*Standard Deviation*		*Correlation Coefficient (r)*
		Consideration	*QWL*	
Managers	151	6.166	72.617	0.3696
Subordinates	247	6.373	79.8834	0.0931

managers. Past research suggests that employee perceptions of leadership behaviour are also directly related to employee attitudes (*Williams et al*, 1992) particularly satisfaction and commitment (*Bass*, 1990).

Jobs high in both intrinsic (e.g., autonomy, challenge) and extrinsic (e.g., opportunities for recognition) rewards have progressively stronger positive effects on the job satisfaction and career satisfaction of individuals with low, moderate and high job involvement, respectively. The results also show differential effects of leadership behaviour on job and career satisfaction and commitment to the organization. The relationship of leadership behaviour to career satisfaction is markedly higher for individuals with low job involvement than those with moderate or high levels of involvement. Leaders need to reduce role conflict and role ambiguity and offer advancement and developmental prospects. Role ambiguity leads to low job involvement and has negative effect on organizational commitment. High levels of job involvement can lead to improved quality of work life.

Greenhaus and Beutell (1985) have proposed that high levels of job involvement and family involvement heighten the level of work-family conflict experienced by individuals and its aversive effects on individuals' well-being.

Table 11.9 summarises correlation between Initiation Component of leadership behaviour description index (LBDQ) and quality of work life (QWL) index as perceived by the Managers and their Subordinates. Here also, a very strong correlation has been noticed between initiativeness of the

TABLE 11.9

Correlation Coefficients to determine Correlation between Initiation Component of Leadership Behaviour Description Index (LBDQ) and Quality of Work Life (QWL) index as perceived by the Managers and their Subordinates

	Sample Size (n)	*Standard Deviation*		*Correlation Coefficient (r)*
		Initiation	*QWL*	
Managers	151	7.478	72.617	0.4001
Subordinates	247	4.844	79.883	0.1252

managers and their Quality of Work Life. Subordinates expressed moderate positive correlation. Thus, subordinates feel that leaders with higher initiativeness generate better quality of work life among the subordinates.

Many factors influence the quality of work life. These include employment relationships:

- work environment
- organizational structures and processes
- job design
- management practices and supervision
- overall business strategy
- organizational culture
- worker attitudes and behaviour

A moderate correlation has been observed between organisational commitment and the quality of work life among both managers and the subordinates (Table 11.10). Thus, those employees have more commitment towards their organisation who feel that quality of work life in their organisation is good, irrespective of whether they are the managers or the subordinates.

TABLE 11.10

Correlation Coefficients to determine Correlation between Organisational Commitment (OC) Index and Quality of Work Life (QWL) index as perceived by the Managers and their Subordinates

	Sample Size (n)	*Standard Deviation*		*Correlation Coefficient (r)*
		QC	*QWL*	
Managers	151	9.102	72.617	0.190
Subordinates	247	11.146	79.8834	0.065

Organizational change also affects employment relationships. It has been noticed that downsizing reduces commitment and trust. Similarly, organisation restructuring negatively affects organisational commitment.

The results of a 1993 meta-analysis of 118 studies looking at work satisfaction in over 15,000 nurses revealed that job satisfaction was associated strongly with reduced work stress, organizational commitment, communication with supervisors, autonomy, employee recognition, fairness, locus of control, years of experience, education and professionalism. This study also found a strong relationship between job satisfaction and QWL (*Blegen*, 1993).

Since the advent of liberalization in India, there has been an increase in the take-up of flexible work practices aimed at improving work and family balance. Despite the increased interest and debate about work and family balance, the survey found that when it comes to balancing work and family life and managing stress levels, organizations need to provide working arrangements that are flexible enough especially for younger age workers. Our survey has shown the relatively high percentage of workers over the age of 35 who indicated dissatisfaction with the level of stress they felt and with their ability to adequately balance work and family time.

However, those managers who exhibit higher affective commitment, i.e. attachment with their organisation also have higher quality of work life. Thus, moral bindings lead to higher perceived quality of work life. In case of subordinates, such correlation between affective commitment and the quality of work life is not very strong, albeit positive. (Table 11.11)

It has been reported that strong employment relationships depend on a healthy and supportive work environment wherein

TABLE 11.11

Correlation Coefficients to determine Correlation between Affective Component of Organisational Commitment (OC) Index and Quality of Work Life (QWL) index as perceived by the Managers and their Subordinates

	Sample Size (n)	*Standard Deviation*		*Correlation Coefficient (r)*
		Affective	*QWL*	
Managers	151	3.431	72.617	0.130
Subordinates	247	4.889	79.8834	0.086

there is interesting work and need-based continuous training and development, besides job security.

Table 11.12 highlights the correlation between Continuance Component of organisational commitment (OC) index and quality of work life (QWL) index as perceived by the managers and their subordinates. This correlation is very moderate in case of managers and is negative in case of subordinates. Subordinates feel that the costs associated with leaving the organisation are not a major factor in perceiving the quality of work life. There are visible effects that work conditions can have in the individual welfare like manifestation of satisfaction in the workplace, growth and development of the employees, etc. Eight items that could enhance quality of work life include wages and benefits, career opportunity, freedom of communication between managers and employees, security in the managers, pride of work and company, interpersonal openness, training and development and innovation in the work system.

TABLE 11.12

Correlation Coefficients to determine Correlation between Continuance Component of Organisational Commitment (OC) Index and Quality of Work Life (QWL) index as perceived by the Managers and their Subordinates

	Sample Size (n)	*Standard Deviation*		*Correlation Coefficient (r)*
		Continuum	*QWL*	
Managers	151	5.638	72.617	0.075
Subordinates	247	5.617	79.8834	-0.045

Workers often perceive training as a reward providing self-actualization and the motivation to learn; career development with increased responsibility, autonomy and likelihood of advancement; and personal psychosocial benefits, including increased confidence, new friendships and better functioning in non-work life (*Noe and Wilk,* 1993).

The correlation between normative component of organisational commitment and quality of work life was also analysed (Table 11.13). A moderate positive correlation exists between these two variables. The relationship is stronger for the managers than the subordinates. Thus, moral obligation towards the organisation also leads to higher perceived quality of work life for the managers. However, such a moral obligation is not that strongly correlated with the quality of work life.

TABLE 11.13

Correlation Coefficients to determine Correlation between Normative Component of Organisational Commitment (OC) Index and Quality of Work Life (QWL) index as perceived by the Managers and their Subordinates

	Sample Size (n)	*Standard Deviation*		*Correlation Coefficient (r)*
		Normative	*QWL*	
Managers	151	4.668	72.617	0.185
Subordinates	247	4.848	79.8834	0.114

Many authors have identified three contributions of autonomy in work to positive self-esteem: (1) autonomy via self-perceptions-allows individuals to take responsibility for their own actions and success; (2) autonomy via reflected appraisals-autonomy is experienced as a reward for demonstrated competence and reliability; and (3) autonomy via social comparison-autonomy as a status indicator in the workplace culture is used for social comparison with other workers. Results of the present study also indicate that, in order for autonomy to have a positive effect on self-esteem, it must be valued by the worker.

Critical analysis of the existing literature supplemented by the findings of the present study has helped to identify factors employees use to evaluate companies as better places to work. Organizations which have higher perceived QWL and instill organizational commitment have following characteristic features :

(a) Generating pride in work and company through its innovative products and ethical orientation.

(b) Freedom of communication between managers and employees, relying more on inter-personal skills.
(c) Career possibility and ample chance of professional ascension.
(d) Interpersonal openness and developing groups cohesiveness.
(e) Security related to the tenures and transparent evaluation systems.
(f) Training and development and continuous need assessment.
(g) Innovation at work system and providing opportunities for "constructive destruction".
(h) Payment and benefits based on merit so as to attract and retain the best talent.

Based on our findings, following recommendations could be offered for building commitment to high quality work environments which instill organisational commitment and develop higher quality of work life:

(a) Making high quality work environments central to corporate values and mission, confirming that employees are assets.
(b) Negotiating roles and responsibilities of professional associations, unions, management and government.
(c) Benchmarking job quality and analyzing impact on results.
(d) Diagnosing areas of strength and weakness and develop suitable strategies.
(e) Continuously evaluating the impact of organizational change on employees and service outcomes.
(f) Building quality work environment goals into business plans, showing links to results.
(g) Providing incentives for managers to contribute to specific job quality goals.
(h) Communicating to general public how high quality work environments improve the quality of their lives so as to attract and retain the best talent.

REFERENCES

Bass, B.M. (1998): *Transformational Leadership: Industrial, Military and Educational Impact*, Lawrence Erlbaum, Mahwah, New Jersy.

Blegen, M. (1993): Nurses' Job Satisfaction: A Meta-analysis of Related Variables. *Nurs Res*, 1993, Vol. 102, pp. 36-101.

Greenhaus, J.H. and Beutell, N.J. (1985): "Sources of Conflict Between Work and Family Roles." *Academy of Management Review*, Vol. 10(1), pp. 76-88.

Noe, R.A. and Wilk, S.L. (1993): "Investigation of the Factors That Influence Employees' Participation in Development Activities". *J. Appl. Psychol.* Vol. 78, pp. 291-302.

Williams, M.L., Podsakoff, P.M. and Huber, V. (1992): "Effects of Group-level and Individual-level variation in Leader Behaviours on Subordinate Attitudes and Performance." *Journal of Occupational and Organizational Psychology*, Vol. 65, pp. 115-29.

CHAPTER

12

Findings of the Exploratory Study

This chapter highlights the salient features of the research undertaken. The research work has been presented in twelve chapters. Effort was made to introduce the topic by developing the conceptual framework in Chapters 1, 2 and 3. Companies generate sustainable competitive advantages by effectively controlling and manipulating their resources and/or capabilities that are: (1) valuable, (2) rare, (3) that cannot be perfectly imitated, and (4) for which no perfect substitute is available. Human resource activities including those that improve employee attitudes on workplace quality meet these four characteristics. As a result, human resource activities can create a competitive advantage by developing a skilled workforce that effectively carries out the company's business strategy. This competitive advantage leads to improved performance, higher profitability and greater market value. Thus, one of the most challenging tasks for an organization is to create, sustain and improve through strategic role of leadership, quality of work life and organisational commitment. The various determinants of leadership were identified, besides different approaches to leadership and leadership styles. Leadership styles as a function of emotional competence was highlighted. Theories of leadership besides leadership behaviour patterns were critically examined. Given the ever-increasing demand to become more competitive and effective, today's employers are not simply interested in ensuring the legal defensibility of their policies, practices and procedures; rather they are also interested in "managing diversity" to ensure that employees reach their full potential. Chapter 2 highlighted the conceptual underpinnings of organisational commitment besides the need and importance of developing organisational commitment among employees. The components and determinants of organizational commitment were also analysed. Similarly, quality of work life has been conceptually analysed in Chapter 3.

Review of existing literature in Chapters 4, 5 and 6 has highlighted the growing recognition in organizations that to manage a diverse employee base, organizational climate must be appropriate. Such a conducive environment is predominantly dependent on the leader's behaviour and is reflected in the improved quality of work life and organizational commitment manifested by the employees. Committed employees are considered necessary to build better relationships with clients and customers, to learn more effectively, to be more adaptable to change and generally to work more efficiently. Strategy scholars have argued that managing knowledge effectively can provide firms with sustainable competitive advantages. Leaders are central to the process of managing knowledge effectively. Managing knowledge includes three key processes: creating, sharing and exploiting knowledge. Successful leaders tend to create a climate within the work environment where they are able to assist employees to set and achieve individual, team and ultimately organizational objectives. With the shift from hierarchical organizations to flatter and team-based structures, the role of leaders has changed so as to become less concerned with the day-to-day work activities and more focused on the procurement of needed resources besides developing and supporting a work environment that facilitates team success. Employees are increasingly working in locations separated by time and geographical location; this presents leaders with a new level of complexity when trying to foster creativity. Leaders who enable employees to participate in decision-making and encourage communication among subordinates generate favourable work culture. QWL among such organizations is highly characterized by less interpersonal conflicts and hostility and less non-cooperative relationships. Today transformational leadership is viewed as the most prominent topic in the current research and theories of leadership.

Organizational commitment is characterized by an individual's: (1) belief in and acceptance of organizational goals and values; (2) willingness to exert effort towards organizational goal accomplishment; and (3) strong desire to maintain organizational membership. Commitment research has shown that people are more likely to develop higher levels of commitment when they can identify with the values and standards of the organization. Organisational and managerial support; commitment to developing individual potential; culture and values alignment as well as organisational competence are the top four drivers for engendering and maintaining employee commitment. Commitment has several components: compatibility of values, pride in the organisation, loyalty, job satisfaction and feeling fairly rewarded. Commitment must also be understood as a two-way process, involving responsibilities on the employer to develop and value employees.

The key concepts captured and discussed in the existing literature include job security, better reward systems, higher pay, opportunity for growth, participative groups and increased organizational productivity among others.

Rationale for the present study was based upon the realization of the researchers that it is a futile quest for universal leadership principles that apply equivalently across all cultures as there are bound to be variations in leadership styles, practices and preferences. Combination of technological advances, larger multicultural samples, enhanced clarification of dimensions of culture and better understanding besides measurement of cognitive processes across cultures may allow us to better understand the role culture plays in the enactment and interpretation of the leadership behaviour.

Leaders may move across different industries and organizations during their career span, yet they may exhibit similar leadership behavioural patterns which may get developed over a period of time. The contemporary leader is expected to make moderate use of visionary, transactional and empowering behaviours while avoiding autocratic behaviours. Exploring the role of leadership styles in converting knowledge into competitive advantage is important to our understanding of leaders and organizations.

Over the past decade, the area of organizational commitment has received considerable attention from both researchers and managers. Of particular interest is the link between this and other constructs such as trust, task performance and turnover. Despite the widespread acknowledgement of the importance and value of organizational commitment, there has been limited research that has specifically addressed the relationship between leader behaviour and employee commitment, particularly in the consumer durable sector. The present study examines the nature of the relationships between organizational commitment and two dimensions of leader behaviour—supportive behaviours and extinction behaviours. There is, however, a considerable body of literature that examines relationships between supervisor behaviour, particularly the level of support provided by supervisors and a range of desired organizational outcomes. It is argued that since employees do not differentiate between supervisors, managers and leaders in any practical sense, supervisory behaviour can be equated to leadership behaviours.

Present study seeks to examine the relationship between perceptions of leader behaviour in the work environment, quality of work life and levels of organizational commitment among employees in a large segment of Indian economy, i.e. white goods industry.

Improving employee retention is a difficult challenge to managers since the bureaucratic cultural norm of most organisations with its hierarchical structures, roles, regulations, with heavy emphasis on measurement of outcomes and costs may not be the culture most conducive to enhancing job satisfaction and commitment. *Accordingly, this study investigates the relationships between leadership behaviour and perceived QWL besides several important job-related variables of organizational commitment.*

It has been argued that the high levels of trust, loyalty and altruism ingrained in oriental cultures mean that Asian employees often display high levels of commitment to their organization. This needs to be cross-examined in Indian context. The study assumes even greater importance as the white goods (consumer durable) industry is dominated with Japanese, Korean and Taiwanese origin companies.

Gaps in existing literature were identified and it was found that the studies involving leadership behaviour patterns and its influences on the subordinates have mostly been done in the developed countries. As it has been conclusively proved that leadership is situational, it becomes important that the studies are conducted in India so as to have direct impact on the management practices. Moreover, the studies have been done on quality of work life as well as organisational commitment *per se*. However, there is scarce literature available highlighting the influence of leadership behaviour on the quality of work life as well as organisational commitment. Hence, the rationale for the present study. *The leadership has also been studied in its various facets like the leadership styles, factors affecting leadership effectiveness, challenges facing leadership, etc.* There is thus a need to study the extent to which leader's behaviour influences organisational commitment among subordinates as well as its impact on quality of work life. It may also be worthwhile to study whether any significant difference exists between organisational commitment exhibited by the subordinates and the leader.

Need for the study was felt as although the concept of job involvement, its antecedents and outcomes have been researched extensively by organizational researchers, little attention has been devoted to exploring job involvement and its relationship to the work experiences and job attitudes of white goods industry personnel. The dearth of research in this area is surprising in light of prior findings that these professionals have high need for achievement and growth and place a high value on interesting work, job challenge and growth opportunities. The job design literature provides extensive evidence that job involvement is associated positively with the five "core" elements, i.e. job characteristics or job scope; need for achievement and growth; job satisfaction; performance and organizational commitment. These factors underscore the importance of examining the work experiences and other factors related to the job involvement of employees and the relationship of involvement with favorable job and organizational outcomes, reflecting their quality of work life. Studies on the antecedents of commitment have shown that job involvement and its relationship to organizational commitment differ significantly across occupational groups. Viewed in conjunction with previous findings, organizational commitment is the most proximal determinant of turnover intentions of employees. Perusal of existing studies has reinforced the importance of investigating the job involvement of employees and the role of involvement in influencing the quality of work life. Thus, the purpose of this study was to examine: (1) the relationship of personal/demographic variables, job characteristics and work experiences with variations in the level of job involvement; (2) the relationship of job characteristics and work experiences with career expectations, job satisfaction, career satisfaction and organizational commitment; and (3) the role played by job involvement in influencing the relationships among these variables.

Systematic evaluation of QWL in the consumer durable industry has not occurred. The existence of rapid environmental changes and competitive pressures in the industry suggested the importance of determining the extent to which QWL activity, if any, existed in the industry. Furthermore, it was deemed desirable to understand which components of working life were perceived as important within different employee groups and with which aspects satisfaction existed.

The salient findings, their managerial as well as organizational implications have been highlighted. The summary of the findings along with their linkages with the existing literature have been presented. Efforts have also been done to suggest suitable strategies at organizational level. These include:

1. The mean scores of managers on the total LBD index are almost similar to the perception of the subordinates about their manager. However, there is a difference on the individual components. Managers perceive

themselves to be high on consideration index whereas the subordinates feel that the managers are high on initiative index and low on consideration. Leaders must concentrate less on "concrete task and performance direction" and more on "framing and guiding the work tasks so that they align with the organisation's mission and focus." Vision and goals, rather than rules and procedures, are seen as key tools for co-ordination and control. Clear vision helps people understand the purpose, objectives and priorities of an organisation, gives work meaning and fosters a sense of common purpose.

2. Comparison of the managerial cadre on the basis of age of the respondents reveals that the managerial cadre below the age of 35 consider themselves to be low on consideration index as compared to managerial cadre respondents above the age of 35, whereas the initiativeness is perceived to be high in managerial cadre above the age of 35 as compared to the managers of lower age bracket. Our respondents have shown that successful change leaders, among other things, communicate a clear vision and enlist other to help achieve it. Thus, managers have an impact in organisations through promulgating vision which attracts commitment and energises people, creates meaning, establishes a standard of excellence and bridges the present with the future. Managers need to conceptualise major work characteristics (i.e. staffing, training, assigning work, appraising performance, allocating rewards, etc.) within a human resource framework, so as to make subordinates aware about their responsibilities regarding work groups. This could be achieved through the decentralisation of power so as to make them responsible for their team functioning in well-adapted working conditions.
3. Managerial cadre with Post-graduate qualifications consider themselves to be high on total leadership behaviour index as well as on both consideration as well as initiative indices compared to managers with only graduate qualifications. These findings reveal that

the main challenges for today's managers are to build a long-term vision, to increase commitment, to build teams and coalitions in order to fully realize the skills of the team. To reach goals of the organization, they should focus on motivating, inspiring and empowering their employees. In work settings, the supervisor is often the most salient person and is therefore likely to both represent the organisation's culture and to exert a direct influence upon subordinates' behaviours. Superiors assigning tasks, specifying procedures and clarifying expectations have been shown to result in reduced role ambiguity and increased job satisfaction among employees. Leaders who are perceived to closely monitor their subordinates in order to prevent mistakes tend to evoke higher levels of emotional exhaustion among their staff as close monitoring may be perceived as a lack of trust in the staff.

4. The leadership behaviour index and its constituent elements (viz., consideration and initiative) were also analysed by applying t-test of significance. It was found that the subordinates consider their managers to be having more initiative than the perception of the managers about themselves. One possible explanation could be the lower involvement of the subordinates in goal setting and decision-making, thereby making employees feel that the manager has more initiative as he takes most of the decisions. Such a perception may lead to poor development of the subordinate as he may not take initiative himself and may look towards the manager for problem-solving.
5. The subordinates have similar perception about their executive as that of the executives themselves on the consideration index. Leadership is a process of social interaction, process that is ultimately founded in cognitive processes. Consideration is a people-related dimension, i.e. the degree to which a leader acts in a friendly and supportive manner by showing concern for subordinates and looks after their welfare. Leaders high on consideration tend to focus on the needs of the stakeholders both physical and psychological.

Conversely, initiating structure behaviours are more task focused and are defined as "the degree to which a leader defines and structures his or her own role and the roles of subordinates toward attainment of the group's formal goals. Leaders high on initiating structure exhibit behaviours, which provide direction and clarify goals. The initiating structure style focuses less on how stakeholders feel and more on creating systems for efficiently performing job tasks. Based on the process of automatic categorization and the general preference for homogeneity, it is conceivable that subordinates in certain industries which have shorter chains of command may evaluate their leaders more readily and optimistically than in other industries which have longer chains of command. This is evidenced by the fact that past research has consistently shown that consideration behaviours, either alone or in conjunction with structuring behaviour is related to job satisfaction. Consequently, a positive employee appraisal lends itself to the consideration style.

6. Comparative analysis was also undertaken to analyse whether there is any significant difference in the perception of the managers in different age groups on the consideration index. Managerial cadre in the age group above 35 years has statistically significant scores on the consideration index than the managers in the age group below 35 years. As the managers reach higher age groups, consideration towards the well being of the subordinates take precedence. Similarly, perception of the subordinates about consideration index of their manager was compared across different age groups. However, no significant difference was noticed. Thus, subordinates across different age groups have no significant difference in their perception about their manager on the consideration index. It may be explained that the subordinates tend to focus on the readily visible and identifiable task-related behaviours of the leader, in turn yielding a greater perception of structuring behaviour. Decision-making may be largely

centralized and procedures may have been highly structured.

7. Difference in managers' perception across different age groups on the initiative index was statistically insignificant. Subordinates across different age groups also had similar opinion about their managers. Thus, managers as well as their subordinates perceive them to have similar level of initiativeness.
8. Another hypothesis tested was whether there is any significant difference on the total Leadership Behaviour Description Index between manager below the age of 35 and those managers above the age of 35. It was found that managers above the age of 35 years consider themselves to have higher Leadership Behaviour score as compared to the managers below 35 years.
9. In order to test whether their subordinates also have similar perception about their superiors, difference on Leadership Behaviour Description Index of the subordinates of different age groups was computed. Subordinates across different age groups have similar opinion about their manager on the total Leadership Behaviour Description Index as no significant difference exists in opinions across age groups.
10. Another hypothesis tested was whether managers of different qualifications differ on the total Leadership Behaviour Description Index. It was found that the managers with Post-graduate qualifications were higher on the total Leadership Behaviour Description Index as compared to the managers with graduate qualifications and this difference was statistically significant.
11. Another hypothesis tested was whether the subordinates with different levels of qualifications also have perceptual difference about the Leadership Behaviour Description Index of their supervisor. However, this difference was not statistically significant. Thus, subordinates have similar opinion about their manager irrespective of their level of qualifications.

12. Another comparative analysis was undertaken on the consideration index between managers of graduate qualifications and the managers with post-graduate qualifications. Managers with higher qualifications had statistically significantly higher consideration index than managers with graduate qualifications. However, subordinates with post-graduate qualifications had no significant difference in their opinion about their manager on consideration index than subordinates with only graduate qualifications. Thus, subordinates have similar opinion about their managers on consideration index irrespective of their level of educational qualifications.
13. Comparative analysis of the managers across educational qualifications was also undertaken on the initiation index. It was found out that the managers with post-graduate qualifications had significantly higher score on the initation index than the managers with graduate qualifications. Analysis of the perception of the subordinates about their manager's initiation index revealed that there is no statistical difference between subordinate across different educational qualifications, i.e. subordinate with graduate qualifications had similar opinion about their manager's initiativeness as that of the subordinates with post-graduate qualifications.
14. It has been recognised that individual, organisational and task characteristics exist which may act as moderators on leadership effectiveness. Among these moderators are *individual characteristics of subordinates* (ability and training; high need for independence; professional orientation; indifference toward organisational rewards), *task characteristics* (methodologically invariant tasks; task-provided feedback; intrinsically satisfying tasks) and finally, *organisational characteristics* (organisational formalisation; organizational inflexibility; highly specified and active advisory and staff functions; cohesive work groups; organisational rewards not within the leader's control; spatial distance between a

superior and subordinates). It can, hence, be concluded that characteristics such as job design, interdependence, team composition, environmental context and process (e.g. workload sharing, communication/cooperation within groups, potency and social support) better account for effectiveness criteria (such as productivity and satisfaction). In an international sample, the influence of cultural factors cannot be ruled out.

15. Perusal of these findings reveals that the non-managerial cadre exhibited higher level of organisational commitment as compared to the managerial cadre. Non-managers scored higher on the affective and continuance dimensions of the organisational commitment whereas managers scored higher on the normative index. Thus, it could be said that the non-managers felt obliged to the organisation and/or felt that the opportunity cost of leaving the organisation may be higher. It could also be due to lack of perceived better opportunities in other organizations. Managers by exhibiting higher scores on the normative index showed their concern toward moral aspects of continuing with the organisation.
16. Analysis was also undertaken on the organisational commitment across different age groups. Managers below the age of 35 exhibited more commitment score than managers above 35 years. On the other hand, non-managers in the higher age groups were more committed. This could be explained for fewer opportunities to elderly personnel at the lower hierarchies.
17. Organisational commitment among managers with graduate qualifications was higher than that of the managers with post-graduate qualifications. This could be explained for lack of many opportunities to non-professionals at upper ladders of the hierarchy. Post-graduate qualifications may open new vistas for growth. Hence, managers with Post-graduate qualifications tend to move from the organizations faster, thereby exhibiting lower organisational

commitment. Non-managers with Post-graduate qualifications scored higher on the organisational commitment index than the non-managers with simple graduate qualifications.

18. It can be argued that developmental prospects are more strongly related to commitment among managers whereas advancement prospects have a positive effect on organizational commitment among the non-managers. Job involvement among the non-manager groups also enhances organisational commitment. It could also be hypothesized that role stressors as well as role conflicts have negative effects on organizational commitment. Organisations need to clearly define areas of operations and reduce role ambiguity so as to ensure higher organisational commitment among the subordinates.
19. Effort was also made to statistically analyse whether there is any significant difference in the organisational commitment levels of the managers and the subordinates. The findings reveal that the difference in the total organisational commitment scores is not statistically significant. The organisational commitment level among the consumer durable industry jobs could be attributed to the higher levels of intrinsic and extrinsic rewards including salary and entail more extensive boundary-spanning activities and greater role stress than the jobs held by employees of other durable industries with low and/or moderate involvement. These experiences are also differentially related to career expectations and indicators of the quality of work life among individuals in this high involvement industry. Moreover, these high-involvement employees display greater commitment to their employing organizations than other industries as reported in the other studies using the same scale. Furthermore, jobs high in both intrinsic (e.g., autonomy, challenge) and extrinsic (e.g., opportunities for recognition) rewards have progressively stronger positive effects on the job satisfaction and career satisfaction of individuals with high job involvement.

The results of previous studies (quoted in the review of literature section) also show differential effects of salary on job and career satisfaction and commitment to the organization.

20. Survey revealed that the non-managers have significantly higher levels of affective commitment as well as continuance commitment as compared to the managers. On the other hand, managers have significantly higher scores on the normative commitment index than the non-managers. It could be explained that the subordinates feel more loyal to the organisation and also have a perception that it may be difficult to get another job having similar level of status and monetary gains as the present one. Managers on the other hand by exhibiting higher normative commitment scores feel they are morally obliged to continue as the organisation may have offered them so much in terms of self-esteem, positions in the hierarchy and involvement in the decision-making. There should be more focus on empowered work groups and a movement away from the traditional rigid, hierarchical system of management in organizations. The researcher is of the opinion that as supervisors assumes the role of "coach" employee involvement and performance will improve. Managerial cadre need to communicate clear performance objectives, provide immediate feedback, assist in developing self-improvement plans, recognize and reward high performance and build warm positive relationships with subordinates. It has been found out that most managers do a good job of performing the technical work of their units, but experience much more difficulty with the human resource management tasks that are necessary to achieve organizational effectiveness (e.g., rewarding and encouraging good performance, handling conduct problems, empowering their staff and involving them in goal-setting and decision-making, etc.). Managers need to develop teams so as to achieve positive business results (i.e.,

improved organizational efficiency and effectiveness) through increased organisational commitment.

21. Comparison on each of the individual constituents of organizational commitment was carried out between employees below and above the age of 35 years. There was no significant difference between managers of different age groups on affective index, whereas subordinates above the age of 35 years had significantly higher scores on the affective index as compared to the subordinates below the age of 35 years. Thus, employees in the higher age groups tend to associate more closely with the organization and its objectives and goals as compared to the non-managerial cadre of lower age groups.
22. Comparative analysis of the managers of different age groups on the continuance index revealed that there is no significant impact of the age on the continuance index. Managers of different age groups have similar scores on the continuance index. On the other hand, senior aged subordinates had significantly higher scores on the normative index as compared to the subordinates of younger age groups. It implies that the subordinates of higher age groups feel it necessitated to continue with the organisation as there may be fewer opportunities of switching the jobs. Thus, compulsion to continue with the present organisation was higher among the subordinates in senior age group.
23. Third dimension of organisational commitment, i.e. normative index was also compared across different age groups. There was no significant difference on the normative index for both managers as well as the subordinates of different age groups. Managers as well as subordinates of different age groups have similar perceived moral need to continue with their present organisation. This may emerge from the industry or organizational features, its mission and goals and their alignment with the employees' own aspirations.

24. Another basis of comparison in the present study was the impact of educational qualifications on the constituents of organisational commitment. No significant difference was among managers with Graduate qualifications from those managers having Post-graduate qualifications on the affective component of organisational commitment. Subordinates also exhibited similar responses. There was no significant difference on the affective index among subordinates having different levels of educational qualifications.
25. Similar impact of educational qualifications on the continuance index of organisational commitment was studied. Here also no significant difference was observed between managers with Post-graduate and the managers with Graduate qualifications. Subordinates also exhibited similar trend as subordinates with Post-graduate qualifications did not significantly differ from the subordinates with Graduate qualifications.
26. The impact of educational qualifications on the normative component of organisational commitment was also studied. Here also no significant difference was observed between Post-graduate or Graduate managers as well as non-managers. Thus, educational qualifications had no significant impact on the normative index. The urge to remain in the organisation due to moral obligations is similar whether managers have Post-graduate or Graduate qualifications. Similar is the response exhibited by subordinates. There is similar feeling of moral responsibility towards organisation in subordinates whether they have Post-graduate or Graduate qualifications.
27. The impact of educational qualifications on the total organisational commitment scores was tested. It was found out that educational qualifications have no significant impact on the organisational commitment level among both managers as well as non-managers. They exhibited similar organisational commitment

scores. It has been noticed that if the organisation is facing rapid change with a requirement for reactivity which alters job characteristic and work-unit values, the "fit" may become a mismatch which might predict a fall in AC scores. As organisational values appear not to influence NC or AC directly one might suggest that internal organisational functioning changes may not impact on these facets of commitment. Literature review has suggested that commitment to an organisation results when individuals publicly commit themselves to a specific course of action, namely to being an employee of a particular organisation and to supporting the goals of that organisation. It has been hypothesized that some employees may become committed to using specific procedures in the pursuit of these organisational goals and is likely to resist actively any changes proposed by management to either the goals or procedures. *Finegan* (2000) studied the influence of personal and organisational values on AC, NC and CC. She found that AC is highest when there is congruence between individual's personal values and those of the organisation. This was not the case for NC, where there was a closer relationship between an individual's personal value system and NC, with the organisational culture playing little or no part in the relationship.

28. The results of this survey were intended to assist decision-makers in identifying key workplace issues, as perceived by employees, in order to develop strategies to address and improve the quality of working conditions for staff within consumer durable industry in particular and business enterprises as a whole. Quality of work life is a dynamic multi-dimensional construct that currently includes such concepts as job security, reward systems, training and career advancement opportunities and participation in decision-making. As such quality of work life has been defined as the workplace strategies, operations and environment that promote and maintain employee satisfaction with an aim to improving working

conditions for employees and organizational effectiveness for employers.

29. The findings reveal that the subordinates perceive their quality of work life to be much better than the perception of the managers. Thus, subordinates rate organizational culture and work environment to be much more conducive than the managers who do not express higher scores on the quality of work life index. Characteristics that describe the overall organization are viewed as part of the behaviour and reward system of the staff working in that setting. Organizational features such as policies and procedures, leadership style, operations and general contextual factors of the setting, all have a profound effect on how staff views the quality of their work life. QWL is an umbrella term which includes many concepts. Therefore, concentrating on only one job characteristic, whether it is wages or management style, is an inadequate approach to assessing QWL. Thus, study was construed as a compendium of three factors, viz., leadership behaviour, organisational commitment and quality of work life. As the perceptions held by employees play an important role in their decisions to enter, stay with or leave an organization, it is important that staff perceptions be included when assessing quality of work life. Critical analysis of the existing literature undertaken has led to different approaches which can be grouped under three main groups or common conceptions as:

    1. Emphasis on well-being and worker satisfaction, concomitant with the concern with the productivity increase, effectiveness and the organizational effectiveness.
    2. Valuation of workers' participation in decision-taking process, at work and questions related to the reformularization of positions.
    3. Emphasis on humanist perspective to think on people, work and organization.

30. One of the most significant findings was the difference in employees' opinion based on the age of respondents. The experiences and expectations of younger workers (those under 35 years) were compared to those of prime age (35 to 45) and to mature age workers (45 and above). To control for the impact of different working time arrangements, only full-time workers were selected for the purpose of age comparisons. Amongst full-time workers there were significant differences on a number of key factors. The most telling concerned the levels of *dissatisfaction* amongst older full-time managers. Within the managerial cadre, younger age group expressed higher QWL scores as compared to the higher age group managers. One possible explanation could be exposures to many different organizations which the elder aged managers have served spanning across their careers thereby having a good idea of working conditions of many organisations, whereas the experiences of the younger managers may have been limited to the few organizations. Another explanation could be higher expectations of the senior aged managers arising out of family compulsions, stress levels arising out of comparative inability to move to different organizations, locational constraints, etc. On the other hand, senior aged non-managers were more satisfied with the quality of work life in their present organisation than the younger aged subordinates. This could arise with the satisfaction and reconciliation with their present status, understanding of the job market imperfections, family liabilities making them more realistic, etc.
31. The Quality of Work Life index was also compared across different levels of educational qualifications. Managers with Graduate qualifications had a higher perceived quality of work life scores compared to the managers with Post-graduate qualifications. Similar pattern was observed for the non-managers. One possible explanation could be the enhanced expectancy levels due to higher qualification, leading to increased

dissatisfaction with present state of affairs. Another reason could be the difficulties in switching jobs which are in consonance with one's academic excellence. While job insecurity and declining working conditions are of paramount importance to employee groups, perceived employee dissatisfaction and the concomitant effects on productivity and on-costs are of concern to employers.

32. Each of the seventeen constituent elements of the Quality of Work Life index were statistically analysed. The comparisons on the basis of age as well as academic qualifications were also undertaken.
33. Relationship between total Leadership Behaviour Description Index (LBDQ) and organisational commitment (OC) index as perceived by the managers and their subordinates about their managers is positive for both managers as well as the subordinates. However, the intensity of correlation is more for the managers as compared to the subordinates. This implies that those leaders who exhibit higher leadership behavioural patterns also have higher commitment towards their organizations. Subordinates feel that those subordinates who work under leaders exhibiting higher leadership behaviour indices are more committed towards their organizations. *Mathieu & Zajac* (1990) in their meta-analysis of antecedent correlates and consequences of organisational commitment reported correlation between organisational commitment, leader initiating structure and leader consideration. *Parrish* (2001) also reported significant and positive relationship between both components of leadership behaviour, consideration and initiating structure and perceived affective commitment in library supervisors. *Rhodes & Steers* (1981), *Banai et al* (2004), *Scandura & Williams* (2004) have reported similar findings.
34. Correlation between consideration component of the Leadership Behaviour Description Index (LBDQ) and organisational commitment (OC) index as perceived by the managers and their subordinates was also

determined. The relationship is also positively correlated. However, the managers feel there is a stronger correlation between these two parameters, whereas subordinates perception is not that stronger. This means that those managers who are more considerate also exhibit more organisational commitment. Subordinates feel that those managers who are considerate instill organisational commitment among the subordinates. Managers need to offer better career prospects, more interesting and satisfying work, greater recognition of efforts and remuneration to generate organisational commitment. Positive correlation was also noticed between initiation component of LBD index and organisational commitment index. This correlation was higher for the subordinates than the managers, implying thereby that the subordinates exhibit more commitment towards their organisation if the manager is initiative-oriented.

35. Correlation between total Leadership Behaviour Description Index (LBDQ) and Quality of Work Life (QWL) index reveal that those leaders having higher leadership behaviour index also have better quality of work life. Positive correlation also exists between these two variables for subordinates, albeit to a lesser extent. Thus, those subordinates who work under leaders exhibiting higher leadership behaviour perceive that they have better quality of work life. Leadership style, in terms of conditional/unconditional feedback impacts one's self-perception as well as one's self-esteem. It is affected by the employee's ability to attribute task results to him/her, depending on whether the leader is autocratic or participative.

36. A moderate correlation has been observed between organisational commitment and the quality of work life among both managers and the subordinates. Thus, those employees have more commitment towards their organisation who feel that quality of work life in their organisation is good, irrespective of whether they are the managers or the subordinates. Organizational change also affects employment relationships. It has

been noticed that downsizing reduces commitment and trust. Similarly, organisation restructuring negatively affects organisational commitment.

Jobs high in both intrinsic (e.g., autonomy, challenge) and extrinsic (e.g., opportunities for recognition) rewards have progressively stronger positive effects on the job satisfaction and career satisfaction of individuals with low, moderate, and high job involvement, respectively. The results also show differential effects of leadership behaviour on job and career satisfaction and commitment to the organization. The relationship of leadership behaviour to career satisfaction is markedly higher for individuals with low job involvement than those with moderate or high levels of involvement.

Many factors have been found to influence the quality of work. These include: employment relationships; work environment; organizational structures and processes; job design; management practices and supervision; overall business strategy; oganizational culture besides workers' attitudes and behaviour.

Since the advent of liberalization in India, there has been an increase in the take-up of flexible work practices aimed at improving work and family balance. Despite the increased interest and debate about work and family balance, present study has found that when it comes to balancing work and family life and managing stress levels, organizations need to provide working arrangements that are flexible enough, especially for younger age workers. Our survey has shown the relatively high percentage of workers over the age of 35 years who indicated dissatisfaction with the level of stress they felt and with their ability to adequately balance work and family time.

Those managers who exhibit higher affective commitment also have higher quality of work life. Thus moral binding lead to higher perceived quality of work life. Correlation between continuance component of organisational commitment (OC) Index and quality of work life (QWL) index as perceived by the managers and their subordinates. This correlation is very moderate in case of managers and is negative in case of subordinates. Subordinate feel that the costs associated with leaving the organisation are not a major factor in perceiving the quality of work life, but visible effects that work conditions have in the individual welfare (e.g., manifestation of satisfaction in the workplace, growth and development of the employees, etc.) were considered more important. A moderate positive correlation exists between normative component of organisational commitment and quality of work life. This relationship is stronger for the managers than the subordinates.

Our findings reveal that eight items that could enhance quality of work life include wages and benefits, career opportunity, freedom of communication between managers and employees, trust in the managers, pride of work and company, interpersonal openness, training and development and innovation in the work system.

Avenues for further Research

Key research themes that have been highlighted in the existing literature include managing the performance paradox, goal setting and self-management, discontinuous information processing, organization learning, organizational change and individual transitions and the implications of these changes for employment relations.

Evidence suggests that work role marginality (e.g., job instability, skill underutilization, downward mobility and promotion opportunities) need to be studied in Indian organizations. Studies need to be undertaken in identifying how autonomy in the work place enhances or constrains the development of self-esteem and self-efficacy among managers and non-managers. Moreover, these studies can effectively address which job conditions impact self-evaluation and life satisfaction the most among different levels of workers.

The relatively higher scores for professional commitment can be accounted for by the high degree of dedication and motivation that employees have towards their profession and their organisation. Organisational commitment scores are lower in comparison with the scores for professional commitment. Efforts could be made to identify how much of the organisational commitment could be due to professional or occupational commitment.

Comparative analysis could also be undertaken on leadership behaviour patterns, quality of work life and organisational commitment among employees of such organizations as cultural diversities of top management may get reflected in their policies and procedures.

As the study was limited to the consumer durable industry, it may be worthwhile to replicate it in the fastest segments of Indian industry, especially the information technology and cellular telephony industry to identify if there is any impact of type of industry on organisational commitment or quality of work life.

Bibliography

Agarwala, T. (2003): "Innovative Human Resource Practices and Organizational Commitment: An Empirical Investigation." *International Journal of Human Resource Management*, Vol. 14(2), pp. 175-97.

Allen, N.J. and Meyer, J.P. (2000): "Construct Validation in Organizational Behaviour Research: the Case of Organizational Commitment." In: Goffin, R.D. and Helmes, E. (Eds.), *Problems and Solution in Human Assessment: Honouring Douglas N. Jackson at Seventy*, pp. 285-314.

Allen, N.J. and Smith, J. (1987): "An Investigation of Extra-role Behaviours Within Organizations." *Proceedings of the Annual Meeting of the Canadian Psychological Association*, Vancouver: British Colombia, Canada, pp. 81-89.

Arnold, J. and Davey, K.M. (1992): "Self-ratings and Supervisor Ratings of Graduate Employees' Competencies During Early Career." *Journal of Occupational and Organizational Psychology*, Vol. 65, pp. 235-50.

Ashforth, R.E. and Humphrey, R.H. (1995): "Emotion in the Workplace: A Reappraisal." *Human Relations*, Vol. 48, pp. 97-125.

Ashkanasy, N.M. and Tse, B. (2000): "Transformational Leadership As Management of Emotion: A Conceptual Review." In: N. Ashkanasy, C.E.J. Hartel and W.J. Zerbe, Editors, *Emotions in the Workplace: Research, Theory, and Practice*, pp. 221-35. Westport, Ct: Quorum Books.

Ashkanasy, N.M. (1989): "Causal Attribution and Supervisors' Responses to Subordinate Performance: the Green and Mitchell Model Revisited." *Journal of Applied Social Psychology,* Vol. 19, pp. 309-30.

Ashkanasy, N.M., Hartel, C.E.J. and Zerbe, W.J. (2000): "Commentary: Emerging Research Agendas." In: N.M. Ashkanasy, C.E.J. Hartel and W.J. Zerbe, Editors, *Emotions in the Workplace,* pp. 272-74. Westport, Ct: Quorum Books.

Ashour, A.S. (1973): "The Contingency Model of Leadership Effectiveness: An Evaluation." *Organizational Behaviour and Human Decision Processes,* Vol. 9, pp. 335-76.

Atwater, L.E. and Yammarino, F.J. (1992): "Does Self-other Agreement on Leadership Perceptions Moderate the Validity of Leadership and Performance Predictions?" *Personnel Psychology,* Vol. 45, pp. 141-64.

Avolio, B.J. and Bass, B.M. (1995): "Individual Consideration Viewed at Multiple Levels of Analysis—A Multilevel Framework For Examining the Diffusion of Transformational Leadership." *The Leadership Quarterly,* Vol. 6, pp. 199–218.

Baker, J. (1993): "Tightening the Iron Cage: Coercive Control in Self-managing Teams." *Administrative Science Quarterly,* Sept, pp. 408-37.

Barley, S. and Cunda, G. (1992): "Design and Devotion: Surges of Rational and Normative Ideologies of Control in Managerial Discourse." *Administrative Science Quarterly,* Sept., pp. 363-99.

Barrett, G.V. (2000): "Emotional Intelligence: the Madison Avenue Approach To Professional Practice." In: R. Page (Chair), *Competency Models and Emotional Intelligence: Are They Useful Constructs?* Symposium Conducted at the Meeting of the Society for Industrial and Organizational Psychology, New Orleans, April.

Bass, B.M. and Avolio, B.J. (1990): "The Implications of Transactional and Transformational Leadership For Individual, Team and Organizational Development." *Research in Organizational Change and Development,* Vol. 4, pp. 231-72.

Bass, B.M. and Yammarino, F.J. (1991): "Congruence of Self and Others' Leadership Ratings of Naval Officers For Understanding Successful Performance." *Applied Psychology: An International Review*, Vol. 40, pp. 437-54.

Baum, J.R., Kirkpatrick, S.A. and Locke, E.A. (1998): "A Longitudinal Study of the Relation of Vision and Vision Communication to Venture Growth in Entrepreneurial Firms." *Journal of Applied Psychology*, Vol. 83, pp. 43-54.

Becker, B. and Gerhart, B. (1996): "The Impact of HRM on Organizational Performance: Progress and Prospects." *Academy of Management Journal*, Vol. 39, pp. 779-801.

Becker, H. (1992): "Foci and Bases of Commitment: Are These Distinctions Worth Making?" *Academy of Management Journal*, Vol. 35, pp. 232-44.

Becker, T.E. and Billings, R.S. (1993): "Profiles of Commitment: An Empirical Test." *Journal of Organizational Behaviour*, Vol. 14(2), pp. 177-90.

Bell, D. (1973): *Coming of Post-industrial Society: A Venture in Social Forecasting*. New York: Basic Books.

Benkhoff, B. (1997): "A Test of the HRM Model: Good For Employers and Employees." *Human Resource Management Journal*, Vol. 7(4), pp. 44-60.

Berson, Y. and Shamir, B. (2001): "The Relationship Between Vision Strength, Leadership Style and Context." *The Leadership Quarterly*, Vol. 12(1), pp. 53-73.

Bhattacharya, D.K. (1993): "Promotion From Within: A Positive Reinforce For Enriching QWL for White Collar Employees." *The Indian Journal of Labour Economics*, Vol. 36(4), pp. 829-39.

Biswas, S.K. (1993): "Quality of Work Life—What It Is?" *The Indian Journal of Labour Economics*, Vol. 36(4), pp. 759-64.

Bochner, S. and Hesketh, B. (1994): "Power Distance, Individualism/Collectivism and Job-related Attitudes in A Culturally Diverse Work Group." *Journal of Cross-cultural Psychology*, Vol. 25, pp. 233-57.

Bohl, D.L., Slocum, J.W. Jr., Luthans, R. and Hodgetts, R.M. (1996): "Ideas That Will Shape the Future of Management Practices." *Organisational Dynamics*, Vol. 25(1), pp. 6-13.

Boisot, M.H. (1998): *Knowledge Assets: Securing Competitive Advantage in the Information Economy*. New York: Oxford University Press.

Borg, M.G. (1990): "Occupational Stress in British Educational Settings: A Review." *Educational Psychology*, Vol. 10, pp. 103-26.

Borghans, L. and De Steur, M. (1999): *Choosing Health Care: A Conceptual Framework*. Den Haag: OSA.

Bourantas, D. (1988): "Leadership Styles, Need Satisfaction and the Organizational Commitment of Greek Managers." *Scandinavian Journal of Management*, Vol. 4(3-4), pp. 121-34.

Bray, S.R., Millen, J.A. (2005): "The Effects of Leadership Style and Exercise Program Choreography on Enjoyment and Intentions To Exercise." *Psychology of Sport and Exercise*, in Press.

Brenner, O.K., Tomkiewicz, J. and Schein, V.E. (1989): "The Relationship Between Sex-role Stereotypes and Requisite Management Characteristics Revisited." *Academy of Management Journal*, Vol. 32, pp. 662-69.

Brower, H.H., Schoorman, F.D. and Tan, H.H. (2000): "A Model of Relational Leadership: the Integration of Trust and Leader-member Exchange." *Leadership Quarterly*, Vol. 11, pp. 227-50.

Bryman, A., Bresnen, M., Ford, J., Beardsworth, A. and Keil, T. (1987): "Leader Orientation and Organizational Transience: An Investigation Using Fielder's LPC Scale." *Journal of Occupational Psychology*, Vol. 60, pp. 13-20.

Burr, R. and Girardi, A. (2001): "The Interaction Between Competence and Commitment as a Predictor of Human Capital within the Firm." *Interactive Papers, Academy of Management Conference*, 510, August, Washington, D.C.

Busch, P. (1980): "The Sales Manager's Bases of Social Power and Influence Upon the Sales Force." *Journal of Marketing*, Vol. 44, pp. 91-101.

Calder, B.J. (1977): "An Attribution Theory of Leadership." In: B.M. Staw and R.G. Salancik, Editors, *New Directions in Organizational Behaviour*, pp. 179-204. Chicago: St. Claire Press.

Campbell, A., Converse, P.E. and Rogers, W.L. (1976): *The Quality of American Life*. New York: Russel Sage Foundation.

Cann, A., and Siegfried, W.D. (1990): "Gender Stereotypes and Dimensions of Effective Leader Behaviour." *Sex Roles*, Vol. 23, pp. 413-19.

Cherulnik, P.D., Donley, K.A., Wiewel, T.S.R. and Miller, S.R. (2001): "Charisma is Contagious: the Effect of Leaders' Charisma on Observers' Affect." *Journal of Applied Social Psychology,* Vol. 31, pp. 2149-59.

Chong, M.L. and Chong, J. (2002): "The Effects of Budget Emphasis, Participation and Organizational Commitment on Job Satisfaction: Evidence From the Financial Services Sector." *Advances in Accounting Behavioural Research,* Vol. 5, pp. 183-211.

Church, A.H. (1994): "Managerial Self-awareness in High Performance Individuals in Organizations." Doctoral Dissertation, Columbia University, 1994. Dissertation Abstracts International, 55-05b, 2028 (University Microfilms No. Aai9427924).

Church, A.H. (1997): "Managerial Self-awareness in High Performing Individuals in Organizations." *Journal of Applied Psychology,* Vol. 82, pp. 281-92.

Cialdini, R.B. and Trost, M.R. (1998): "Social Influence: Social Norms, Conformity and Compliance." In: Gilbert, D.T., Fiske, S.T., and Lindzey, G. (Eds.), *The Handbook of Social Psychology* (4th Ed.), Vol. 2, pp. 151-92. Boston, MA: McGraw-hill.

Conger, J.A. (1999): "Charismatic and Transformational Leadership in Organizations: An Insider's Perspective on These Developing Streams of Research." *Leadership Quarterly,* Vol. 10, pp. 145-69.

Conger, J.A., and Kanungo, R.N. (1994): "Charismatic Leadership in Organizations: Perceived Behavioural Attributes and Their Measurement." *Journal of Organizational Behaviour,* Vol. 15, pp. 439-52.

Cook, J.D., Hepworth, S.J., Wall, T.D. and Warr, P.B. (1981): *The Experience of Work: A Compendium and Review of 249 Measures and Their Use.* New York: Academic Press.

Costa, P.T., Jr. and Mccrae, R.R. (1980): "Influence of Extraversion and Neuroticism on Subjective Well-being." *Journal of Personality and Social Psychology,* Vol. 38, pp. 668-78.

Cox, T., Boot, N., Cox, S. and Harrison, S. (1988): "Stress in Schools: An Organizational Perspective." *Work and Stress,* Vol. 2, pp. 353-62.

Cribben, J.J. (1981): *Leadership: Strategies for Organizational Effectiveness,* New York.

Czander, W. and Lee, D.H. (2001): "Employee Commitment: A Psycho-social Perspective on Asian and American Culture and Businesses." In: J. Kidd, L. Xue and F. J. Richter (Eds.) *Maximizing Human Intelligence Deployment in Asian Business.*

De, N.R. (1982): "Interlinkage Between Quality of Work Life and Quality of Life." *Productivity,* Vol. 22(4), pp. 89-91.

De, N.R. (1984): "Quality of Life and Quality of Work Life; Towards An Appreciation." *Productivity,* Vol. 25(2), 129-41.

Delongis, A., Coyne, J.C., Dakof, G., Folkman, S. and Lazarus, R.S. (1982): "Relationship of Daily Hassles, Uplifts and Major Life Events To Healthy Status." *Health Psychology,* Vol. 1, pp. 119-36.

Delongis, A., Folkman, S. and Lazarus, R.S. (1988): "The Impact of Daily Stress on Health and Mood: Psychological and Social Resources As Mediators." *Journal of Personality and Social Psychology,* Vol. 54, pp. 486-95.

Deluga, R.J. (2001): "American Presidential Machiavellianism: Implications For Charismatic Leadership and Rated Performance." *The Leadership Quarterly,* Vol. 12, pp. 339-63.

Diener, E., Emmons, R.L.A., Larsen, R.J. and Griffin, S. (1985): "The Satisfaction With Life Scale." *Journal of Personality Assessment,* Vol. 49, pp. 71-75.

Doherty, A.J. (1988): "Psychological Morale: Its Conceptualization and Measurement." *The Doherty Inventory of Psychological Morale (Dipm). Educational Studies,* Vol. 14, pp. 65-75.

Driscoll, V. (1978): "Trust and Participation in Organizational Decision-making As Predictors of Satisfaction." *Academy of Management Journal,* Vol. 21, pp. 44-56.

Dunham, R.B., Grube, J.A. and Castaneda, M.B. (1994): "Organizational Commitment: the Utility of an Integrative Definition." *Journal of Applied Psychology,* Vol. 79, pp. 370-80.

Durkin, H. (1964): *The Group on Depth.* New York: Seaview/ Putnam Press.

Dzinkowski, R. (2000): "The Measurement and Management of Intellectual Capital: An Introduction." *Management Accounting,* February, pp. 32-36.

Eagly, A.H., Wood, W. and Diekman, A.B. (2000): "Social Role Theory of Sex Differences and Similarities: A Current Appraisal." In: Eckes, T. and Trautner, H.M. (Eds.), *The Developmental Social Psychology of Gender*. London: Erlbaum.

Eby, L.T., Freeman, D.M., Rush, M.C. and Lance, C.E. (1999): "Motivational Bases of Affective Organizational Commitment: A Partial Test of An Integrative Theoretical Model." *Journal of Occupational and Organizational Psychology,* Vol. 72, pp. 463-83.

Erez, M. and Earley, P.C. (1993): *Culture, Self-identity, and Work.* New York: Oxford University Press.

Feather, N.T. and Rauter, Kartrin, A. (2004): "Organisational Citizenship Behaviours in Relation to Job Status, Job Insecurity, Organizational Commitment and Identification, Job Satisfaction and Work Values." *Journal of Occupational and Organizational Psychology,* Vol. 77, pp. 81-94.

Ferris, G.R., Bhawuk, D.P.S., Fedor, D.F. and Judge, T.A. (1995): "Organizational Politics and Citizenship: Attributions of Intentionality and Construct Definition." In: M.J. Martinko, Editor, *Advances in Attribution Theory: An Organizational Perspective,* St. Lucie Press, Delray Beach, Fl, pp. 231-52.

Fry, L.W. (2003): "Toward a Theory of Spiritual Leadership." *The Leadership Quarterly,* Vol. 14(6), pp. 693-727.

Galton, F. (1860): *Hereditary Genius.* Imprint By Meridian Books, Cleveland, OH, 1962.

Gani, A. (1993): "Quality of Work Life in a State Setting: Finding of An Empirical Study." *The Indian Journal of Labour Economics,* Vol. 36(4), 817-24.

Gardiner, M., and Tiggemann, M. (1999): "Gender Differences in Leadership Style, Job Stress and Mental Health in Male- and Female-dominated Industries." *Journal of Occupational and Organizational Psychology,* Vol. 72, pp. 301-15.

George, J.M. (2000): "Emotions and Leadership: the Role of Emotional Intelligence." *Human Relations,* Vol. 53, pp. 1027-55.

George, M.J. and Gareth, J.R. (1996): "The Experience of Work and Turnover Intentions: Interactive Effects of Value Attainment, Job Satisfaction, and Positive Mood." *Journal of Applied Psychology,* Vol. 81, pp. 318-25.

Gibson, C.B. (1995): "An Investigation of Gender Differences in Leadership Across Four Countries." *Journal of International Business Studies,* Vol. 26, pp. 255-79.

Graen, G. and Uhl-bien, M. (1995): "Development of the Leader-member Exchange Theory of Leadership Over 25 Years: Applying A Multi-level Multi-domain Perspective." *Leadership Quarterly,* Vol. 6, pp. 219-47.

Greenleaf, R. (1988): *Spirituality As Leadership*. Greenleaf Center For Servant-leadership, Indinapolis.

Griffeth, R.W., Hom, P.W. and Gaertner, S. (2000): "A Meta-analysis of Antecedents and Correlates of Employee Turnover: Update, Moderator Tests and Research Implications For the Next Millennium." *Journal of Management*, Vol. 26(3), pp. 463-88.

Grinnell, J.P. (2003): "An Empirical Investigation of CEO Leadership in Two Types of Small Firms." *Sam Advanced Management Journal,* 22 Sept.

Grothe, C.M (1991): "Is the Work Force Vanguard to the 21st Century A Quality of Work Life Deficient-prone Generation?" *Journal of Business Research,* Vol. 23(1), pp. 67-82.

Guest, D. (2002): "Human Resource Management, Corporate Performance and Employee Well Being: Building the Worker Into HRM." *Journal of Industrial Relations,* Vol. 44(3), pp. 335-58.

Haire, M., Ghiselli, E.E. and Porter, L.W. (1966): *Managerial Thinking: An International Study*. New York: John Wiley.

Halpern, J. and Halpern, I. (1995): *Re-engineering the Corporation*. New York: Harper.

Halpin, A.W. and Winer, B.J. (1957): "A Factorial Analysis of the Leader Behaviour Descriptions." In: Stogdill, R.M. and Coons, A.E. (Eds.). Leader Behaviour: Its Description and Measurement: Res. Monographs. Bureau of Business Research, Ohio State University, Columbus, Ohio (U.S.).

Harris, M.M. and Schaubroeck, J. (1988): "A Meta-analysis of Self-supervisor, Self-peer and Peer-supervisory Ratings." *Personnel Psychology,* Vol. 41, pp. 43-62.

Hart, M.P. (1994): "Teacher Quality of Work Life: Integrating Work Experiences, Psychological Distress and Morale." *Journal of Occupational and Organisational Psychology*, Vol. 67(2), pp. 109-32.

Hart, P.M., Conn, M. and Carter, N. (1992): *The School Organizational Health Questionnaire: Manual*. Unpublished Manuscript, Department of Psychology, University of Melbourne.

Hartog, D.N. and Verburg, R.M. (1997): "Charisma and Rhetoric: Communicative Techniques of International Business Leaders." *The Leadership Quarterly*, Vol. 8(4), pp. 355-91.

Headey, B. (1983): "Quality of Life Studies: Their Implications For Social and Market Researchers." *European Research*, April, pp. 56-67.

Headey, B., Holmstrom, E. and Wearing, A.J. (1984): "Well-being and Ill-being: Different Dimensions?" *Social Indicators Research*, Vol. 14, pp. 115-39.

Helgesen, S. (1990): *The Female Advantage: Women's Way of Leadership*. New York: Doubleday.

Hemphill, J.K. and Coons, A.E. (1950): *Leader Behaviour Description Questionnaire*. Personnel Research Board, Ohio State University, Ohio, Columbus (U.S.).

Hemphill, J.K. and Coons, A.E. (1957): "Development of the Leader Behaviour Description Questionnaire." *Journal of Social Issues*, Vol. 12, pp. 41-49.

Hemphill, J.K. (1955): "Leadership Behaviour Associated With the Administrative Reputation of College Department." *Journal of Educational Psychology*, Vol. 46(7), pp. 38-51.

Hepworth, W. and Towler, A. (2004): "The Effects of Individual Differences and Charismatic Leadership on Workplace Aggression." *Journal of Occupational Health Psychology*, Vol. 9(2), pp. 176-85.

Hewett, T.T. and O'brien, G.E. (1974): "The Effects of Work Organization, Leadership Style and Member Compatibility Upon the Productivity of Small Groups Working on a Manipulative Task." *Organizational Behaviour and Human Performance*, Vol. 11(2), pp. 283-301.

Holahan, C.J. and Moos, R.H. (1986): "Personality, Coping and Family Resources in Stress Resistance: A Longitudinal Analysis." *Journal of Personality and Social Psychology*, Vol. 51, pp. 389-95.

Holdnak, B.J., Harsh, J. and Bushardt, S.C. (1993): "An Examination of Leadership Style and Its Relevance To Shift Work in an Organizational Setting." *Health Care Management Review*, Vol. 18, pp. 21-30.

Hoque, M.E. and Rahman, A. (1999): "Quality of Work Life and Job Behaviour of Workers in Bangladesh: A Comparative Study of Private and Public Sectors." *Indian Journal of Industrial Relations*, Vol. 35(2), pp. 175-84.

Howell, J.M. and Hall-merenda, K.E. (1999): "The Ties That Bind: the Impact of Leader-Member Exchange, Transformational and Transactional Leadership and Distance on Predicting Follower Performance." *Journal of Applied Psychology*, Vol. 84, pp. 680-94.

Howell, J.M. and Frost, P.J. (1989): "A Laboratory Study of Charismatic Leadership." *Organizational Behaviour and Human Decision Processes*, Vol. 43(2), pp. 243-69.

Howell, J.M. and Higgins, C.A. (1990): "Champions of Technological Innovation." *Administrative Science Quarterly*, Vol. 35, pp. 317-41.

Ingber, D. (1981): "Computer Addicts." *Science Digest*, July, pp. 114-21.

Irgens, O.M. (1995): "Situational Leadership: A Modification of Hersey and Blanchard's Model." *Leadership and Organizational Behaviour*, Vol. 16(2), pp. 36-39.

Jacobs, T.O. and Jaques, E. (1987): "Leadership in Complex Systems." In: Zeidner, J. (Ed.) *Human Productivity Enhancement*, New York: Praeger, Vol. 2, pp. 7-65.

James, S. and Hendry, B. (1991): "The Money Or the Job: the Decision to Leave Policing." *Australia and New Zealand Journal of Criminology*, Vol. 24, pp. 169-89.

Johnson, C. (1993): "Gender and Formal Authority." *Social Psychology Quarterly*, Vol. 56, pp. 193-210.

Johnson, J. (2000): "Differences in Supervisor and Non-supervisor Perceptions of Quality Culture and Organizational Climate." *Public Personnel Management*, 1 April.

Katz, D. and Kahn, R.L. (1978): *Social Psychology of Organization*, (2nd Edition). New York: John Wiley and Sons.

King, R.C. and Sethi, V. (1997): "The Moderating Effect of Organizational Commitment on Burnout in Information Systems Professionals." *European Journal of Information Systems*, Vol. 6, pp. 86-96.

Kirby, E.L. and Harter, L.M. (2001): "Discourses of Diversity and the Quality of Work Life." *Management Communication Quarterly*, Vol. 15(1), pp. 121-27.

Klenke, K. (1993): "Meta-analytic Studies of Leadership: Added Insights or Added Paradoxes." *Current Psychology: Developmental, Learning Personality, Social*, Vol. 12, pp. 326-43.

Kluckhohn, C. (1951): "The Study of Culture." In: Lenèr, D. and Lassell, H.D. (Eds.) *The Policy Science*. Stanford, CA: Stanford University Press.

Kochan, Katz and Mckersie (1989): "The Transformation; Clair Brown and Michael Reich, When Does Cooperation Work? A Look at Nummi and Van Nuys," *California Management Review*, Summer, pp. 26-44.

Kouzes, J.M. and Pozner, B.Z. (1995): *The Leadership Challenges: How To Keep Getting Extraordinary Things Done in Organisations*. San Francisco: Jossey-bass.

Kristof, A.L. (1996): "Person-Organization Fit: An Integrative Review of Its Conceptualizations, Measurements and Implications." *Personnel Psychology*, Vol. 49, pp. 1-49.

Kunda, G. (1992): *Engineering Culture, Control and Commitment in A High-tech Corporatio*. Philadelphia: Temple University Press.

Lagace, R.R. (1991): "An Exploratory Study of Reciprocal Trust Between Sales Managers and Salespersons." *Journal of Personal Selling and Sales Management*, Vol. 11, pp. 49-56.

Larre, E.C. (1999): "Equity-based Compensation at High-growth Companies: Responding to Long-term Stock Price Declines." *Compensation and Benefits Review*, Vol. Sept.-Oct., pp. 44-53.

Lawler, E., Ledford, G. and Mohnnan, S. (1992): "Employee Involvement and Total Quality Management." *Practice and Results in Fortune 1000 Companies*. San Francisco: Jossey-bass Publishers.

Lazarus, R.S. (1990): "Theory-based Stress Measurement: Psychological Inquiry." *International Journal of Peer Commentary and Review,* Vol. 1, pp. 3-13.

Leana, C. and Florkowski, G. (1992): "Employee Involvement Programs: Integrating Psychological Theory and Management Practice." *Research in Personnel and Human Resources Management,* Vol. 10, pp. 233-70.

Levering, R. and Moskowitz, M. (1994): *The 100 Best Companies to Work For in America,* New York: Penguin Group.

Levine, D. and Tyson, L. (1991): "Participation, Productivity and the Firm's Environment." In: Alan Blinder (Ed.) *Paying For Productivity,* pp. 183-224. Washington: the Brookings Institution.

Licht, W. (1991): "Studying Work: Personnel Policies in Philadelphia Firms, 1850-1950." In: Sanford Jacoby (Ed.), *Masters To Managers,* p. 57, New York: Columbia University Press.

Likert, R. (1961): *New Patterns of Management.* New York: McGraw-Hill.

Lincoln, J.R. and Miller, J. (1979): "Work and Friendship Ties in Organizations: A Comparative Analysis of Related Networks." *Administrative Science Quarterly,* Vol. 24, pp. 181-99.

Mabe, P.A. and West, S.G. (1982): "Validity of Self-evaluation of Ability: A Review and Meta Analysis." *Journal of Applied Psychology,* Vol. 67, pp. 280-96.

Maccoby, M. (1984): "Helping Labour and Management Set Up A Quality-of-Worklife Program." *Monthly Labour Review,* pp. 28-32.

Man, T.W.Y., Lau, T. and Chan, K.F. (2002): "The Competitiveness of Small and Medium Enterprises: A Conceptualization with Focus on Entrepreneurial Competencies." *Journal of Business Venturing,* Vol. 17, pp. 123-42.

Mann, R.D. (1959): "A Review of the Relationship Between Personality and Performance in Small Groups." *Psychological Bulletin,* Vol. 56, pp. 241-70.

Marcoulides, G.A. (1995): "The Invariance of Leadership Styles Across Four Countries." *Journal of Managerial Issues,* 22 June.

Martinko, M.J. (1995): "The Nature and Function of Attribution Theory within the Organizational Sciences." In: Martinko, M.J., Edt., *Advances in Attribution Theory: An Organizational Perspective*, St. Lucie Press, Delray Beach, Fl, pp. 7-14.

Mathieu, J. and Zajac, D.M. (1990): "A Review and Meta-analysis of the Antecedent, Correlates and Consequences of Organizational Commitment Among Professionals and Non-professionals." *Journal of Vocational Behaviour*, Vol. 34, pp. 299-317.

Mccracken, M.J.A. and Kaynak, H. (1996): "An Empirical Investigation of the Relationship Between Quality and Productivity." *Quality Management Journal*, Vol. 3(2), pp. 36-51.

Mehta, P. (1978): "Objective and Subjective Factors in Employees Satisfaction in Life and Work." *Indian Journal of Industrial Relations*, Vol. 13(4), pp. 433-44.

Meyer, J.P. and Allen, N.J. (1988): "Links Between Work Experiences and Organizational Commitment During the First Year of Employment: A Longitudinal Analysis." *Journal of Occupational Psychology*, Vol. 61, pp. 195-209.

Monga, M.L. and Maggu, A. (1981): "QWL: A Study of Public Sector in India," Asci, *Journal of Management*, Vol. 19(4).

Nowack, K.M. (1992): "Self-assessment and Rater-assessment as a Dimension of Management Development." *Human Resource Development Quarterly*, Vol. 3, pp. 141-55.

O'reilly, C.A., Caldwell, D. and Barnett, W. (1989): "Work Group Demography, Social Interaction and Turnover." *Administrative Science Quarterly*, Vol. 34, pp. 24-37.

Onne, J. (2000): "Job Demands, Perceptions of Effort Reward Fairness and Innovative Work Behaviour." *Journal of Occupational and Organizational Psychology*, Vol. 73(3), pp. 287-302.

O'reilly, C. (1989): "Corporations, Culture and Commitment: Motivation and Social Control in Organizations." *California Management Review*, Vol. 31(4), pp. 9-25.

Organ, D.W. (1990): "The Motivational Basis of Organizational Citizenship Behaviour." In: Staw, B.M. and Cummings, L.L. (Eds.), *Research in Organizational Behaviour*, pp. 43-72. Greenwich, Ct: Jai Press.

Parker, S.K. (1998): "Enhancing Role Breadth Self-efficacy: The Role of Job Enrichment and Other Organizational Interventions." *Journal of Applied Psychology*, Vol. 83, pp. 835-52.

Peters, T. (1990): "The Best Managers Will Listen, Motivate, Support: Isn't that Just Like a Woman?" *Working Woman*, Vol. Sept., pp. 216-17.

Pfeffer, J. and Salancick, G.R. (1978): *The External Control of Organizations*. New York: Harper and Row.

Pfeffer, J. (1998): *The Human Equation: Building Profits By Putting People First*. Boston, MA: Harvard Business School Press.

Porter, L.W., Crampon, W.J. and Smith, F.J. (1976): "Organizational Commitment and Managerial Turnover: A Longitudinal Study." *Organizational Behaviour and Human Performance*, Vol. 15, pp. 87-89.

Powell, G.N. (1988): *Women and Men in Management*. Newbury Park, CA: Sage.

Pruijt, H. (2003): "Performance and Quality of Working Life." *Journal of Organisational Change Management*, Vol. 13(4), pp. 389-400.

Rice, R.W. (1981): "Leader LPC and Follower Satisfaction: A Review:" *Organizational Behaviour and Human Performance*, Vol. 28, pp. 1-25.

Rice, R.W. (1978): "Construct Validity of the Least Preferred Co-worker Score." *Psychological Bulletin*, Vol. 85, pp. 199-237.

Ropo, A. and Hunt, J.G. (1995): "Entrepreneurial Processes As Virtuous and Vicious Spirals in a Changing Opportunity Structure: A Paradoxical Perspective." *Entrepreneurship Theory and Practice*, Vol. Spring, pp. 91-111.

Rosin, H. and Korabi, K. (1995): "Organizational Experiences and Propensity to Leave: A Multivariate Investigation of Men and Women Managers." *Journal of Vocational Behaviour*, Vol. 46, pp. 1-16.

Rosin, H.M. and Korabik, K. (1991): "Workplace Variables, Affective Responses and Intention To Leave Among Women Managers." *Journal of Occupational Psychology*, Vol. 64, pp. 317-30.

Rusbult, C.E. and Farrell, D. (1983): "A Longitudinal Test of the Investment Model: The Impact on Job Satisfaction, Job Commitment and Turnover of Variations in Rewards,

Costs, Alternatives and Investments." *Journal of Applied Psychology*, Vol. 68, pp. 429-38.

Ryan, G.M. (1995): *Theoretical Basis For the QWL Concept*. University of Siena: Quality, (Esprit Project 8162) (Working Paper).

Sanford, J. (1991): "Employing Bureaucracy; Jacoby, Masters to Managers." *Historical and Comparative Perspectives on American Employers*, New York, Columbia University Press.

Sanyal, A. and Singh, B.R. (1982): "Improving the Quality of Work Life." *Lok Udyog*, pp. 27-35.

Savery, L.K., Soutar, G.N. and Weaver, J.R. (1991): "Organizational Commitment and the West Australian Police Force." *The Police Journal*, Vol. 64, pp. 168-77.

Sayeed and Parkash (1981): "The Quality of Work Life in Relation to Job Satisfaction and Performance in Two Organizations." *Managerial Psychology*, Vol. 2(1).

Schein, V.E. and Mueller, R. (1992): "Sex Role Stereotypes and Requisite Management Characteristics: A Cross-cultural Look." *Journal of Organizational Behaviour*, Vol. 13, pp. 439-47.

Schein, V.E., Mueller, R. and Jacobson, C. (1989): "The Relationship Between Sex Role Stereotypes and Requisite Management Characteristics Among College Students." *Sex Roles*, Vol. 20, pp. 103-10.

Sekaran, U. (1985): "The Perceived Quality of Working Life in Banks in Major Cities in India." *Prajnan*, Vol. 14(3), pp. 273-84.

Selznick, P. (1957): *Leadership in Administration: A Sociological Interpretation*. Berkeley, Ca: University of California Press.

Sgro, J.A., Worchel, P., Pence, E.C. and Orban, J.A. (1980): "Perceived Leader Behaviour as a Function of Leader's Interpersonal Trust Orientation." *Academy of Management Journal*, Vol. 23, pp. 161-65.

Sheldon, M.E. (1971): "Investments and Involvements As Mechanisms Producing Commitment to the Organization." *Administrative Science Quarterly*, Vol. 16, pp. 143-50.

Sheridan, J.E., Vredenburgh, D.J and Abelson, M.A. (1984): "Contextual Model of Leadership Influence in Hospital Units." *Academy of Management Journal*, Vol. 27(1), pp. 57-78.

Sims, H.P. Jr. and Manz, C.C. (1996): *Company of Heroes: Unleashing the Power of Self-leadership*. Wiley, New York.

Singh, J.P (1982): "Improving Quality of Working Life in the Indian Context." *Productivity*, Vol. 22(4), pp. 13-20.

Singh, J.P. (1983): "QWL Experiments in India—Trails and Triumphs." *Abhigyan*, Vol. Autumn, pp. 23-37.

Singhal, S. and Upadhaya, H.S. (1972): "Psychology of Men at Work: The Employee Perception of Job Incentives." *Indian Journal of Industrial Relations*, Vol. 8(1), pp. 17-30.

Singhal, S. (1983): "Quality of Work Life: A Reexamination of Assumptions." Hyderabad: National Symposium on Quality of Working Life, Mimeographed, pp. 25-26.

Sinha, J.B.P (1993): "Quality of Work Life: A Continuing Concern." *The Indian Journal of Labour Economics*, Vol. 36(4), pp. 745-53.

Smith, P.B. and M.F. Peterson (1988): *Leadership, Organization and Culture*. Newbury Park: Sage.

Snyder, M. (1974): "Self-monitoring of Expressive Behaviour." *Journal of Personality, and Social Psychology*, Vol. 30, pp. 526-37.

Stevenson, H.H. and Jarillo, L.C. (1990): "A Paradigm of Entrepreneurship: Entrepreneurial Management." *Strategic Management Journal*, Vol. 11, pp. 17-27.

Stordeur, S., D'hoore, W. and Vandenberghe, C. (2001): "Leadership, Organizational Stress and Emotional Exhaustion Among Nursing Hospital Staff." *Journal of Advanced Nursing*, Vol. 35(4), pp. 533-42.

Thomas, D.C. and Ravlin, E.C. (1995): "Responses of Employees to Cultural Adaptation By A Foreign Manager." *Journal of Applied Psychology*. Vol. 80, pp. 133-46.

Velsor, V.E., Taylor, S. and Leslie, J.B. (1993): "An Examination of the Relationships Among Self-perception Accuracy, Self-awareness, Gender and Leader Effectiveness." *Human Resource Management*, Vol. 32(2&3), pp. 249-63.

Venkata, C.J. and Velayudhan (1999): "Impact of Advanced Technology on Quality of Work Life. A Study of Steel Plant." *Management and Labour Studies*, Vol. 24(4), pp. 249-55.

Verma, J. (1993): "Quality of Work Life and Quality of Life: An Indigenous Approach." *The Indian Journal of Labour Economics*, Vol. 36(4), pp. 765-69.

Warr, P., Barter, J. and Brownbridge, G. (1983): "On the Independence of Positive and Negative Affect." *Journal of Personality and Social Psychology*, Vol. 44, pp. 644-51.

Watson, D. and Tellegen, A. (1985): "Toward A Consensual Structure of Mood." *Psychological Bulletin*, Vol. 98, pp. 219-35.

Watts, C.N. and Levy, P.E. (2004): "The Mediating Role of Affective Commitment in the Relation of the Feedback Environment To Work Outcomes." *Journal of Vocational Behaviour,* Vol. 65(3), December, pp. 351-65.

Zenger, T.R. and Lawrence, B.S. (1989): "Organization Demography: The Differential Effects of Age and Tenure on Technical Communication." *Academy of Management Journal*, Vol. 32, pp. 353-76.

Zhang, J.J., Jensen, B.E. and Mann, B.L. (1996): "Modification and Revision of the Leadership For Sport Scale." *Journal of Sport Behaviour*, Vol. 19(4).

Index